# THE LOST GOSPEL

# THE LOST GOSPEL

## THE QUEST FOR
## THE GOSPEL OF
## JUDAS ISCARIOT

## HERBERT KROSNEY

NATIONAL GEOGRAPHIC

WASHINGTON, D.C.

ISBN-10: 1-4262-0047-1
ISBN-13: 978-1-4262-0047-2

All photographs by Kenneth Garrett, except image of Codex Tchacos insert page 1, courtesy of Florence Darbre. Insert page 2: The Taking of Christ by a follower of Caravaggio/Private Collection/© Lawrence Steigrad Fine Arts, New York/ The Bridgeman Art Library.

Timeline images: Judas by Leonardo Da Vinci, The Royal Collection © 2005, Her Majesty Queen Elizabeth II; Jesus and St. Peter courtesy of St. Catherine's Monastery, Sinai.

Scripture quoted by permission. Quotations are from the Net Bible ® copyright © 1996–2006 by Biblical Studies Press, L.L.C. http://www.bible.org/. All rights reserved.

Founded in 1888, the National Geographic Society is one of the largest nonprofit scientific and educational organizations in the world. It reaches more than 285 million people worldwide each month through its official journal, National Geographic, and its four other magazines; the National Geographic Channel; television documentaries; radio programs; films; books; videos and DVDs; maps; and interactive media. National Geographic has funded more than 8,000 scientific research projects and supports an education program combating geographic illiteracy. For more information, visit nationalgeographic.com.

*Interior design by Melissa Farris.*

*For Bernard Krosney*

# THE LOST GOSPEL

## DEFINING TIME PERIODS

Many scholars and editors working today in the multicultural discipline of world history use terminology that does not impose the standards of one culture on others. As recommended by the scholars who have contributed to the National Geographic Society's publication of the Gospel of Judas, this book uses the terms BCE (before the Common Era) and CE (Common Era). BCE refers to the same time period as B.C. (before Christ), and CE refers to the same time period as A.D. (anno Domini, a Latin phrase meaning "in the year of the Lord").

JESUS

JUDAS

ca 30
Crucifixion
of Jesus of
Nazareth

100-130
Rise of Christian
Gnosticism

ca 180
Irenaeus, Bishop
of Lyon, condemns
Gnostic teachings
and calls **Gospel
of Judas** "fictitious
history"

275-300
Familiar Christian
views become
dominant among
believers

**EARLY CHRISTIAN HISTORY**

| A.D. 1 | 100 | 200 | 300 |
|---|---|---|---|

TEXTS

49-62
Paul writes first
letters—earliest
New Testament
(NT) texts

65-95
Gospels of Mark,
Matthew, Luke,
and John (NT)

110-150
Gospels of
Thomas and
Peter (not in NT);
II Peter, latest
book of NT;
Gospel of Mary
(Gnostic?)

ca 150
**Gospel of Judas**
written, Gospel of
Truth, Secret Book of
John (all Gnostic)

ca 150-200
Mark, Matthew,
Luke, and John first
recognized as the
authoritative Gospels

ca 200-230
Second Discourse
of Great Seth
(Gnostic)

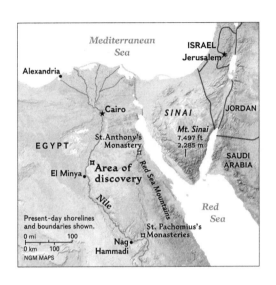

**367**
Athanasius,
Bishop of
Alexandria,
first to list 27
books of New
Testament

**375**
Epiphanius,
Bishop of
Salamis,
condemns
**Gospel of
Judas**

**ca 380**
Christianity
becomes
official
religion of
Roman
Empire

**1844-1859**
Codex Sinaiticus,
containing one
of the earliest
New Testaments,
found in Sinai

**1945**
Nag Hammadi
library (52 texts,
many Gnostic),
Egypt

**1990s**
Gospel of the
Savior translated
from fragments
found in Egypt

**400**  **1800** MODERN DISCOVERIES  **1900**  **2000**

**300s**
Estimated date
of surviving
copy of **Gospel
of Judas**

**1886**
Gospel of
Peter, Egypt

**1896**
Gospel of
Mary, Egypt

**1947**
Dead Sea
Scrolls,
Israel

**1970s**
Bound
manuscript
containing
**Gospel of
Judas**, Egypt

**2001-2006**
**Gospel of
Judas** restored
and translated
into English

PETER

# CONTENTS

# BART D. EHRMAN

In fall 2004 I received several unexpected and rather mysterious phone calls. The first was from a professional friend of mine, Sheila, who has for years worked on biblical archaeology in Israel. After a brief chat about her next dig, she raised the question that had prompted her call: Had I ever heard of a Gospel of Judas?

I had only a vague recollection of the book: It was one of the gospels that was mentioned by some of the early church fathers, but that had evidently been destroyed, or at least lost, many centuries ago. It is included in none of the standard reference works of the early Christian "apocrypha"—that is, the surviving gospels, acts, epistles, and apocalypses that were not included in the New Testament. I wasn't able to tell Sheila much more about it.

Her question struck me as odd—why would she be asking me about a gospel that hardly anyone had ever heard of, and that no one had ever seen? I decided to reread the ancient discussions of the Gospel of Judas, just to refresh my memory. It did not take long, as the gospel is mentioned in only a couple of ancient sources.

The earliest is the church father Irenaeus, who in 180 CE wrote a five-volume refutation of different Christian "heretics" (that is, those who held to the "wrong beliefs"), especially groups of gnostics. The gnostics believed that the way to salvation was not through belief in the death and resurrection of Jesus, but through the secret knowledge (*gnosis* is the Greek word for knowledge) that Jesus delivered, not to the crowds but to his inner circle. This secret knowledge revealed how people can escape the prisons of their material bodies to return to the spiritual realm whence they came. Some gnostic groups had highly esoteric and mysterious views of the world. In one of the most important archaeological discoveries of the twentieth century, a collection of gnostic writings was uncovered in 1945 near the Egyptian town of Nag Hammadi. These Nag Hammadi documents included a number of previously lost gospels—including the Gospel of Thomas and the Gospel of Philip—but they did not contain a copy of the Gospel of Judas.

In any event, Irenaeus does indicate that the Gospel of Judas was used by a group of gnostics called the Cainites. These people believed that the world had been created not by the One True God, but by a lesser, ignorant deity—the God of the Old Testament, who was not to be trusted or followed. The true God was above the inferior God of the Jews. And so, according to the Cainites, anyone who opposed the God of the Jews by breaking his law—as done, for example, by Cain, the first fratricide, and the men of Sodom and Gomorrah—was actually standing for the truth. The Cainites allegedly had a gospel that supported their rather peculiar theology. This gospel was written in the name of Judas Iscariot, known throughout Christian history as the traitor, the one disciple of Jesus who had turned evil and betrayed his master. According to the Cainites, however, what Judas had done was not evil. He alone was the one who understood the mysteries of Jesus and did Jesus' will. All the other disciples, who worshiped the false Jewish God, failed to understand the truth of Jesus.

After doing this research on the lost Gospel of Judas, I received a second phone call. This one was from a woman who worked for the National Geographic Society. She too wanted to know about the Gospel of Judas. This time I was better prepared and could tell her all that we knew—or that I thought we knew—about the gospel. After a brief discussion, she wanted to know if I thought it would be a significant discovery if the Gospel of Judas were to turn up. I wondered, of course, why she was asking. Rarely does anyone call a scholar to pose a purely hypothetical question about an unlikely discovery. Had the book been found?

I was cautious in my response. In my opinion, if the Gospel of Judas turned up, it would undoubtedly be very interesting for scholars of ancient Christianity. But would it be headline news? It depended entirely on what was *in* the gospel. If, for example, the gospel was like most of the writings discovered near Nag Hammadi, a book that explained how the world came into existence and how people might escape their entrapment in matter, that would further our knowledge about early Christian gnosticism—obviously a very good thing, but not earth-shattering. If, on the other hand, this gospel included an ancient version of the story of Jesus from the perspective of Judas himself and embraced a view at odds with the one that became "orthodox" throughout the history of the Christian church—a discovery of that kind would be absolutely phenomenal. It would be one of the most significant archaeological discoveries of modern times, certainly the most important of the past sixty years.

She thanked me for the information and we ended the call.

A few days later, she called back with stunning information. As it turns out, the Gospel of Judas had turned up in Egypt, in a manuscript written in Coptic (the ancient Egyptian language that the Nag Hammadi documents were also written in). It was in the possession of a group in Switzerland called the Maecenas Foundation, which was interested in involving National Geographic in the publication and dissemination of the text. In response, the Society was concerned, first off, to learn if this was the real thing or a later forgery.

There was a range of interrelated questions: Was this new discovery the gospel that Irenaeus and other church fathers had castigated as a gnostic creation, telling the story of Jesus from Judas's perspective? How old was the manuscript that contained the gospel? And when was the gospel itself originally composed? National Geographic needed an expert to verify the discovered text and wanted to know if I could help.

To say I was thrilled would be a profound understatement. Few scholars have the chance to be on the ground floor of a significant discovery. And this might be just that. Of course, it might also be a hoax. Hence the need to verify the facts.

I agreed to help. What the Society wanted was my expertise on early Christianity, to help them see the broad historical significance of a text like this. They were also planning to secure the services of a scientist who could provide a carbon-14 dating of the manuscript. I told them that they would also need a Coptologist—someone whose expertise was in ancient Coptic (my own research specialty is ancient Greek manuscripts). A good Coptologist could examine the text and give an estimate of its date simply based on the style of handwriting. And so, a three-person team was assembled: Tim Jull, director of the National Science Foundation–Arizona Accelerator Mass Spectrometer Facility in Tucson, the expert in carbon-14 dating; Stephen Emmel, an

American-born professor of Coptic at the University of Münster in Germany; and myself, historian of early Christianity.

We flew to Geneva in December 2004 and under secretive conditions were shown the documents. They surpassed even our most sanguine expectations. There was no doubt in my mind that this was the real thing. Even though my expertise is Greek rather than Coptic, I have read enough ancient manuscripts to know one when I see one. The form of the manuscript and the style of writing looked very similar to what you can find in Greek manuscripts of the fourth century. My best guess at first glance was that this was from that period. Could it be a modern forgery? Not a chance.

Everyone on the team had lots of questions. Foremost for me was the content of the document. Turning to the final page, I could see the title (titles come at the end of documents in ancient texts): *Peuaggelion Nioudas*, Coptic for "The Gospel of Judas." And I could make out a bit of the Coptic at the conclusion where the text indicates that "he handed him over to them." But what was the rest of it about? Was it a gospel that took Judas's side in the story of the betrayal, answering why he had done it? Or was it another gnostic text filled almost entirely with mystical reflections about the divine realm and about how this world came to be, with Judas playing at best a minor role? The significance of the document hung on these questions.

There were yet other pressing questions. Where was the text found? Who discovered it? When? Where had it been in all the years since its discovery? Why had none of us heard about it? Who so far had seen it? How did it come to be in the possession of the Maecenas Foundation, the group that evidently owned it? Could they be trusted to make the text available to the rest of the world, scholars and nonscholars alike? How would they publish it? Who would translate it? And so on.

These questions are answered in the present book—a riveting account by Herb Krosney, who first alerted the National Geographic Society to the existence of the document and convinced the Society to consider seriously its possible publication. More than anyone else, Herb has pursued the question of the document's discovery some three decades ago and its very peculiar pilgrimage in the intervening years. With the tenacity of a top-flight investigative reporter, he pursued every facet of the discovery and reclamation of the text. With an uncanny knack for piecing together isolated data, Herb has provided us with scores of details that, were it not for his efforts, would have been lost forever. This book provides far more information about the discovery, fate, and ultimate publication of the Gospel of Judas than we have for any other archaeological discovery of modern times—including such significant finds as the Dead Sea Scrolls and the Nag Hammadi library.

The most significant factor, of course, is the content of the newly discovered document. As it turns out, my highest hopes have been realized. For this is a gospel that tells the tale of Jesus from the viewpoint of Judas Iscariot himself, the one who allegedly betrayed him. As one might expect, this perspective is completely different from what one finds in the canonical accounts of the New Testament Gospels. In the books of Matthew, Mark, Luke, and John, Judas is the villain. In this newly discovered gospel, he is the hero.

It is worth noting that even though the Gospels of the New Testament agree in vilifying Judas, they do not agree on many of the details of his betrayal. The first Gospel to be written was that of Mark, from about 65 or 70 CE (35–40 years after the death of Jesus), and in that account, there is no clue given as to why Judas decided to turn Jesus over to the authorities, leading to his trial and crucifixion. Written somewhat later (80–85 CE), the Gospel of Matthew indicates that Judas did it for money: He was paid thirty pieces of silver for his foul deed. But when he saw that Jesus was condemned, Judas repented and hanged himself out of remorse. Written at about the same time as Matthew, the Gospel of Luke suggests that Judas was inspired by the Devil, so the betrayal was a Satanic act against the Son of God. The final Gospel to be written was John's, in which Judas himself is said to have been "a devil."

In all these accounts, Judas is the fallen disciple, the one betrayer of the cause, the traitor. Yet there are details within these accounts that are difficult—well nigh impossible, in fact—to reconcile with one another. For example, among the Gospels, only Matthew indicates that Judas killed himself. The author of the Gospel of Luke, however, also wrote the Book of Acts, and there we have a different version of Judas's death—we are told that he fell headlong and his "bowels burst open." Moreover, in Matthew's gospel the "blood money" that Judas had returned to the priests out of remorse was used to buy a field to bury strangers in—hence it was called the "Field of Blood" (having come from blood money); in the account in Acts, it is Judas himself who bought the field, which was given its name because he poured out his blood on it.

My point is that each of the individual authors of the New Testament had his own perspective on Judas and told the stories about him in light of that perspective. That continued to be true after the time of the New Testament, as legends about Judas circulated widely. Among the most nefarious of these legends are the ones that paid close attention to the name "Judas," a name etymologically related to the word *Jew*. Judas, by the Middle Ages, became synonymous with the "faithless Jew"—the one who was a greedy, money-hungry, thieving, deceitful, treacherous "Christ-killer."

Some modern scholars have tried to resuscitate the reputation of Judas, but on rather unconvincing textual evidence. Our early records all portray him as the villain in the story of Jesus. But what if there were other portrayals of Judas available that cast him in a more positive light, that interpret his actions differently from the way they are portrayed in the four Gospels that happened to make it into the New Testament?

Now we do have a different depiction.

The Gospel of Judas is a gnostic document, and as such explains in some detail how our evil material world came into being and how we came to be entrapped here. This explanation is understood to be mysterious and secret—it is not for everyone to hear, only the insiders. But the Gospel of Judas is more than simply an additional gnostic text. It is an early gospel that provides an alternative understanding of Jesus, told from the point of view of his betrayer. In this account, Judas is the consummate insider, the one to whom Jesus delivers his secret revelation. Judas is the one faithful disciple, the one who understands Jesus, the one who receives salvation. The other disciples, and the religion they represent, are rooted in ignorance.

As these brief remarks should make clear, this gospel does not conform to traditional Christianity as it emerged in the early centuries to become the most important religious movement in the history of Western civilization. It is an alternative vision of what it means to follow Christ and to be faithful to his teachings.

In this book we learn about how, when, and where this vision was discovered, how it came into the hands of antiquities dealers and how it finally ended up with competent experts who have spent years piecing together the fragmentary text and making it available to us in a modern translation. All of us should be grateful not only for the superb efforts of the translator of this text—

the Swiss Coptic scholar Rodolphe Kasser—and the work of the National Geographic Society for putting in the time and expense to make it widely available, but also to Herb Krosney, who has made the story of the Gospel's discovery and history now accessible to everyone.

# WHO'S WHO IN *THE LOST GOSPEL*

ANCIENT
Jesus
Judas Iscariot
St. Irenaeus, *early church father and author of* Against Heresies
St. Athanasius, *bishop of Alexandria*

MODERN
Am Samiah (pseudonym), *Egyptian villager*
Hanna Asabil (pseudonym), *antiquities dealer, Egypt*
Ludwig Koenen, *papyrologist, U.S.*
Nicolas Koutoulakis, *antiquities dealer, Switzerland*
Yannis Perdios, *antiquities collector, Greece*
James M. Robinson, *early Christianity scholar, U.S.*
Stephen Emmel, *Coptic scholar, Germany*
Boutros (pseudonym), *Egyptian villager*
Frieda Tchacos Nussberger, *antiquities dealer, Switzerland*
Father Gabriel Abdel Sayed, *Coptic priest, U.S.*
Hans P. Kraus, *rare book dealer, U.S.*
Joanna Landis (pseudonym), *Alexandria resident, Egypt*
Roger Bagnall, *classics scholar, U.S.*
Martin Schoyen, *antiquities collector, Norway*
Bruce Ferrini, *antiquities dealer, U.S.*
William Veres, *antiquities dealer, U.K.*
James Ferrell, *antiquities collector, U.S.*
Mario J. Roberty, *lawyer, Switzerland*
Michel van Rijn, *antiquities blogger, U.K.*
Rodolphe Kasser, *Coptic scholar, Switzerland*
Florence Darbre, *papyrus conservator, Switzerland*
Charles Hedrick, *Coptic scholar, U.S.*
Bart D. Ehrman, *early Christianity scholar, U.S.*
A. J. Timothy Jull, *radiocarbon-dating scientist, U.S.*

*Truly, truly I say to you, the man who betrays the Son of God,*
*it is better that he had never been born.*
—THE BOOK OF MATTHEW

He's one of the most hated men in history—the apostle who betrayed Jesus Christ. Judas Iscariot. For centuries, his name has been synonymous with treachery and deceit.

In the mid- to late 1970s, hidden for more than fifteen hundred years, an ancient text emerged from the sands of Egypt. Near the banks of the Nile River, some Egyptian peasants, *fellahin,* stumbled upon a cavern. In biblical times, such chambers had been used to bury the dead. The peasants entered the cave, seeking ancient gold or jewelry, anything of value that they could sell. Instead, among a pile of human bones, they discovered a crumbling limestone box. Inside it, they came upon an unexpected find—a mysterious leather-bound book, a codex. The illiterate peasants couldn't decipher the ancient text, but they knew that old books fetched a good price in Cairo's antiquities markets. This one was made of papyrus, ancient Egypt's form of paper.

The fellahin had no idea that what they were holding was one of the greatest prizes of biblical archaeology: A document stained by the label "heresy" and condemned eighteen hundred years ago.

In April 2000, approximately twenty-two years later, antiquities dealer Frieda Tchacos Nussberger was headed to John F. Kennedy International Airport in New York when she received some stunning news. She'd recently bought the ancient codex from an Egyptian dealer and had taken it to Yale University to have it examined. Now, on her cell phone, a manuscripts expert at Yale dropped a bombshell. "Frieda, it's fantastic!" he said in an extremely emotional voice. "This is a very important document. I think it's the Gospel of Judas!"

For Nussberger, it was the payoff for years of pursuit. She had become obsessed with the mysterious codex without ever knowing what it contained. Could there really be a Gospel of Judas?

Oddly, for someone so notorious, we know very few facts about Judas Iscariot. He was one of the Twelve Apostles. He most likely came from Judea, not Galilee like Jesus and the others. Judas was the apostles' treasurer and, by some gospel accounts, Jesus' most trusted ally, making his betrayal all the more contemptible.

But if the details of his life are murky, there's no question about Judas's place in history. "He's the one who handed over his friend," Marvin Meyer, one of the translators of the newly discovered gospel, explained. "He's the one who brought about the Crucifixion, and he's the one who's damned for all time." In Dante's *Inferno*, Judas is condemned to the lowest pits of hell, where he is eaten, head first, by a giant raptor belonging to Lucifer himself.

"Generally today people think of Judas principally as the betrayer of Jesus, somebody who was a traitor to the cause," scholar Bart Ehrman, noted for his studies of early Christianity, remarked recently. "Often they think of him as somebody who was greedy, avaricious, and who was more interested in making money than in being faithful to his master."

"The word itself is despised," Dr. William Klassen added. "I think virtually throughout the Western world, you wouldn't even call your dog that. And in Germany, of course, it is illegal to name your child Judas."

Christ and his apostles were all observant Jews, Orthodox by today's standards. But in time Judas's dark deed came to represent the supposed villainy of their entire faith. "Traditionally in Christian circles, Judas in fact has been associated with Jews," Ehrman notes. "Not just because of his name, but also because of these characteristics that became stereotypes for Jews in the Middle Ages—this stereotype of being traitors, avaricious, who betray Jesus. And this portrayal of Judas, of course, also leads then to horrendous acts of anti-Semitism through the centuries."

The stain that marks him is based on just twenty-four lines in the Gospels. As C. Stephen Evans, professor of philosophy at Baylor University, said: "Judas Iscariot in the New Testament doesn't appear much, and I think it's because he's an embarrassment. What little is said about him is very sinister, so he's portrayed in increasingly villainous terms as a thief who steals from the money box. Indeed, even as a person who was influenced by Satan."

History, however, records that there was once another written source of information about Judas Iscariot. Around 180 CE, Irenaeus, a church father in what is now France, wrote a scathing attack against a Greek text entitled the Gospel of Judas. "This gospel was about the relationship between Jesus and Judas, and indicated that Judas didn't actually betray Jesus, but did what Jesus wanted him to do, because Judas was the one who really knew the truth, as Jesus wanted it communicated," Ehrman said.

This version of Judas's story was too controversial for early Church leaders like Irenaeus. By condemning it, they erased it from history, never to be seen again.

But never is a long time, and the gospel was suppressed only until it could be found again. At least one copy of it had survived, laying dormant in a lightless vault in the arid Egyptian desert for most of two millennia until it was suddenly brought forth again, eventually finding its way decades later into Frieda Nussberger's custody.

This codex—one of the greatest discoveries in Judeo-Christian archaeology—did not head straight to a museum, nor even to the library of a rich collector. The gospel's removal from its burial place was just the beginning of a bizarre cloak-and-dagger journey. The Gospel of Judas, treated like a piece of merchandise, would be shopped around on three continents over the course of the next twenty-five years, its contents glimpsed only a few times between long periods of inactivity in far from ideal storage conditions. Every step of the way the precious document would deteriorate, until much of it was reduced to fragments of papyrus fibers.

The people who discovered it, bound together with three other texts, knew only that it was very old and would be worth good money. They sold it to a dealer in Cairo, who couldn't read the ancient Coptic either, but knew that it was extremely valuable if only he could find the right buyer.

The humid air of Egypt's capital city contrasts sharply with the arid climate of the desert where the codex was found, and humidity, combined with heat, is a factor that contributes greatly to the deterioration of perishable matter. The papyrus documents would languish while the dealer demanded millions of dollars for their purchase.

The manuscripts were then stolen and landed in Europe—more precisely, Switzerland—where, exposed to the Alpine air, the process of deterioration would continue. Not for the last time, the texts were left to molder in a bank vault. They were subsequently examined by experts who flew in from the United States to determine their authenticity. Already at that stage, warnings were raised about their state of deterioration. The scholars wanted the damage brought under control through careful management and the provision of proper environmental conditions, but that would be years in coming.

The codex next journeyed to the United States for a possible sale. A famous manuscript dealer in New York examined the text yet again but, uncomfortable with the Egyptian seller's price and the cost of restoration, decided against buying them. Despairing, the Cairo dealer finally put the documents in a bank vault on suburban Long Island, where no one had any idea of their condition or even their existence. There they would deteriorate for sixteen long years.

At last, Nussberger rescued them from the bank vault and turned them over to Yale University for inspection. There, a scholar identified the subject of the texts and some of what they said. For a brief period it seemed the codex—its importance discovered—had found a home at last. Yet Nussberger has spoken of the text as "a curse," and it did seem that way. The stigma of the great betrayer would linger on long after the discovery of the manuscript. It was almost as though the text didn't want to be read.

Despite the fact that they contained the fabled Gospel of Judas, Yale was worried about possible legal issues and declined to buy them. Instead they were sold to an antiquities dealer in Ohio.

They disintegrated further when they were briefly stored in the freezer compartment of a refrigerator.

A botched sale led to the manuscript's return to Nussberger and Switzerland, where they would finally find a home where ambient conditions would be adjusted to ensure their future preservation. By this time the fragile papyrus had deteriorated dramatically, with fragments dropping off at the touch. Not only that, but scholars found that pages of the priceless texts were missing, ripped out, possibly to be sold separately.

Each stage of this journey had brought additional damage. Each stage caused the increasingly frail strands of papyrus to deteriorate further, threatening the loss of additional letters, words, and sentences of the ancient texts. Each stage of the journey might cause this voice of Judas Iscariot, now arisen from a centuries-old tomb, to be degraded to the point where it might never be heard.

From the moment Frieda Tchacos Nussberger had learned from the Yale experts what was contained in the mysterious codex, she had been in a race against time to find a buyer who would be able to preserve its pages before they turned to dust. She eventually turned it over to the Maecenas Foundation of Ancient Art in Basel, Switzerland, which specializes in supporting archaeological study projects in ancient cultures or antiquities such as this. Together with Maecenas she engaged Rodolphe Kasser, one of the world's preeminent translators and scholars of Coptic, the rare and ancient language in which the text is written. Seeing how badly it had deteriorated, he joined forces with a superb document restorer, Florence Darbre.

In 2002, in her studio in Switzerland, Darbre opened the box containing the Gospel of Judas for the very first time. "I had to look at it. I had to open and close the box several times," she said. "One often needs to have nerves of steel in order to touch certain objects." In thirty years of work, she had never seen an ancient document in such bad condition. Its fragile papyrus pages had broken into thousands of fragments. "Whatever document you work with, there is always a story. One always wonders who wrote it, where did it go, who had it, and who read it?"

To get answers, Kasser and Darbre would begin a painstaking process of piecing together the fragments—fragments that tell a story early church fathers had successfully suppressed. But even in its decrepit state, one line begged for an explanation: its title, *Peuaggelion Nioudas*, in Coptic—"the Gospel of Judas."

It was one of the most complex puzzles ever contrived by history. The gospel was written on thirteen sheets of papyrus both front and back—twenty-six numbered pages, from pages 33 to 58 in the codex—but the papyri were now in myriad pieces. If a fragment fit on one side, it must also fit on the other. Kasser put the immense difficulties of reconstructing it into perspective: "If you take a nine- to ten-page typed document and rip it up into tiny pieces, throw away half the pieces, and try to reconstruct the other half, you will see how difficult this process is."

To avoid touching the actual document until they have to, they have devised an ingenious plan. First, using photographs of both the fragments and the pages, Kasser looks for a match. Then, working with photocopies, he cuts and pastes the pieces together. "Each time that we are able to place a fragment," Kasser explains, "I bring a photocopy of it to Madame Darbre who uses it to place the fragment within the original." Then Darbre tests whether Kasser was right. "We fathom the meaning of the codex little by little, thanks to these victories," Darbre says. "The more fragments are added, the more we can read, and the more the story is revealed."

Another scholar, Gregor Wurst, devised a computer program to help identify the papyri fibers so the pieces could more easily fit together. There are hundreds of fragments left to place, but what they've revealed is already dramatic. The text tells a story of the last days of Jesus Christ—one that could challenge some of Christianity's most deeply held beliefs. In it, the betrayer becomes a hero, and Jesus Christ arranges his own execution. The text matches the document Irenaeus railed against eighteen hundred years ago. The proof is in some of its most chilling lines, where Jesus gives Judas his mission of betrayal, saying: "You will exceed all of them. For you will sacrifice the man that clothes me."

American scholar Stephen Emmel, who was one of the first to see it, observes, "It could be explosive for a lot of people. It could create a crisis of faith." Professor Kasser adds, "It is certainly one of the greatest discoveries of this century. It is a great discovery because it is an authentic testimony."

CHAPTER ONE

# A DESERT GRAVE

*Jesus told Judas, "Lift up your eyes and look at the cloud
and the light within it and the stars surrounding it.
The star that leads the way is your star."*
—THE GOSPEL OF JUDAS

The Jebel Qarara hills rise dramatically out of the Egyptian
desert. They are only a few minutes' walk from the Nile River,
but the climate in the barren hills is drier than in the river valley.
Up in the heights, arid winds sweep down regularly onto the sand-
scalloped plains. In their journeys they whistle past the caves that
puncture the stark cliffs of the Jebel Qarara.

The *fellahin* came upon the burial place by accident. These peasants were probably like many in the area, poor farmers who had to
scratch out their sustenance from the earth. They were willing to
do whatever they had to do to provide for their families. For many,
that meant exploring the local area for hidden antiquities. Grave
robbing has been practiced in Egypt since the days when the first
pyramids were built, and although those pharaohs' tombs have

long since been stripped clean, many other remains can be gleaned from the four thousand years of Egypt's glorious past. Because the market for antiquities is underground—like the places where many antiquities come from—it can be highly profitable.

The burial cave was located across the river from Maghagha, not far from the village of Qarara in what is known as Middle Egypt. The fellahin stumbled upon the cave hidden down in the rocks. Climbing down to it, they found the skeleton of a wealthy man in a shroud. Other human remains, probably members of the dead man's family, were with him in the cave. His precious books were beside him, encased in a white limestone box.

The peasant and his friends recognized that the cache was ancient. Perhaps it was even from the time of the pharaohs. Whatever period the box came from, it was an answer to their prayers. They had found treasure. They were winners of one of the great lotteries of Egypt. The sum they could fetch for it would provide them a week or a month or a year of the basics of daily life, depending how clever they were in selling their wares.

They immediately contacted Am Samiah, a local scout. Such agents acted as middlemen, selling the antiquities to dealers in Cairo, Egypt's capital city. The lucky fellahin brought Am Samiah to the cave to see the valuable cache. The job of sorting out the treasure had to be done discreetly. Not only did they fear the police but also other local peasants who might try to steal away their prize.

Two caskets were set near the entrance. As they were handling the sarcophagus, it broke, and part of it shattered. Inside they discovered a skeleton. Alongside it were a number of glass flasks of Roman manufacture, encased in a wrapping of straw or papyrus.

Last of all, they uncovered the texts. Their discovery was a gift of great fortune. Am Samiah was, like the fellahin, a working man whose principal interest was not the manuscripts' value to humankind. He did not care particularly what the manuscripts said, or in which language they were written. He was primarily concerned with how much he could sell them for to help support his family. Sadly, this has been the case with other artifacts found in Egypt. If fellahin have any interest in scholarship, it stems from the fact that if the scholars value an artifact highly, it will sell for a higher price. Those antiquities that end up in museums sell for the best price of all.

At first, the dealers who later examined the manuscripts thought that the writing might be in the ancient and traditional language of the Jews, Hebrew. That was not the case. The primary text is in Coptic, the ancient language of the people who lived in this great valley, who adopted the letters of the Greek alphabet as part of their writing system. Coptic is the ancestral tongue of the many Christians who live in the area. Some Copts speculated that the text was a testament of Saint Mark, the venerated evangelist. That, too, was not the case, although the papyrus texts were written by someone familiar with those gospels that would become the "canon," or official literature, of the Christian church.

Unbeknownst to Am Samiah or the fellahin, the papyrus cache would turn out to be one of the greatest discoveries of the twentieth century. Such a treasure trove had not been unearthed since the historic discovery at Nag Hammadi, farther down the Nile River, where in December 1945, a group of farmers found fifty-two documents stored in a clay jar—an immense find that rivals the discovery of the Dead Sea Scrolls. The world of biblical study was blown wide open by the Nag Hammadi library, because the cache included many gnostic texts, condemned by some early church fathers as heresy. Yet these books also had spread the good news of Jesus, and what they had to say often differed radically from the texts included in the New Testament.

The white limestone sarcophagus discovered by the Qarara peasants contained texts that spoke of Jesus but had not been accepted by the orthodox church. One in particular would excite scholars' interest: the Gospel of Judas. This twenty-six-page papyrus manuscript hinted at a secret plan Jesus had for Judas. He had asked his most trusted disciple to undertake the greatest sacrifice of all: to betray him and hand him over for execution in order to liberate his soul from the confines of his body and to thus fulfill destiny. The book gave clues to where this man really stood among the apostles who loved Jesus—a disciple who would be despised because of the task Jesus entrusted to him.

The narrative these papyrus pages recounted offered a startling new twist to the ancient narrative that was holy to millions of Christians throughout the world. Sometime in the distant past, a scribe of a Christian sect had written this gospel. Judas's side of the familiar narrative had never been told before. Whoever wrote it believed, in contradiction to all that had been recounted elsewhere, in the betrayer's goodness and in his unique understanding of Jesus' message. Now those words from centuries past could once more be read. Judas, or whoever wrote about him, was able at long last to tell the betrayer's side of the story.

Any exploration of Christianity in Egypt rightfully should start in the fabled city of Alexandria. The Christian Coptic Orthodox Church claims a lineage stemming from the teachings of St. Mark, who wrote the oldest Gospel in the New Testament. According to the Copts' account, Mark came to Alexandria during the reign of Emperor Nero in the 50s CE, and later he was killed there during a Jewish revolt against Roman soldiers trying to suppress their religious practices in 68.

The city was originally named after Alexander the Great, who, as a dashing young man, led his Macedonian armies through western Asia and united the known world under his rule. He founded this city as his gift to the gods and his people. It would flourish as the capital of Egypt for the next three hundred years under Ptolemy, one of Alexander's generals, and his successors. Alexandria's library became the largest of ancient times, and its lighthouse was one of the Seven Wonders of the Ancient World. It was also, according to popular myth, where Cleopatra seduced Julius Caesar, and after his assassination, seduced Mark Antony.

Alexandria today is the second largest city in Egypt, with six million inhabitants. Its fabled corniche along the Mediterranean Sea extends a dozen miles, while the city itself stretches southward for miles from the shore. Fittingly, given the city's strong Greek historical ties, the corniche offers a breathtaking vista north over blue waters in the direction of Crete and the Greek mainland a few hundred miles away. Here its British colonial exterior remains, recalling the storied days of early twentieth-century rule chronicled so vividly by Lawrence Durrell in his celebrated *The Alexandria Quartet*. Yet, on closer look, the houses resemble much of the rest of Egypt, broken down and deteriorated. Along the celebrated corniche, as well as inland, splendid houses have been replaced by faceless multistory apartment buildings. Alexandria is in the process of becoming an overcrowded metropolis, a city now remote from its Greek origins and defined by both the modernistic architecture of its newly rebuilt library and the increasing popularity of the Islamic faith, as evidenced by the growing number of women wearing the modest head coverings of the believer.

The city's link to the Gospel of Judas is Joanna Landis, one of the inhabitants of this bustling seaport, because Am Samiah took her to a remote location on the east bank of the Nile where an intriguing find had been made. Alexandria is a primary center for Egyptian exports, including Egyptian folk art and ancient objects. Ancient Egypt was one of the greatest of the early civilizations, and the wonders of Tutankhamun's tomb are only the most spectacular of the finds from a past that has spanned five thousand years. On a more common level, Egypt is filled with small-time traders ready to do whatever is necessary to earn an extra pound or an extra dollar, whether it is selling a trinket, amulet beads, a local piece of handicraft—or, with great luck, a major sculpture or papyrus text from antiquity.

Joanna was a dabbler in folk crafts and art objects who made occasional visits south to Middle and Upper Egypt. Her trips were also spiritual journeys into the past of the country she loved. Joanna was enthralled by ancient Egypt and how the centuries rolled by one after the other as she drove along the Nile River. The word *nile* comes from the Greek *nelios*, meaning "river valley," and the inhabitants on its banks believe that the Nile is the source of all prosperity. And they have good reason, since its thousand-mile ribbon cuts through a country otherwise dominated by the Sahara desert. The Nile Delta in the north is so fertile that it was the granary for the Roman Empire.

On those riverbanks that were once flooded every summer, Joanna could see a panorama of life, with the peasant villages and the never-changing ways of farming the land. Interconnecting canals divert the river and provide channels of irrigation for miles inland. At harvest time in late April, horse-drawn carts pull wagons loaded with green shoots of wheat and a green grass for animal feed that the Arabs call *bersim,* which is a kind of clover. The miles and miles of wheat waving gently in the Egyptian sun are dotted with scarecrows, most wearing a *galabiya*, an Egyptian robe, to frighten away hungry birds.

Driving south from the coast, the sights of the Nile Delta are soon replaced by the teeming urban mélange that is Cairo. The capital of Egypt and the largest city in Africa, with a population that has swelled in recent years to sixteen million, Cairo spreads across both banks of the Nile, covering an area of more than 175 square miles. Numerous suburbs extend outward from it. South of downtown is Old Cairo, the home of the Coptic Christian community and a number of Coptic churches with their distinctive crosses rising from their cupolas. Old Cairo lies across the river from the Sphinx and the three famous pyramids of Giza, tombs of ancient Egyptian pharaohs. To the south stretch miles of additional pyramids, rising on the western bank of the Nile Valley. In Saqqara stands the famous Step Pyramid, and in Danshur rise the massive Bent Pyramid and the Red Pyramid, two of the earliest ever built, as far back as 2600 BCE.

One destination of Joanna's forays was in Al Minya province, located in an area commonly referred to as Middle Egypt, where many Egyptian Christians still live. She would pass small farm villages marked by mud-brick hovels until reaching one of the northernmost towns in Al Minya, Maghagha, 120 miles south of Cairo. Pronounced Mu-RAIR-a, Maghagha is a dirty, busy town in which Coptic Christians compose some 15 percent of the population. Coptic churches, with their ornate crosses, are scattered throughout the area.

Christianity spread down the Nile Valley during the centuries of Roman rule. Egypt is the the place where the idea of a lone man, a hermit, living in isolated contemplation while he attained a state of holiness, may have started, at least in the Western world. It is also the home of the first Christian monasteries, and it may be that the scribe who copied the Gospel of Judas into Coptic did so in one of these monasteries.

The area brims with religious history. In the southern reaches of Middle Egypt lies Tell el-Amarna. In the fourteenth century BCE, Pharaoh Akhenaten declared Aten, the sun god, as the only true god, a precursor to monotheism. To ensure Aten's dominance over all other Egyptian gods, he built a new capital at Amarna, replete with fabulous white temples. Aten's reign would perish, however, with Akhenaten's death, and the capital was moved back to Thebes, where his son, the glittering Tutankhamun, would soon rule.

On one trip to Maghagha in 1978, Joanna sought out Am Samiah, a native of the village who she thought might help her locate some interesting pieces. She knew he was always on the lookout for artifacts that could be sold to contacts in the bazaars of Cairo or Alexandria. On this occasion, Am Samiah told her of ancient documents he had found and recently sold. At the time, Joanna did not participate in the market for ancient papyri and she could not know the incalculable significance of that find, so she had no interest in acquiring these documents herself. Yet Am Samiah did take her to the place where the cache had been found.

As Joanna later recalled, Am Samiah "lived there with his numerous young children and wife in an unfinished two-story brick house. In his 'garage' was a beautiful ... camel, to whom he was feeding *foul* [the Egyptian grain staple], sometimes by hand. Am Samiah always wore galabiyas, like the three Magi of the Epiphany, with a lot of shawls around his head, but plastic sandals in summer or winter on his feet."

Am Samiah was, like many in Maghagha, a garlic farmer. Garlic is Maghagha's specialty. Fed by the Nile water and blazing Egyptian sunshine, the garlic is strongly flavored, although very small in size.

Also like many of the residents of Middle Egypt, Am Samiah was a member of the Christian Coptic Orthodox Church of Egypt. "He was a Copt by religion," Joanna continued. "You would know it immediately from the pictures of saints hanging in the waiting room of his house. That was a room, rather clean, with narrow benches all around, where visitors, mostly men, sit with their feet on the benches. He served *shai*, or tea, well boiled, in small cups with the little gold label of the shop still on, very tasty and strong with a lot of sugar and *nana*. Then *araq balah* [alcohol made from dates] in the evening."

Like Christians all across the Roman Empire, the Egyptian Christians were sometimes subjected to persecution during the first three centuries after Jesus, until Emperor Constantine legalized Christianity in 313. In the meantime, the new faith spread irrepressibly through Alexandria and all along the settlements of the Nile River.

When the Arabs conquered the country in the seventh century, they converted everyone they could to their new religion, Islam. The Arabs called the Egyptian natives Gypt, from the Greek word *Egyptos,* which in turn derives from Ha-Ka-Ptah, the name for Memphis, the capital of the ancient Egyptian empire. The word Copt, a corruption of "Gypt," thus means Egypt.

These Egyptians adopted the Greek alphabet to their language, but since it was lacking certain sounds, they added seven characters and wound up with an alphabet of thirty-two letters. With mounting frequency, they told the tales of their new religion and old culture in the native language and dialects of the regions of

Egypt where they lived. That combination of local language with Greek lettering became known as "Coptic."

The Copts claim that they are the pure Egyptians, and this designation is accepted by most Egyptian Muslims. The Muslim population of Egypt still refer to themselves as "Arabs" as well as Egyptians. The Coptic religion flourished even after the Arab conquest of Egypt in 641. Today roughly one out of every eight Egyptians is a Coptic Christian.

Joanna's remembrances of Am Samiah and what he told her revolved about the centuries-long history of the Nile Valley, where the same way of life is passed down from generation to generation. "The dry desert air that blows on the village carries the smell of home-baked bread. They bake on the roofs of their houses, the women sitting on the floor, and chitchat around the *tableya* [the low table on which they open the bread], their fingers tap-dancing on the dough, to make the Arab *regiff*. And the smell of the dry corn stalks, which they spread on the roof. If you eat one fresh-baked bread and fried eggs with *samna baladi* [cooked butter] you are ready to start business."

A hard worker, Am Samiah was persistent, warmhearted, open, and always hospitable to visitors. Besides garlic, Am Samiah, with his camels and his children, planted beans and wheat and sugar-cane and the animal feed that the local peasants call *barsim*. Nonetheless, he made only a meager living from the land. In order to supplement his income, he, like others in his region, searched for whatever he could buy and sell with a profit in the markets in Al Minya or those beyond, in Cairo or Alexandria. Most of the time, these objects were trinkets or amulet beads. Some were valuable, some not.

One major source of revenue was a number of ancient textiles, which Am Samiah and others began to discover in the area, both around Maghagha and in the hills across the Nile in the town called Qarara. The arid desert is a hospitable environment for the preservation of such fragile heirlooms. From the late 1960s to the early 1980s, Coptic textiles from the fourth and fifth century were found and exported.

"Am Samiah told me about a textile, an embroidered Coptic textile, that he had found and sold, Joanna recalled. "He was impressed, because it depicted el Adra—the Virgin Mary."

Joanna discovered in long talks with Am Samiah how he worked. He was not a digger or an excavator. He was a scout, seeking out whatever might be of value in his area of Egypt. He required mobility but couldn't afford a car, so a good friend proved a big help. Mahmoud, a worker in a government office near Maghagha, had a small car, and he became Am Samiah's colleague and even his partner in a number of the transactions.

The local Coptic villages in Middle Egypt were inhabited by people who were often illiterate, like Am Samiah, and they needed connections to sell the treasures of the past to dealers in Cairo or Alexandria. Am Samiah and Mahmoud, who was a Muslim, drove from place to place, contacting local jewelers. These jewelers have shops that are far more diverse than what a Westerner would think of as a store to buy jewelry. Sometimes they don't have any jewelry at all. They collect trinkets and amulets and icons and textiles and anything else that might have value. Some of the jewelers Am Samiah visited had shops in Cairo, or at least had connections with dealers whom they trusted in Cairo or Alexandria.

Naturally, each step of the process brought a markup. The Egyptian villagers—including the jewelers—did not participate in the markups that followed their initial one, but because they knew no language other than the local dialect, they needed middlemen who could take the goods to a wider market. The three-hour drive from Maghagha to Cairo brought a significant markup. Am Samiah could sell a valuable item for robust prices—as much as a thousand Egyptian pounds, the equivalent of three hundred dollars at the time, although most he sold for much less. The dealer in Cairo or Alexandria, with his connections, would slap on another price increase. If a connection could be made with wealthy European or American dealers, the price would be marked up yet again. When those dealers in turn sold the items to a museum, a wealthy private collector, or a university, that would entail still another markup.

The trade is as ancient as civilization itself. Art and old objects, along with agriculture and other goods, have been part of commerce in the eastern Mediterranean for at least three millennia. In the nineteenth century, Western explorers rediscovered Egypt and its ancient riches. Some of the country's greatest treasures, such as the Rosetta Stone, were either excavated or bought and then shipped to Europe and beyond, where they went on exhibit in museums from St. Petersburg to Berlin to London to Los Angeles.

The trade was of great benefit to Egypt. The antiquities were displayed in major institutions throughout the Western world. The exhibits in the West helped stimulate interest in Egyptian civilization and attracted visitors to the country—so much so that tourism increasingly became the country's major industry and principal source of hard currency. Many Egyptian leaders, however, saw the trade as a one-way affair, with their side on the short end.

After World War II, when the country gained full independence, the government almost immediately began to impose restrictions on the antiquities trade in an attempt to control it. This culminated in a 1983 law that, building on prior Egyptian legislation dating back to 1951, was designed to impose strict government regulation on the selling and export of antiquities. The law gave antiquities dealers six months in which to register certain objects in their possession and restricted their sale or export. Partly due to nationalism and the desire to protect what it considers its cultural heritage, the Egyptian government has sought to assert as much control over the industry as it can, including putting tough restrictions on exports. The governmental leaders want to supervise and control sales and revenues and to block anyone—Egyptian nationals included—from participating independently in the trade and profiting from it.

That attitude has hardly stopped the trade, however, although it has become increasingly illegal and far more difficult to pursue. The trade is fueled largely by the fact that a reservoir of potentially valuable goods is still buried in a country where it is often tough to eke out a living, and a diminishing but lucrative market for these goods exists wherever antiquity and ancient culture can be sold or displayed. The antiquities trade continues to be a moneymaker, though it now has to be pursued with much more cunning than in the past.

By the early 1980s, the issue of provenance had risen to the fore, and that is no less true today. As Egyptologist Robert Bianchi observed, "An object today is considered guilty until proven innocent." If an object of antiquity was exported from Egypt after the legislation regulating exports of antiquities became effective, the Egyptians may go after it with whatever legal force they can muster.

Egypt, with several other originating countries, has also attempted to reclaim objects that were exported from the country decades or even more than a century earlier. Negotiations and sometimes court cases between the originating countries for antiquities and some of the world's leading museums—such as the Getty Museum in Los Angeles, the Metropolitan Museum in New York, and the British Museum in London—have made newspaper headlines. Some of the goods are clearly stolen artifacts. In one stunning example, a top New York art dealer, Frederick Schultz, was convicted in 2002 for conspiring to receive stolen Egyptian antiquities, including a bust of a pharaoh that he later sold for $1.2 million—an object that British dealer Jonathan Tokely-Parry smuggled out of Egypt as a cheap souvenir.

During Joanna's visit to Maghagha in 1978, Am Samiah took her to the other side of the river to view the spot where the ancient codex, a bound group of texts, had been found. They crossed the Nile by boat, a typical handmade wooden felucca with unfurled sails and several oars thrown on board in case of an emergency. The sails had many patches to cover the tears, she remembered. The boatmen were experienced Nile sailors and guided the small craft through strong currents and shallow waters, heading for a lagoon on the eastern side.

"His wife and two children came along," Joanna recalled. "In her basket she carried some paraphernalia. But as we reached the middle of the river, she took out of her *zenbil* [basket] two cups and offered me the Nile water [*maya assleya*, the authentic water], scooped out of the river from the side of the boat. I was scared to drink [because of] *bilharzia*, but she insisted." Tasting the waters of the Nile is considered a blessing, though there is danger of serious infectious disease. "I must say, it was so sweet, I still have the taste in my mouth."

When they came to the other side, Joanna entered a new world. "A feeling of eternity befell me. Little children splashing water on their baby donkeys, their shiny sunbaked bodies glittering under the sun. It was a different world, no stress, no hurry, little donkeys were driven by children to the Nile, to be washed and stilled. It was as if two thousand years had never elapsed."

After disembarking, Joanna and Am Samiah walked on a dirt road up a hill. She could not recall how long they walked, but it was not far. The children who followed them (children and flies follow you everywhere in Egypt, Joanna noted) had slipped behind, raising a small cloud of dust. She saw a fortress-like building with thick mud walls. Joanna wondered if the walls were to protect the inhabitants from the oppressive summertime heat of the region or from outside enemies.

"We entered a courtyard, where chicken and dogs, children and goats lived happily together. We entered in the guest room, where tea was served ... sweet and hot with mint. Then Am Samiah got up and asked me to follow him: *Yialla al magara* [let's go to the cavern]; that is how he called the place we were heading to."

The site where Am Samiah wanted to take her was a series of catacombs. As far as she knew, they were unknown to Western archaeologists or any of the many Egyptologists who visited the area. "The amazing part of the trip was the catacombs," she said, "carved in the limestone slopes of the mountain. Big square pillars supported the alcoves, and they seemed endless. They reminded me of the Alexandrian catacombs in their style.

"A hole appeared suddenly in front of us, they lifted a big

stone, and we slid to an underworld of silence. It was an airy gallery, with many square columns, all of it cut out of the limestone rocks. We could stand and walk around easily. The only light streamed through the hole through which we entered. The place was clean, not smelly. The air was dry."

Another extraordinary revelation awaited her.

"On this occasion Am Samiah told me about the books. He told me a little—that they were found in a box, which he had sold not long ago. I asked him if it was in Greek. But he was illiterate. He didn't know which language it was, or whether it was one language or many. I asked him where he found it, and he answered, 'Fel gabal,' in the mountain."

Am Samiah told Joanna that he had sold the books some time before. He intimated that his dealer in Cairo had found the texts intriguing, and Am Samiah had made a good profit. He could look forward to better times. He could feed his family for many months. Possibly he would now buy his own car.

Standing in that cave, Joanna experienced a sudden feeling of fear and foreboding, almost mystical in its depth. She left that cave in a state of semi-panic, scrambling out of it, glad to see the light of day. But she would often wonder later what had really happened in Jebel Qarara and what had been found.

Joanna's tale is a unique testimony because Am Samiah wanted to tell her more, but was reluctant to do so, whether out of fear or discretion. Hers is so far the only account of a spectacular discovery. Some time afterward, Am Samiah died. The local scout who had played such an important role in bringing the Gospel of Judas to light took much of his knowledge of the find to his grave.

☥

Twenty-seven years later, Joanna tried to discover where exactly the codex had been found. After a considerable time spent searching, she managed to obtain a telephone number for Mahmoud, the man she understood to be connected to Am Samiah.

Mahmoud remembered her immediately. He was excited to hear from her after so much time. In his initial enthusiasm, he said he could help her gather details of the discovery. He told Joanna that he had been to the cave and knew precisely where the ancient texts had been found. It was where Joanna had visited. Mahmoud described the cave to Joanna in broad detail. He recalled a number of baskets with Roman glass flasks enclosed inside, that had found their way to the big city markets in Cairo and Alexandria.

However, he also issued a few warnings. The Egyptian authorities still did not know of the catacombs' existence. The opening had long since been covered up. The village people were worried about the *raffir,* the wardens, who now patrolled the general area. Mahmoud was willing to take her to the cave, but it would have to be at night, so they could evade the wardens and enter the cave. It would take some digging to get inside, and they would have to cover their tracks when they came out. She should bring along a friend. It could be a full night in the desert hills of Jebel Qarara.

There was another cautionary note. A second group had entered the cave after Am Samiah had been there, according to Mahmoud. They had emptied the cave of additional materials, beyond the texts that had been found in the first two caskets near the entrance. They were not such nice people. In fact, it was far better for one's health to be extremely wary about crossing them. They were the kind of people who would try to exact retribution if they were exposed.

Joanna set up a meeting with Mahmoud. They would meet a month later, after schedules could be arranged.

But in that month, things changed. Problems arose. In a follow-up phone call, Mahmoud told Joanna that, unfortunately, the burial place had been left much as the second group had left it, totally ransacked. There were skeletons scattered all about. The place was a mess. It looked like what it was: a burial site that had been plundered. All the objects were out of it; they had long since been sold in the markets of Cairo and Alexandria. Mahmoud had nothing to do with these later sales, but he had heard about them.

When at last the proposed meeting took place, Mahmoud greeted Joanna wearing a T-shirt rather than a galabiya. He was an athletically built, handsome fellow with a ready smile. His hair was cut short, and he had an intelligent, inquiring face. Yet Mahmoud began to pull back even further from his earlier statements. He was less precise about the catacombs' location. He told Joanna that the site was extraordinarily difficult to find for any outsider. The Antiquities Authority people did not know about it, and only he and several other local fellahin could find it.

His backpedaling continued. Yes, the texts were found in Jebel Qarara, but not exactly where Joanna had been, he now contended. The real cave was some five kilometers away. He reiterated that he was concerned about the raffir. He was prepared to take Joanna, but only if he was paid, and only if Joanna and her colleagues would assume all responsibility.

Presumably, by "responsibility" he was referring to a series of possible expenses: the legal bills that might be incurred in the event of arrest, the *baksheesh* required to bribe the group's way out of difficulty, or whatever might be required to pay off the second group for what they might consider as incursions on their "property." That is where negotiations broke down.

The idea of trespassing in an antiquities site in Egypt without proper permits was unappealing enough. In normal circumstances, eight different permits from eight different Egyptian ministries are required for every "sensitive" location, and all of Al Minya Province was in that category. In addition, such an expedition would require extraordinary preparation. There was genuine danger. Al Minya Province, a part of Egypt where a number of terrorist incidents initiated by Islamic terrorists had occurred, was considered a problematic security area. In the end, Mahmoud's offer was declined.

The manuscript's early trail has now gone cold and is reliably known only after it surfaced in Cairo. The Gospel of Judas was still an unknown quantity to its handlers. The Egyptian peasants who had taken it from its catacomb had no idea even what language it was written in. The dealer in Cairo to whom Am Samiah sold the codex would eventually learn slightly more, but would never realize what the Coptic words said. The fragile papyrus manuscript had begun its wayward journey toward an increasingly perilous future.

# CHAPTER TWO

# A KING'S RANSOM

*From what I've seen here, this is one of the greatest historical discoveries*
*of the twentieth century, assuming the dating bears out its origins. It's*
*certainly the greatest discovery of the last sixty years—since Nag*
*Hammadi and the Dead Sea Scrolls.*
—BART D. EHRMAN

Soon after its discovery in the Jebel Qarara tomb, the codex traveled north in Am Samiah's possession from Al Minya Province
to Cairo. Here it was sold to an antiquities dealer named Hanna
Asabil. Under his stewardship, the Gospel of Judas would undergo its most alarming phase of deterioration.

The documents were probably wrapped in newspaper for their
trip to the city, as they were later during inspections in Europe and
America. That is the way Egyptians transfer precious goods. Yet
papyrus can be soiled and destroyed by vermin or by damp. It can
be scorched by a searing sun or burned by fire. Though the documents could be worth millions of dollars, their value depended on
their staying intact.

Such neglect stems from the neglect that marks so many items in the Egyptian antiquities market. At the bottom end of the scale, papyrus can be found in flea markets such as Souq al-Goma'a, which attracts thousands of Cairo's poor every week. A factor in having a country so rich in artifacts is that the determination of their price is often set by the seller, whose knowledge is usually that of a shrewd businessman, not an academic.

Further complicating the picture is the secrecy that prevails in the world of Egyptian antiquities. Dealers rarely tell the whole truth to clients and, if forced to do so, do it sparingly. The truth can often get them in trouble. Ludwig Koenen, a professor at the University of Michigan and a noted papyrologist, put it succinctly: "When I lived in Egypt, I learned that you cannot trust what the seller or the dealer tells you."

Exaggerating, deceiving, and even outright lying are all part of negotiating in the Egyptian souk. It's simply part of the game, an essential element in the give and take that has gone on for generations. All means are justified to make an object appear valuable or authentic. An additional dictum is specific to antiquity dealing: protect your source. Exposing a source is a serious and even dangerous business. In the case of dealers, that also means never exposing exactly where your goods come from nor, necessarily, to whom you are in the process of selling.

Penalties can be harsh for betrayal. There are stories of Egyptian dealers killing one of their own for indiscreetly chatting about where someone else was getting his goods. Anyone who talks is considered a traitor to the whole profession.

Hanna would never tell where he was buying an object or to whom he was selling. What if his source had more items in the future? What if there were other potential buyers? Revealing who these buyers or sellers were did not increase the money paid. Any piece of information could lead only to harm, the least of which was to open up the deal to possible competition. That Hanna bought the codex manuscripts from Am Samiah was a secret, to be protected in the same way that Bob Woodward and Carl Bernstein hid the identity of Deep Throat for three decades after Watergate.

Hanna had a number of stories about how the codex was found and came to be in his possession. In one, he and his family had actually inherited the precious manuscripts from his father. The documents in all their variety had been passed down from father to son for generation after generation—no one could quite recall how many. As an embellishment to this story, Hanna sometimes related that his father had been a farmer at Beni Mazhar, north of the city of Minya. His father had collected the texts shortly after World War II—that is to say, certainly sometime before 1951, the date when several Egyptian laws governing antiquities were first enacted into law. The only problem with this tale is that no one believes it.

On one visit to a potential client, Hanna told a dealer colleague a second account of how the books were discovered. Two farmers were plowing their fields near Maghagha. The ground suddenly gave way, and they stumbled onto a tomb. There, they found the manuscripts wrapped in linen alongside a dead body—Hanna used the word "mummy" in Arabic, as well as the word "sarcophagus." This narrative is remarkably similar to how the famous codices were discovered at Nag Hammadi in 1945. No doubt Hanna was familiar with accounts of the famous Nag Hammadi find that was well covered in the Egyptian press.

Yet another version of the codex's origin comes from well-known Italian papyrologist Manfredo Manfredi, who was an acquaintance of Hanna in the early 1970s. Manfredi, a distinguished professor at the University of Florence in Italy, was a frequent visitor to Cairo. Hanna once told him that the manuscripts were found in a closed room, probably a tomb, in Hermopolis, which is located ten miles south of Al Minya. Whether that version has any validity is unknown.

In May 2004, Hanna reminisced that a number of manuscripts had found their way into his possession, some in Greek, some in Coptic (although it is doubtful whether Hanna could tell the difference). Those in Coptic were found near Maghagha, he said, probably in the Jebel Qarara hills just across the river. Those in Greek were found at a location in or around Beni Hassan, a historic site in the area.

Whatever the manuscripts' provenance, Hanna was in partnership with several Egyptian colleagues and had to share the profits with them. A friend and business associate of one of them, Boutros, told yet another account of those events of only a quarter century ago that still seem to lack form or clarity, much like the Egyptian mist that hovers over the river early in the morning before it is quickly burned away by the sun. Like several of the other versions, it is not without self-interest.

At 60, Boutros is a cautious, thin man with a slight pencil mustache and an occasional quick smile. According to Boutros, one of Hanna's colleagues, not Hanna himself, had initially bought the books from Am Samiah. The two came from the same area; the colleague lived in a town next to Maghagha called Sandafa el Far. He met the farmer by chance in a church only five or six miles from Maghagha—the Ambar, otherwise known as St. Samuel Church, is a monastery and famous Coptic place of religious worship.

Am Samiah invited that colleague to his house in Maghagha. At his house, Am Samiah showed him a portrait on a wall that depicted a Coptic personality: A saint, or possibly the Holy Family in Egypt—he could not remember precisely which.

That was during "the tenth month of the year 1981," according to Boutros. This date is at variance with all other dates gathered during this investigation, but other aspects of the story have the ring of truth.

Two months later, Am Samiah contacted the colleague and offered him the codex. According to Boutros, the colleague had "some shops in Cairo and also in Sohag in Upper Egypt." Hanna and his associates had been in business together and worked in a sort of loose partnership. The colleague took the books to Hanna in Cairo. Hanna was extremely pleased and took possession of them, hoping to make a fortune for himself and his family.

However, Hanna later cheated the colleagues, according to Boutros, by not splitting the sale of the manuscripts with them and giving them their rightful commissions. Boutros was angry—on his friends' behalf—and he wanted to collect his money. Boutros sought to arrange proper payment of the commission. No one could have believed that Hanna would cheat in such a manner, Boutros contended, and yet that is what happened. Hanna's defense through the years is that he supported his colleagues in other ways.

"He is the son of a dog," Boutros said bitterly about Hanna, years after the events.

Another possibility is that Hanna never knew precisely where the manuscripts were found. Am Samiah was an excellent "runner"—also referred to by the French *fournisseur,* a supplier—and just like Hanna, Am Samiah would not have been likely to reveal his sources unnecessarily. That could only lead to trouble.

Several danger points existed for Am Samiah at the time he possessed the manuscripts, requiring discretion and secrecy. First of all, competitors might go back to the same source and obtain similar manuscripts or documents (and, according to Mahmoud's account to Joanna, this in fact did happen). Second, he had to worry about law enforcement officials and how they might react. Third, somewhere up the line in Egypt might come requests for baksheesh, and some kind of payoff that would have to be made.

Discretion is the better part of valor. It is better not to say too much when conducting business in the antiquities market.

Hanna Asabil was short and stout and some thought him ugly because he had a goiter in his neck, which led to the nickname "Gwat." In addition, he was a chain-smoker. He often wore a light tan business suit that hung clumsily on his body. In the 1970s, Hanna was still a bachelor and, notwithstanding his goiter, an eligible one in the Coptic community in Cairo; though already more than forty years old, he was capable of earning a good living and supporting a family in style.

As soon as he saw Am Samiah's papyri, Hanna knew immediately that "the book," as he referred to the codex, was an item of potentially great value. He was ready to pay a high price for it. That sum was agreed quickly: 8,000 Egyptian pounds, a lucrative deal for Am Samiah, who was eager to sell. At the time, 8,000 Egyptian pounds was the equivalent of several thousand dollars, a number Hanna also confirmed to an intermediary. His partners in the deal, according to Boutros, gave Am Samiah's wife a few presents, including three gold bracelets, as a goodwill gesture.

Hanna is a devout Coptic Christian and a regular churchgoer. He is also a powerful "jeweler," in the Egyptian fashion of brokers who buy whatever local people have that is of potential value. Hanna and the many dealers like him are, in effect, linkage points to the outside world for the villagers. The connection with Hanna, among others, had enabled Am Samiah to become one of the more prosperous villagers in Maghagha.

The reason many antiquities are sold in Cairo is simple: It is one of the biggest markets in the world, for all sorts of goods. The city is as populous as Tokyo, with its sixteen million in the inner metropolitan area swelling to twenty million in daytime when workers and executives pour in from the outlying suburbs by train, car, bicycle, and even foot.

The city is famous for its constant noise—the honking of cars and other traffic sounds, the sellers hawking their merchandise. The street markets are everywhere. The largest one is the Khan el Khalili souk, a bazaar that is more than six centuries old. It operates much as it did during medieval times. A wide and enticing variety of goods is available: spices, perfumes, gold, silver, carpets, brass, leatherworks, glass both ancient and modern, ceramics, high-quality museum reproductions, classic vases, papyrus, and more. It is constantly crowded. The hawkers look for unsuspecting tourists or anyone else who might be considered a soft touch.

Unlike the jewelry stores in the provinces—where each store features a selective hodgepodge of merchandise—the shops in Cairo tend to be far more specialized. The goods come mainly from within Egypt, but they can also include imports from elsewhere.

The Khan el Khalili market was so plentiful in ancient days, pungent with the pleasant scents of the spices of the East, that some have suggested it played a role in the decision of Columbus and his sponsors to look for an alternative route to India.

The truly valuable items are not on display. True treasures, such as the manuscripts from Al Minya, had their own special place and would only be offered to special customers. It was reported that sometime in the 1970s the ancient texts, including the Gospel of Judas, were offered in a shop in Cairo. While it is doubtful that Hanna would have ever permitted a public display, the suggestion is not totally without merit.

If so, the texts would have been examined by serious customers in a small, dark space where the general crowd was not permitted. The visitor would have entered a shop and proceeded to a back room. The key might have been turned to lock the door behind seller and buyer. He would have been served coffee or *shai*, tea. Then the text would have been furtively brought out so that it could be examined, giving the potential buyer a brief opportunity to try to determine when it might have been written or what it might say. No one would be allowed to dwell too long. This was a sale, not a scholarly inspection.

Hanna, who originally came from Al Minya Province, had done well in Cairo. He was an able seller of precious items, though known in the marketplace for his high prices and a streak of stubbornness. It was said that he had bought several buildings in Cairo, including the multistory apartment house in which he lived in the well-to-do Heliopolis section northeast of the city. That he tried to sell items of antiquity out of his apartment is confirmed by dealers who dealt with him.

Hanna Asabil's apartment was not ostentatious. Like many others in Cairo at the time, it was part of a series of dilapidated structures that conveyed a seedy elegance. Like much of the city, the building was in urgent need of renovation.

Even though Hanna owned the entire building, the interior of his own apartment was not especially attractive or elegant. The narrow entrance was also a reception room. The living room was small, with a hard-cushioned sofa pushed against one wall. In front of the sofa was a rectangular table with a glass top, with ashtrays full of cigarette butts. A naked lightbulb hung from the ceiling. The kitchen and bathroom were tiny and so dimly lit one visitor who came to see Hanna needed to carry a flashlight.

Hanna kept a few of his treasures in a safe hidden in his apartment and in other flats that were owned by relatives or to which he had access; he would never, of course, tell where. The valuables included some archaeological objects, a gold necklace, some papyrus fragments or scrolls, a number of ancient coins, and some cash.

One of the visitors to Hanna's apartment was antiquities dealer Frieda Tchacos Nussberger. Tough and temperamental, she did her studies and started a career in Paris, but later married a Swiss artist and jeweler named Werner Nussberger and became an art dealer in Zurich. She met Hanna during the 1970s when she used to visit Cairo. "Hanna was receiving his clients in a small apartment in Heliopolis," she remembers. "Second floor. He owned the whole building. You would recognize his door by several locks attached to it. It was a typical Arabic Coptic apartment.

"Hanna was never alone. [One of his relatives] would appear behind a door, while Hanna would offer a tea or a Sinalco. When he was expecting us, he often prepared our favorite meal, *melocheya*—a kind of specially prepared Egyptian green—with baby pigeons, which he would serve on his table after having spread newspapers instead of a tablecloth on his bare table. We ate with aluminum cutlery, and we ripped the pigeons apart with our hands. The melocheya with the rice was worth the trip."

Eating was the prologue to business. After the meal, out came the items Hanna was offering that day. "After having washed our greasy hands in the uninviting bathroom, we sat and were ready to see what the house [that is, Hanna] had to offer. Out from under the beds came cartons, looking like crates, bound together with strings."

Sometimes the goods were attractive, sometimes not. There was never any certainty as to the real value of any single item. Hanna played his cards close to the vest.

What struck Frieda is that none of the better Cairo dealers had their own library or were particularly knowledgeable about objects of antiquity from an academic standpoint. None pursued the provenance of any single item through research in academic reference books to determine what an object actually was or what it might be worth. It was virtually unheard of to find a dealer visiting the Cairo Museum. "Hanna was no better than all the rest," Frieda recalled.

She found him a curious fellow—a good dealer with several really great items and many objects of little value. He was unafraid to ask astronomical prices and wait for months or even years if the response was no.

Frieda was surprised to learn, years later, that one of Hanna's specialties was papyrus texts. She did not believe Hanna had the knowledge or sophistication to evaluate an ancient manuscript. Someone—most likely, a scholar—must have advised Hanna.

If so, one possibility was a German professor, Ludwig Koenen, who had been associated with the University of Cologne in

Germany but was transplanted to the United States and became a professor at the University of Michigan in the mid-1970s. For Cairo's genuine dealers in antiquities, Koenen became the best-known of the Europeans or Americans who either lived in or visited Cairo. He was known by local Arabs as "Koenig," which means "king" in German, but it could be that this nickname was coincidental—they may simply have had trouble pronouncing his name. According to local Cairenes, he not only bought for himself and his universities but also taught a whole generation of Egyptian dealers what to look for and how to value papyrus.

Koenen was a familiar figure in the antiquities shops of Cairo and in any of the places where ancient papyri could be found throughout Egypt. He had begun visiting Cairo in the late 1950s. According to Professor Roger Bagnall of Columbia University, a noted classicist and papyrologist in his own right, "Ludwig was buying left and right. Yale University was also buying, both through a New York dealer, H. P. Kraus, and directly. It was the last great period when there was papyrus on the market. By the early seventies, the market was declining."

Typical of many seekers, Koenen loved to wander the shops and probe the sellers with questions about ancient papyri that might have been discovered in some remote site. Koenen was particularly interested in fragments of inscribed papyri, which were found inside the cartonnage sarcophagi from the Ptolemaic and Roman periods. The books, such as the Gospel of Judas or a number of the codices found at Nag Hammadi, had bindings that held the quires of the papyri together. Papyri fragments were often glued inside the cartonnage masks. The material was considered expendable in antiquity, but has considerable value in modern times. The fill inside the bindings often offers significant clues about when a book of papyrus was created, or may provide historical evidence of all sorts concerning the setting and provenance of a papyrus document. Koenen showed the dealers how to examine the interior of the cartonnage, and then how to carefully detach the fragments, which had been glued into place by the ancient Egyptians.

"I believe it was Koenen who opened the eyes of the dealers in Cairo," a fellow dealer observed. "Nobody knew about these hidden treasures before. Or that they were valuable." In correspondence, Koenen acknowledged knowing Hanna, but did not recall that Hanna had said anything to him about "the book," the particular texts that included the Gospel of Judas, in the early or mid-1970s.

Another name mentioned as being a possible source of Hanna's expertise was Italian papyrologist Manfredo Manfredi. "Hanna knew of the Manfredis and the Koenens, and he developed an instinct for these pieces of inscribed fragments of papyri," the dealer elaborated. "He knew that we dealers were not capable of appreciating such a treasure trove, but he was trying to use us to bring him in contact with a potential buyer."

Manfredi was not a Coptologist, a scholar of the ancient Copts, and he had no particular interest in buying Coptic books. Still, by helping Hanna, he thought he might be able to arrange better deals on the fragments of papyri he was acquiring for his own collection. In a phone call, Manfredi acknowledged that he had known Hanna in Cairo, but said that he had not actually seen him since 1974 or 1975. Manfredi seemed to know about the codex, however, which he understood had come from Hermopolis, near Jebel el Tuna. When asked more precise questions, trying to jog his memory, Manfredi became reticent.

In 1979, although Hanna was already a wealthy man by Egyptian standards, he believed that the papyrus manuscripts he had acquired through Am Samiah would make his fortune. Still, he did not know what the documents said and could not really know what they were worth in either monetary or scholarship terms. Nevertheless, he believed that he held in his hands one of the great treasures of modern times.

In a secret meeting conducted in Cairo in January with one of Hanna's associates, it was said that Manfredi was the person who offered Hanna specific advice on pricing the ancient texts. The number suggested by Manfredi, according to this colleague, was $3 million.

As a devout Coptic Christian, Hanna would have been delighted to learn that the documents were ancient books telling the story of Jesus in the historic language of his community, although the orthodox Copts throughout the years adhered to canonical teachings and adamantly rejected gnosticism.

Several sections of the Bible, in both the Old Testament and the New, resonate strongly with Egyptian believers—especially those who live in Cairo, because several of the most important sites of the Coptic faith are located in the city. The first is related to the story of Moses. According to Coptic beliefs, the Avraham Ibn Ezra synagogue, situated directly adjacent to several Coptic churches in Old Cairo, is the place where the earnest young Moses came to pray that the Lord stop the plagues that were inflicting misery upon the Egyptian people.

As the Christian message spread among them, Egyptians warmly embraced the narrative of the biblical Hebrews who had been slaves for them and with whom they readily identified. The Copts believe firmly in the Christian God, but they have also incorporated the Old Testament into their own belief system.

"Blessed be Egypt my people," they relate, referring to a quotation from Isaiah 19:25, which continues "upon Assyria the work of my hands, and upon Israel my possession." The part of the quotation pertaining to Egypt is used in much of their literature. It graces the back cover of a beautifully produced book called *The Holy Family in Egypt,* which was published in the workrooms of one of the leading Coptic monasteries, Al Mina, located in the Nile Delta not far from Alexandria.

Also in Isaiah, it is predicted that there will "be an altar to the Lord in the center of the Land of Egypt" (Isaiah 19:19). The passage continues: "The Lord will make himself known to the Egyptians; and the Egyptians will know the Lord on that day, and will worship with sacrifice and burnt-offering, and they will make vows to the Lord and perform them" (Isaiah 19:21). The Copts claim to have identified the place where the altar of the Lord is to be located. They commemorate it at the Al-Muharraq Monastery at Assiut in Upper Egypt.

Just as they have incorporated Old Testament narratives into their belief systems, the Copts have amplified on passages in the New Testament that relate to Egypt. Copts celebrate the passage in the Gospel of Matthew where the Holy Family comes to Egypt to escape Herod's killings of firstborn children. Joseph and Mary fear the census has been designed in order to inflict harm or death upon the young Messiah. "An angel of the Lord appeared to Joseph in a dream and said, 'Get up, take the child and his mother, and flee to Egypt, and remain there until I tell you; for Herod is about to search for the child, to destroy him'" (Matthew 2:13).

Though the Bible does not specify their path, the Copts have elaborately attempted to reconstruct the route taken by the Holy Family during their trek in Egypt. The Coptic account of the journey is extremely detailed. According to this tradition, the Holy Family traveled overland to Egypt along Sinai's northern route, via El Arish. Much of the Holy Family's journey then traversed the Nile Valley, from north to south, from Alexandria down to Assiut. Several beautifully produced Coptic books have been published depicting the Holy Family's journey in Egypt, the most handsome of them displaying a picture showing Joseph, "the hardened old carpenter, who was Mary's betrothed, striding ahead, leading the donkey by its leash into the untracked paths of a wilderness dark as the desert nights, and unending as the mother of never-ending horizons."

The Monastery of Al-Muharraq near Assiut is also in the area where the Holy Family stayed for six months, according to Coptic belief. The place was so hallowed, says the literature, that the Copts of Egypt called the place "the Second Bethlehem." It was at the site of this monastery that an angel of the Lord appeared to Joseph, as recorded in Matthew 2:20, and told him, "Get up, take the child and his mother, and go to the land of Israel, for those who were seeking the child's life are dead." With that instruction, based on a dream, Joseph, Mary, and the young Jesus returned to the Holy Land of Israel.

The Coptic religion further teaches that miracles are being carried out today just as in yesteryear. The Virgin Mary has made repeated appearances in their land, they assert. One famous visit occurred in 1968. The Virgin appeared at the top of the Church of St. Mary, in the Zeitoun section of Cairo, and remained there for several days. Another visit occurred in 1980 near Ramses Square in the heart of Cairo. Then, in August 2000, the Virgin Mary came home, so to speak. She was sighted at the church inside the Al-Muharraq Monastery, the Holy Family's last stop in Egypt before returning to the province of Judea.

Now Hanna Asabil had in his possession a document that told another key story of his Lord—if only he could have read it. For the time being, it was just another item to be sold to the highest bidder.

☥

Hanna often sat at his favorite coffeehouse, chain-smoking, drinking coffee, playing *trik-trak*—the local form of *shesh-besh*, or backgammon—and noshing on a kind of black almond that is standard coffeehouse fare in Cairo. Among Hanna's visitors were a select and highly knowledgeable group of Western visitors who liked to wander the Cairo shops, searching for hidden treasure among all the fakes. He often met his visitors not at his shop or his apartment but at a coffeehouse such as this one or perhaps at the Nile Hilton.

The European dealers visiting Cairo at the time used to stay at the Hilton, the best hotel in town. Entering its lobby was like making a landing at the exclusive George V Hotel in Paris, or a university club in New York, where all the guests knew each other or of each other. It was a common meeting spot for the traders of antiquities.

The manuscripts were kept well hidden elsewhere. Hanna did not offer them to many of his customers. Hanna was a moderately successful local dealer, but he needed a connection in order to make a sale of the magnitude he was asking. After all, he spoke no English, French, or German, common European languages in scholarship concerning Egypt. He spoke only Arabic, and that was not going to help the papyri get sold to a moneyed foreign client.

This kind of sale required the best connections possible to catch the attention of the world's greatest museums, universities, and wealthiest private collectors. Hanna lacked that kind of influence and contacts. He needed to choose someone out of this conundrum of gospel seekers, academics, buyers, sellers, voyeurs, and visionaries to help him make the best possible sale.

One obvious candidate was the man many believed had the right connections in London, Paris, and New York. It was a man with whom Hanna, and many other Egyptian dealers, had already done considerable business. He was the greatest of all the Near East antiquities dealers, considered the doyen of the pack, the most successful buyer and seller in the post–World War II years.

His name was Nicolas Koutoulakis.

CHAPTER THREE

# BETRAYING JESUS

*Jesus said to Judas: "You will exceed all of them.*
*For you will sacrifice the man that clothes me."*
—THE GOSPEL OF JUDAS

The papyrus manuscripts in Cairo contained a version of history's most momentous betrayal that turned the interpretation of the facts, as believed by most people, upside down. An essential element in Christian religious belief has been that Jesus was crucified because one of his own disciples betrayed him. The shocking contention of the newly discovered gospel is that Judas did only what his master asked him to do.

There is little reason to doubt that some kind of betrayal took place. Bart Ehrman, author of *Lost Christianities,* observes, "Jesus was almost certainly turned in to the authorities by Judas Iscariot. The reason historians think that this is true is because it's not the sort of story that any Christian would have made up. The fact that it's in all of our traditions, and the fact that no Christian made it up, shows us that there really was a betrayer of Jesus, who must have come from the inner circle. What it was that Judas betrayed, and why Judas betrayed what he betrayed, is a question that theologians and historians have wrangled over for many years."

The word *betrayal* in the context of the New Testament is itself at issue. As theologian William Klassen argues in *Judas: Betrayer or Friend of Jesus?*, the Greek word primarily used to describe Judas's actions in the New Testament, *paradidomi,* should not be translated as simply "to betray" but rather "to hand over," "to transmit," or "to surrender." It may lack the aspect of moral condemnation that is associated with it in English translations of the word.

The manuscript found in Jebel Qarara was potentially explosive. The Gospel of Judas provided a fresh witness to one of history's defining events, leading up to the Crucifixion and Resurrection of Jesus Christ. It was as close to a contemporary account of what had happened as many other accounts of Jesus. It was supposedly the gospel, or good news, of one of the chief actors in the epic account of the last days of Jesus.

The significance of the new papyri lay in that they were genuine. The gospel had been mentioned in history as early as the second century, but there were thought to be no surviving copies. As Professor Rodolphe Kasser explained, "It is certainly one of the greatest discoveries of this century. It is a great discovery because it is an authentic testimony."

The contours of ancient Jerusalem curve through the rocky landscape marked by scrubland and scraggly olive trees. The walk descends down from the elegantly reconditioned Jerusalem Cinematheque through the picturesque Hinnom Valley, descending to where the valley meets the Valley of Kidron. These two principal valleys separate the hilltop centers of ancient Jerusalem. The City of David—where the legendary King David reigned and made Jerusalem the capital of the unified kingdoms of Judea and Israel—is just above, sloping northward to the Temple Mount.

The midday sun burns out all color, leaving the city a scorched brown with streaks of dark rock. This is where the walls of the long-destroyed First Temple are believed to have been—the temple built by David's son, King Solomon.

Many have walked among these hills, Jesus among them. Down in the valley is the traditional Aceldama—"field of blood," in the Aramaic language of biblical times. This is the spot where Judas killed himself with his own hand because of his remorse, according to the accounts in the New Testament Gospels.

All of the famous holy sites are close. From Aceldama, a visitor can walk up a steep hill to arrive at Mount Zion, the site where the Last Supper is thought to have taken place. A room in a building built by the Crusaders has been set aside for the commemoration of the famous meal.

A half mile away, a visitor reaches the still-standing outer retaining walls of the Second Temple, built by Herod to serve as the center of Jewish worship in the time of Jesus. The Second Temple was a magnificent structure that housed the "holy of holies." It was where the rabbis debated the principles of law—and where Jesus cursed the money changers. The Western Wall of the Temple is today considered the holiest site in Judaism because it commemorates the Romans' destruction of the Temple in 70 CE.

The eastern side of the Temple Mount leads to the Garden of Gethsemane a few hundred yards away, where the famous "kiss of betrayal" took place. The word *Gethsemane* comes from the Hebrew for "olive press." Today the modern site houses a beautiful grove with ancient olive trees cared for by Roman Catholic Franciscan fathers.

On the hill above is the ridge known as the Mount of Olives. It has a commanding view of the city of Jerusalem. At its pinnacle is the site of the holiest of all Jewish cemeteries, placed there because Jews historically have believed that it is the place on Earth closest to the heavens and that from here the soul can make a quick departure from the body to reach the desired final resting place. In this general area, Jesus himself is believed to have ascended to heaven.

All these historic locales demonstrate the closeness of Judaism and the Jewish people to the religion to which it gave birth, Christianity. Jesus was a Jew, as were the apostles. Jesus' status as the Messiah was justified in the New Testament with Old Testament prophecy. It was incumbent on Jesus to be of the House of David and come from Judea, the region from Jerusalem southward, including Bethlehem. That Jews long afterward would be vilified as Christ killers is one of the sad legacies of the betrayal by Judas.

"For the most part, the name Judas is equivalent to the demonic," writes Klassen. "At times, Judas is portrayed as the epitome of evil in the form of hypocrisy, greed, unfaithfulness, ingratitude, and, above all, betrayal.... In many writings about him, authors spare themselves the effort of using Judas's name and refer to him mainly as 'the traitor,' implying thereby that his act of betrayal of Jesus is what made him stand out among the twelve apostles. His deed, they judge, stands unique in perversity in the annals of human history."

The stakes are higher than they would first seem. The story of the betrayal is an integral part of the Christian narrative, the essential step that led to the trial, condemnation, crucifixion, and resurrection of Jesus. "If Judas didn't betray Jesus," Ehrman explains, "then that would change how Christians understand their relationship, not only to the betrayer but also to the people whom the betrayer is thought to represent, mainly the Jews. So, throughout the course of Christian history, Christians have blamed the Jews for the death of Jesus and Judas is emblematic of the Jew who betrayed Jesus. If in fact Jesus and Judas were in agreement about Judas's mission, that would change the understanding of the relationship of Jews and Christians."

He continues: "If it turns out that Judas didn't betray Jesus, but simply did what Jesus wanted him to do, then this would show that Jesus was a continuation of Judaism rather than somebody who is representing a break with Judaism. And if historically Jesus didn't represent a break with Judaism, then that would have a significant impact on the relationship of Jews and Christians today, because these wouldn't represent historically two different religions, these would represent the same religion."

What is really known about Judas Iscariot? The references to him in the New Testament are meager. His name is mentioned four times in the Gospel of Matthew, three in Mark, four in Luke, and eight in John.

What we really know about Judas Iscariot has to be approached gingerly. There are no physical descriptions of the man. He could have been short or tall, thin or fat, bearded or clean shaven. He could have had long or short hair. He could have worn local garb or the latest white robe. He could have had distinguishing marks on his face. No one knows.

Judas was evidently trusted by his fellow disciples. He was

their keeper of the purse. That honor accorded to him made the betrayal all the more painful. He was also the odd man out among the twelve disciples. While the others came from Galilee—as did Jesus himself, who though born in Bethlehem, grew up in Nazareth—Judas is thought to be the only disciple from Judea, the harsh mountainous region south of Jerusalem which then gave its name to the entire Roman province. The word *Jew* originally meant simply a person who came from Judea.

Judas's name also had its roots in Judea. Most scholars believe that the name Iscariot indicates that he was from the village of Keriot, since in Hebrew, "ish" equals man, making him Ish-Keriot, "a man from Keriot." Keriot is believed to have been a village in the Judean mountains or foothills overlooking the Dead Sea, not far from the modern Israeli city of Arad.

A secondary school of thought attributes the name Iscariot not to a geographical place but to the Sicarii, or Zealots, a Jewish sect fiercely resistant to Rome who were the last opposition to Roman power. It was the Zealots who famously committed mass suicide at the final stronghold of Masada when the Romans completed their reconquest of the province in 74 CE.

As far as the story of Judas's betrayal goes, the narratives in the four canonical Gospels differ only in the extent and nature of some of the details. A closer look at each shows similarities but also some significant differences.

For many years the Gospel of Matthew was believed to have been written first among the Gospels that became accepted in the New Testament. Some modern scholars have questioned that judgment, contending that passages from Matthew stem from similar ones in the Gospel of Mark, which must have been written before. Still, Matthew is the first of the four Gospels in all translations of the New Testament.

Although early Church histories point to a Gospel of Matthew written in Hebrew or Aramaic, the Gospel of Matthew that has come down through the centuries is thought to have been written originally in Greek. A copy of the original Gospel of Matthew was later said to have been found by St. Jerome and translated into Latin. Not much is known about Matthew himself. In Matthew 9:9 he appears as a tax collector or public official who is called to follow Jesus: "As Jesus was walking along, he saw a man called Matthew sitting at the tax booth; and he said to him, 'Follow me.' And he got up and followed him." In similar passages in Mark (2:14) and Luke (5:27), the name of the tax collector is given as Levi, but most scholars believe them to be the same person.

Judas enters the Gospel when Jesus is in the midst of "proclaiming the good news of the kingdom, and curing every disease and every sickness" (Matthew 9:35). Jesus called to his twelve disciples and "gave them authority over unclean spirits, to cast them out, and to cure every disease and every sickness" (Matthew 10:1). Matthew 10:2–4 names Jesus' followers: "These are the names of the twelve apostles: first, Simon, also known as Peter, and his brother Andrew; James son of Zebedee, and his brother John; Philip and Bartholomew; Thomas and Matthew the tax-collector; James son of Alphaeus, and Thaddaeus; Simon the Cananaean, and Judas Iscariot, the one who betrayed him."

Judas Iscariot assumes a major role in the book of Matthew only in the final days of Jesus' life on Earth. In Matthew 26:2, two days before Passover, Jesus predicts: "You know that in two days' time it will be Passover, and the Son of Man is to be handed over for crucifixion."

At the house of Simon the leper in Bethany, located just on the other side of the Mount of Olives, a woman pours ointment on Jesus' head. His disciples who are there criticize what they regard as an extravagant and pointless act: "But when the disciples saw it, they were angry and said, 'Why this waste? For this ointment could have been sold for a large sum, and the money given to the poor.' But Jesus, aware of this, said to them, 'Why do you trouble the woman? She has performed a good service for me. For you always have the poor with you, but you will not always have me. By pouring this ointment on my body she has prepared me for burial. Truly I tell you, wherever this good news is proclaimed in the whole world, what she has done will be told in remembrance of her'" (Matthew 26:8–13).

Immediately thereafter, the story of Judas's betrayal of Jesus begins to unfold. Though it is not specifically mentioned in the narrative, Judas somehow leaves the other disciples who are with Jesus. The story continues:

"Then one of the twelve, called Judas Iscariot, went unto the chief priests. And he said unto them, 'What will ye give me, and I will deliver him unto you?' And they covenanted with him for thirty pieces of silver. And from that time he sought opportunity to betray him" (Matthew 26:14–16).

Jesus and his twelve disciples then eat what has become known as the Last Supper (Matthew 26:21–25). While eating, Jesus foresees the betrayal that will lead to his crucifixion: "Truly I tell you, one of you will betray me."

The disciples react with great sorrow. Each of them questions Jesus, "Surely not I, Lord?"

He answers, "The one who has dipped his hand into the bowl with me will betray me."

The narrative of betrayal continues with the only outright condemnation, assuming it is a condemnation, of Judas by Jesus in this Gospel. Jesus says, "The Son of Man goes as it is written of him, but woe to that one by whom the Son of Man is betrayed! It would have been better for that one not to have been born." This passage is open to interpretation in light of the Gospel of Judas; perhaps the condemnation is not so much condemnation as a lament for all that the betrayer must soon experience.

Judas in his turn then asks, "Surely not I, Rabbi?" and Jesus answers simply, "You have said so."

After supper, Jesus goes to pray at the garden at the base of the Mount of Olives named Gethsemane. Foretelling the future once more, Jesus predicts that he will rise from the dead and meet his disciples soon in Galilee. He then asserts that Simon Peter will deny him three times—which Simon Peter, to his great distress, actually does in the next passages.

After the disciples have slept, Jesus tells them, "Are you still sleeping and taking your rest? See, the hour is at hand, and the Son of Man is betrayed into the hands of sinners. Get up, let us be going. See, my betrayer is at hand" (26:45–46).

Now comes the story of betrayal (26:47–56). Judas had somehow slipped away again. Without forewarning, Judas reappears. This time he is not alone: "While he was still speaking, Judas, one of the twelve, arrived; with him was a large crowd with swords and clubs, from the chief priests and the elders of the people."

Judas has a signal that he has arranged with the high priests. He will identify Jesus by kissing him. That kiss of the traitor will live on in infamy. "Now the betrayer had given them a sign, saying, 'The one I will kiss is the man; arrest him.' At once he came up to Jesus and said, 'Greetings, Rabbi!' and kissed him. Jesus said to him, 'Friend, do what you are here to do.' Then they came and laid hands on Jesus and arrested him."

Jesus is now on the path to crucifixion. He is on his path to destiny. Without Judas, he would not have met his fate.

Judas's role would seem to have ended, but the Gospel of

Matthew goes on to record his terrible destiny. By the next morning, Judas seems to have been overcome with remorse. He repents for the act of treachery that he had committed the day before: "When Judas, his betrayer, saw that Jesus was condemned, he repented and brought back the thirty pieces of silver to the chief priests and the elders. He said, 'I have sinned by betraying innocent blood.' But they said, 'What is that to us? See to it yourself.' Throwing down the pieces of silver in the temple, he departed; and he went and hanged himself" (27:3–5).

After a discussion among themselves, the chief priests refuse to keep the money. "But the chief priests, taking the pieces of silver, said, 'It is not lawful to put them into the treasury, since they are blood money.'" Instead of using that money for their own purposes, they go out and buy an outlying piece of property, which they designate as a cemetery for unknown persons—Aceldama, the field of blood. "After conferring together, they used them to buy the potter's field as a place to bury foreigners. For this reason that field has been called the Field of Blood to this day" (27:6–8).

The role of Judas is now finished. He has killed himself by his own hand, apparently out of shame.

The following two Gospels, Mark and Luke, do not significantly alter the narrative of Judas and the betrayal. They provide a similar account of Jesus' life and crucifixion with only additional or somewhat differing detail.

The Gospel of Mark adds little new to the Judas narrative, which makes sense if it is the source of Matthew and Luke as is now speculated. The treatment of Judas's decision to betray Jesus is brief here, even cursory: "Then Judas Iscariot, who was one of the twelve, went to the chief priests in order to betray him to them. When they heard it, they were greatly pleased, and promised to give him money. So he began to look for an opportunity to betray him" (Mark 14:10–11).

At the Last Supper, Jesus proclaims, as in the Gospel of Matthew, that one of his disciples will betray him: "'Truly I tell you, one of you will betray me, one who is eating with me.' They began to be distressed and to say to him one after another, 'Surely, not I?' He said to them, 'It is one of the twelve, one who is dipping bread into the bowl with me'" (14:18–20).

Jesus then again condemns the disciple who would betray him in a passage that can be read in two ways, as either expressing anger and condemnation or sorrow and anguish for the person who would have to perform the betrayal: "The Son of Man goes as it is written of him, but woe to that one by whom the Son of Man is betrayed! It would have been better for that one not to have been born" (14:21). That passage could indicate that it was a horrible burden to have to betray Jesus.

The similarities continue at the Mount of Olives. As in the Gospel of Matthew, Judas is not alone. Along with him was "a crowd with swords and clubs, from the chief priests, the scribes, and the elders." The betrayal is once again sealed with a kiss: "Now the betrayer had given them a sign, saying, 'The one I will kiss is the man; arrest him and lead him away under guard.' So when he came, he went up to him at once and said, 'Rabbi!' and kissed him" (14:43–45).

There is no further mention of Judas or his role. The balance of Mark tells the story of the trial, the Crucifixion, and the Resurrection.

Many of the same similarities can be found in the Book of

Luke. Like the Acts of the Apostles, it is dedicated to the "most excellent Theophilus that you may know the truth concerning the things of which you have been informed." That makes sense, since Luke and Acts were written by the same author.

The explanation given here for Judas's betrayal is theological: "Then Satan entered into Judas called Iscariot, who was one of the twelve; he went away and conferred with the chief priests and officers of the temple police about how he might betray him to them. They were greatly pleased and agreed to give him money" (Luke 22:3–5).

The Gospel of John is believed to be the last written of the four canonical Gospels. It is not one of the synoptic gospels, but seems to have had independent sources. It is also the harshest in its condemnation of Judas and of the Jews as a group, regarding the Jews as separate from the true believers. By the time it was written, in the late first century or possibly even well into the second century, Jesus' story clearly no longer was aimed solely at converting Jews but was meant to instruct a wider audience. By that time, Jesus as the Savior was accepted by many in the gentile world as well.

The first mention of Judas is in chapter 12, six days before the Passover, when Jesus comes to Bethany. This time, the visit includes details about the miraculous story of Lazarus, whom Jesus raised from the dead. At the home of two sisters, Mary and Martha, the story of the ointment contains a significant variation: Judas asks the question concerning the price of the ointment: "But Judas Iscariot, one of his disciples (the one who was about to betray him), said, 'Why was this perfume not sold for three hundred denarii and the money given to the poor?'" (John 12:4–5).

We know that Judas Iscariot was in charge of the apostles' money, so it is perhaps not unusual for him to assess the cost of this ceremony. Yet the narrative is scornful of his comments and severely rebukes him: "He said this not because he cared about the poor, but because he was a thief; he kept the common purse and used to steal what was put into it." Jesus concludes the episode by telling Judas and the disciples: "Leave her alone. She bought it so that she might keep it for the day of my burial. You always have the poor with you, but you do not always have me" (12:6–8).

At the Passover feast, the story continues its harsh judgment of Judas: "The devil had already put it into the heart of Judas son of Simon Iscariot to betray him" (13:2).

Jesus says to the twelve: "'Very truly, I tell you, whoever receives one whom I send receives me; and whoever receives me receives him who sent me.' After saying this Jesus was troubled in spirit, and declared, 'Very truly, I tell you, one of you will betray me.' The disciples looked at one another, uncertain of whom he was speaking" (13:20–22).

Simon Peter asks him who the betrayer is. "Jesus answered, 'It is the one to whom I give this piece of bread when I have dipped it in the dish.' So when he had dipped the piece of bread, he gave it to Judas son of Simon Iscariot. After he received the piece of bread, Satan entered into him. Jesus said to him, 'Do quickly what you are going to do'" (13:24–27).

Jesus clearly knows what Judas is about to do. The narrative notes: "Now no one at the table knew why he said this to him. Some thought that, because Judas had the common purse, Jesus was telling him, 'Buy what we need for the festival'; or, that he should give something to the poor. So, after receiving the piece of bread, he immediately went out. And it was night. When he had gone out, Jesus said, 'Now the Son of Man has been glorified, and God has been glorified in him'" (13:28–31).

After supper, Jesus goes outside, crosses over the Kidron Valley, and comes to the Garden of Gethsemane. Judas knows the place because, the narrative notes, Jesus often met there with his disciples (18:1–2). In John, additional details and names emerge, but the story of the betrayal is essentially the same.

When Jesus is brought before Pontius Pilate, he is ridiculed as the "King of the Jews." But Pilate concludes to the assembled Jewish crowd: "Take him yourselves and crucify him; I find no case against him" (19:6). The Gospel of John continues:

> The Jews answered him, "We have a law, and according to that law he ought to die because he has claimed to be the Son of God."
>
> Now when Pilate heard this, he was more afraid than ever. He entered his headquarters again and asked Jesus, "Where are you from?" But Jesus gave him no answer. Pilate therefore said to him, "Do you refuse to speak to me? Do you not know that I have power to release you, and power to crucify you?" Jesus answered him, "You would have no power over me unless it had been given you from above; therefore the one who handed me over to you is guilty of a greater sin." (19:7–11)

That is the final reference to Judas, although John does not specifically name Judas at that point. The passage can be interpreted as releasing Pilate from sin, but also Judas, since both are functioning within a divine plan.

John does not mention the suicide or shame of Judas, or for that matter, the remembrance of Judas in the "Field of Blood."

The one other place in the New Testament that recounts a part of the story of Judas's demise is in Acts 1:16–20. The version of Judas's disastrous end in Acts differs markedly from that in the canonical Gospels. Judas himself is more specifically named as the "guide for those who arrested Jesus." The author of Acts expresses a mixture of sorrow, wistful regret, and considerable anger at Judas's betrayal "for he was numbered among us and was allotted his share in this ministry."

In Acts, unlike the account in Matthew, the high priests from the Temple do not buy the field of blood; instead, Judas himself buys the plot of land with his ill-gotten gain: "(Now this man acquired a field with the reward of his wickedness; and falling headlong, he burst open in the middle and all his bowels gushed out. This became known to all the residents of Jerusalem, so that the field was called in their language Aceldama, that is, Field of Blood.)"

The author of Acts is unsparing in his denunciation of Judas. "For it is written in the book of Psalms: 'Let his homestead become desolate, and let there be no one to live in it.'"

☥

That is the story of Judas as presented in the first five books of the New Testament. The narrative of Judas's betrayal—though it differs in its details in the different Gospels and the Book of Acts—supplies only the barest details. Yet Judas's saga has resounded through history, becoming more symbol than story as its meaning evolved over time.

"From the Middle Ages down to the modern times, Judas is thought to represent Jews," Bart Ehrman explains. "Jews have this stereotype of being traitors who betray Jesus. That's what Judas was—he's responsible for the death of Jesus."

Yet there is a major objection to this traditional anti-Semitism as it developed through the centuries. The deed committed by Judas—for whatever motivation—was *foretold* by Jesus. Christ was going to die and rise from the grave to new life as a result of the betrayal. The betrayal was the necessary forerunner of whatever came next.

"The New Testament has an ironic view of Jesus going to his death," Ehrman continues, "because on the one hand, Jesus knows that he is going to die and he knows why he is going to die, and he knows that he has to die. And it is God's will that he dies. On the other hand, the people who are responsible for his death are vilified. Judas, of course, is vilified because he's the one who turns him over. But one might ask, if Jesus was supposed to die anyway, then Judas of course had to turn him over, and isn't that God's will, and isn't Judas doing Jesus a favor?"

CHAPTER FOUR

# POWER BROKERS

*Trade and commerce, if they were not made of India-rubber,*
*would never manage to bounce over the obstacles which legislators*
*are continually putting in their way.*
—HENRY DAVID THOREAU

Switzerland has become a primary home for a number of the biggest and best antiquities dealers. The mountain republic, with its snow-topped peaks and pure water running down Alpine streams, is an art aficionado's paradise. Its centuries-long tradition of political neutrality, which managed to keep it out of Europe's constant warfare between contentious nations, has helped establish an invisible financial wall around its frontiers.

Inside that wall is a haven not only for money but also for the comfortable lifestyle that money can bring. Swiss citizens enjoy a superb social welfare system, extremely high wages relative to the rest of Europe, world-class universal health care, and five- and six-week vacations as part of normal job compensation. It would be an exaggeration to say that Switzerland is a utopian society, but it is not far from being one. There are no urban slums and little poverty among Swiss citizens. Its currency, the Swiss franc, is one of the world's most unshakable. Generally, Switzerland is a very proper country where privacy, property, and propriety merit respect to the point of veneration.

World War II played a crucial role in the development of modern Switzerland. During the war, the country's banks continued their discretionary policy that protected clients, whoever they might be. They accepted money both from desperate Jews hiding their wealth from Nazi depredation and from Nazi officials trying to stash away their newly seized fortunes. After the war, Switzerland evolved into a haven where people from other countries parked their—sometimes ill-gotten—money and assets. The country has capitalized on its famously neutral political status to establish itself as a thriving financial center.

Swiss respect for private property made it a growing center for the art and antiquities trade as well. This has had both good and bad consequences. Along with Great Britain, Switzerland has long been considered a hub of antiquities traffic. Although both countries have taken strong measures to combat the illegal aspects of the trade, a reputation for impropriety has developed. In one of the more outstanding cases, Swiss police in 1995 raided four bonded warehouses in Geneva, seizing a large number of artifacts allegedly smuggled from Italy. As reported by *Archaeology* magazine, the Carabinieri, Italy's national police force, stated that the warehouses contained 10,000 artifacts worth 50 billion lire (about $35 million), making the raid one of the largest antiquities seizures ever.

Egyptian antiquities have also been funneled through Switzerland. In 2002, Egyptian and Swiss authorities signed a security agreement designed to stop illicit trafficking, and within a year, in 2003, Swiss authorities handed over to the Egyptian government two mummies, sarcophagi, and masks that were among nearly three hundred objects discovered in a duty-free customs warehouse in Geneva. A primary figure in the wave of Egyptian arrests that followed was Tariq al Suwaysi, the head of Egypt's National Democratic Party's Giza office, who for years had worked with some of Switzerland's best and most important dealers, including Nicolas Koutoulakis. The Egyptians arrested included former police officers and customs and antiquities officials, who were charged with exporting the objects by identifying the objects as replicas found in the Khan el Khalili bazaar, Cairo's largest market.

The legacy of Switzerland as a conduit for nefarious transactions casts a shadow over the perfectly respectable antiquities dealers that abound in the country. In the postwar era, one group of dealers specializing in antiquities based themselves in Basel, on Switzerland's northern border. The group featured, among others, Herbert Cahn, whose son Jean-David now runs the gallery; a Greek gentleman named George Zakos, who had spent part of his life in Istanbul; and possibly the best of the lot, Elie Borowski, who miraculously escaped the Holocaust in his Polish homeland after a stint in that country's army and survived the war in Switzerland, where he became a self-taught genius of antiquity finds. A Jew and a Zionist, Borowski's superb private collection, gathered in the decades after World War II, was later made the basis of the beautiful Bible Lands Museum in Jerusalem, which recounts the cultures of the Near East region during biblical and prebiblical times.

Zurich, another Swiss center of this market, became the base of dealer Frieda Tchacos Nussberger. Born in Egypt, Frieda was a citizen of both Switzerland and Greece. She came to Europe as a young student in her late teens and was educated in Geneva at the École d'Interprètes and in Paris at the École du Louvre. After a considerable period in Paris, she bought and then built up the

Nefer Galerie in Zurich. The attractive dealer was a rarity: a female among denizens of a male world. Dealers are a tough breed, and few women have made it into the ranks of the elite.

Frieda knew the Egyptian market well. She had one great advantage when trading with Egyptians or with Arabs from other countries: She spoke Egyptian Arabic fluently—in addition to Greek, English, French, Italian, and passable German. Active internationally, she was a recognized dealer for many museums in Europe, the United States, and Japan and sold to numerous private collectors, as well.

Geneva, located in the French-speaking part of Switzerland, had its own great art dealers. In particular, it was home to the man who became known as the dean of all the antiquities dealers active in the Arab world and beyond: Nicolas Koutoulakis. His dealings brought many of the world's great treasures either to or through Switzerland on their way to museums and private clients in North America and Europe.

Burly and balding, Koutoulakis was born in Crete and often referred to that island of Minoan heroes as his homeland. He reminded some of his colleagues of Zorba the Greek. He somehow had an eye severely injured as a child; the story other dealers believed was that his brother had shot an arrow and hit little Nicolas in the eye, but his son Manolis related that it was actually a stone from a slingshot that caused the injury. Yet the remaining good eye was keen enough to make discerning purchases that netted Koutoulakis millions of dollars. He was known for carrying large amounts of cash at all times, and when he bought an item, he paid promptly. That was one reason for his enormous popularity among local dealers throughout the lands of antiquity in the Near East.

Frieda had met Koutoulakis when she was newly arrived in Paris, beginning her studies in Egyptology at the École du Louvre.

Her father had asked Koutoulakis to bring some gifts from the Middle East to Frieda. Koutoulakis delivered the gifts and invited Frieda out to one of the trendiest bistros in Paris, Restaurant Ruc, where he feted her with champagne and oysters. He then invited her to a cabaret. The evening made an indelible impression on Frieda. "He wanted to excite me," she explained. "That was the way he worked. I was only nineteen years old at the time."

Frieda later opened a gallery in Paris and became a successful dealer. Koutoulakis, more than thirty years her senior, soon saw her as a rival and could not understand how a young and highly attractive Greek woman could be a serious competitor. The differences between them were plain: She had a command of six languages, while Koutoulakis got by on his village-accented Greek, poor French, and mostly rudimentary English. He never invited her to his comfortable villa in Geneva.

Koutoulakis had entered the antiquities trade like many uneducated Greek youngsters. He was a relative of a dealer, Manolis Segredakis, who had an eponymous shop in one of Paris's best areas. The shop featured various antiquities and knickknacks. Nicolas apprenticed with his uncle and, when the older man died without an heir, the shop passed to the young Koutoulakis.

Koutoulakis was a clever trader, and he swiftly became successful, not only taking the shop over but even managing to pay off its debts. Segredakis was a shop with a large, dusty glass window. Inside, it was dark. Stairs led to a mezzanine, and second-rate antiques and unpacked crates usually crowded the hallway. After he achieved a measure of success, Koutoulakis moved to Geneva with his wife, Mireille, and their three children. There, he worked from his home. His daughter Daphne later opened the Galerie Khnoum in Geneva's old city; the gallery was named after the ancient Egyptian god Khnoum, who had the body of a man and the head of a ram. Khnoum was a guardian of the sources of the Nile and controlled the river's annual floods.

Nicolas Koutoulakis was shrewd, a rough-hewn Greek who was both intuitive and smart, with a charm that led to successful deal making. Every year he would take off on an annual hunt for treasure. His first stop was often Italy, still a fertile source of antiquities. He would then pass through Greece and Cyprus, and after that, fly to Syria, eventually making a stop in Tehran and Istanbul, and finally landing in Cairo. Operating with a flair and cunning necessitated by his dealings with the clever brokers of Egypt, Turkey, and Mesopotamia, he developed the discerning eye of a professor and the negotiating skills of a Greek sheep monger.

Certain Cairo dealers called Koutoulakis *louchi,* or cross-eyed— though not to his face. "You had to be careful when dealing with him," one dealer recalled. "We never knew where he was looking." Even so, Koutoulakis developed dozens of contacts among small-time dealers—people like Hanna Asabil in Cairo—*fournisseurs,* runners, all eager to do business with him, feeding him as many artifacts as they could find.

Koutoulakis was unparalleled in his ability to trade advantageously. His competitors marveled at his ability to buy cheap and sell dear. He could purchase an object in Cairo (or Syria or Turkey or Iran) for 200 Egyptian pounds—less than $50 at the time—and sell it for $3,000, a 6,000 percent markup. Today some of those objects can fetch $500,000 at auction.

Nicolas Koutoulakis was part of a small coterie that shaped much of the Middle East antiquities trade in the post–World War II era, enabling local dealers in a number of countries to sell to the West. He had good contacts in the capitals of Europe and the United States, where substantial value was attached to the goods he sold, and in the Middle East as well. In some cases, he was the inheritor of contacts with natives of the Levant and Egypt that went back centuries. Koutoulakis was valued by the Arab sellers for the good prices he paid them and the fact that he paid in cash with no questions asked. He neither liked to give nor take receipts. Some colleagues applied a French phrase to the way he did business: *"Ni vu, ni connu."* Neither seen, nor known.

Postwar dealers like Koutoulakis were united by common factors. They were largely without formal education. They had sensitive noses that could detect an artifact and a great bargain. They were tough fighters. As one observer put it, "Everybody in business in those years didn't have the most delicate stance toward competitors."

An example of the blurred lines within which antiquities dealers operated in those days is demonstrated by the discovery of an 18th-dynasty royal coffin in the Valley of the Kings in 1907. *Archaeology* magazine reported that it was sent to the Egyptian Museum in Cairo, but sometime between a restoration of the objects in 1914 and a museum inventory in 1931, the main part of the sarcophagus, including slivers of gold from its bottom half, was stolen, with only the lid remaining in Cairo. The piece was reportedly acquired around 1950 by Koutoulakis. Efforts to sell it during the 1970s proved unsuccessful, and it was sent to the Egyptian Museum of Art in Munich for restoration around 1980. According to an article in Egypt's *Al Ahram Weekly,* the chief curator at the museum, Dietrich Wildung, told Egyptian authorities about it and offered to return it, suggesting "as recompensation a loan of objects from the Cairo Museum." In 1994, Koutoulakis's daughter officially donated it to the State Museum of Egyptian Art in Munich. Negotiations about the object continued, and it eventually found its way back to the Egyptian Museum in Cairo with the cooperation of the Koutoulakis family.

Later in his career, in order to enhance his dealing in Cairo, Koutoulakis hired a bright youngster, someone much like himself, a kid with street smarts. Tariq al Suwaysi had grown up in Cairo and knew his way around. He was already employed at one of the principal shops in Cairo, but he was looking to make tips and money on his own.

Tariq's status was menial—"He was basically sweeping Koutoulakis's floor," said one colleague—and his job was to keep Koutoulakis informed. If there was an ancient piece worth buying, Tariq's job was to sniff it out. He was willing to pay for information and it flowed in, to Koutoulakis's benefit. Tariq's main duty was to go to a pay phone at the Cairo post office and call Koutoulakis in Greece or Paris or Geneva whenever he got wind of a valuable antiquity making the rounds in Cairo.

"Tariq was not nice at all, but had a lot of personality," reported the colleague. "He was tall, aloof. He could express himself well. He was nicely dressed and knew how to make connections. Later, he became rich through his own dealings, and he thought he would become a minister in the Egyptian government." Tariq married well—far beyond his station, for his bride was his employer's wife's sister. From being a servant and employee, he became a partner.

In Egypt, a hand is always outstretched, a fact of life in making deals, and Tariq knew how to grease the palms of those hands with considerable agility. He was well connected in the highest Egyptian circles. "Tariq was clever. But he was not clever enough to keep a low profile, and he later offended people."

Years later, as mentioned earlier, Tariq would be arrested and brought to trial as one of thirty-one people involved in a massive antiquities smuggling ring that allegedly removed nearly three hundred pharaonic, Coptic, and Islamic artifacts from Egypt to Switzerland. Convicted in 2003, he was sentenced to thirty-five years in prison, a sentence that has been appealed. The general feeling was that, although he was a political figure and had extensive connections within Egyptian society, he had overstretched himself in his antiquities dealings.

☥

All of the scandals in the antiquities trade need to be placed in perspective. The dealers of that era stood between two sides in a looming war. They were the middlemen, the link between buyer and seller—between consumers in the countries of the West and the governments and private individuals in the countries where the artifacts had originated. The last two decades of the twentieth century saw increased pressure on dealers, primarily from the countries where ancient objects originated.

The trade wasn't a new phenomenon, however; it is as ancient as civilization itself. In the words of Robert Bianchi, an Egyptologist and consultant to major museums such the Brooklyn Museum, the Metropolitan Museum of Art, and the Bible Lands Museum in Jerusalem: "Everything has been fluid in the antiquities market— at least, since Greek and Roman times. The West has been trading actively in antiquities since the time of Napoleon."

Among the more ancient objects moved from site to site in ancient times are at least fifteen ancient obelisks that were taken from Egypt back when the Roman Empire flourished. These obelisks are still standing in Rome. In another striking example, the Crusaders took many Egyptian and other objects of antiquity, believing they had the power to cure disease. The authorities controlling Egypt often cooperated. For example, as *Al Ahram Weekly* writer Nevine El Aref points out, French king Louis Philippe traded a clock from the Citadel to Mohammed Ali Pasha in Egypt for the obelisk now in the Place de la Concorde in Paris.

Several removals of major antiquities from their homelands are astounding in retrospect. Soldiers in Napoleon's army, for example, found the famous Rosetta Stone in Egypt in 1799. Napoleon was then defeated by the British, and the item became the property of England after the Treaty of Alexandria was signed in 1801. The Stone was taken to Britain and has resided proudly in the British Museum virtually ever since. It is one of the world's most valuable objects of antiquity, of such infinite value that no earthly sum can be assigned to it. The Egyptian government has asked that it be returned, a request that has been steadfastly rejected by the British government and the British Museum.

Another breathtaking instance that has been considered "plunder" was the removal of the Elgin Marbles from the Parthenon in Greece. Thomas Bruce, the seventh Earl of Elgin, was the British ambassador at Constantinople. He formed a team of architects and painters and, at a time when the Ottoman Turks were the sovereign power in the eastern Mediterranean and exercised control over Greece, obtained from the sultan in Constantinople a permit to remove the marble friezes. Elgin oversaw from afar the removal of sculptures and other objects of antiquity from the Parthenon in massive quantities. "Whatever I can say of their value will not suffice," the man in charge at the site, Giovanni Battista Lusieri, wrote Elgin. "There is nothing in the world more perfect than these pieces." The systematic operation lasted for a number of years, and the objects wound up, like the Rosetta Stone, in the prestigious British Museum. The government of Greece wants the marbles to be returned and also has demanded that the Louvre in Paris, France's greatest museum, turn over the celebrated statue "Winged Victory," which was taken from the island of Samothrace.

A third example of cultural patrimony carted away was the removal of a First Temple–period inscription in King Hezekiah's tunnel in Jerusalem. Diggers working in a shaft of the tunnel found an ancient Hebrew inscription that commemorated the meeting of the teams that had originally dug the tunnel from different ends. The inscription was taken away en bloc and shipped to the Istanbul Museum, where this valuable memento, specifically related to Jewish history and having nothing to do with the Ottoman Turks, still rests. The Israelis have longed to have it returned as a national cultural treasure, but have understood that "legality," such as it is, resides with the government that inherited the many archaeological treasures from throughout Ottoman lands that made their way to modern Turkey.

An example of disputed cultural patrimony comes from South America—specifically, the Inca citadel of Machu Picchu in the Peruvian Andes. In 1911, a Yale University historian named Hiram Bingham, guided by locals, discovered the ancient city, and, along with the National Geographic Society, made three more expeditions and excavated a number of artifacts and remains. The Peruvian government has recently threatened a lawsuit against Yale to recover the artifacts taken during these expeditions. As Danna Harman of the *Christian Science Monitor* writes, the site is "well-preserved ... complete with palaces, baths, temples, tombs, sundials and agricultural terraces," but "the bowls, tools, ritual objects and other objects have been removed to New Haven [Connecticut, site of Yale]." Professor Bingham claimed he acted with the approval of the president of Peru, but today Peru is claiming that the objects were expressly provided as loans. Yale responded in a December 2005 letter, "The civil code of 1852, which was in effect at the time of the Bingham expeditions, gave Yale title to the artifacts at the time of their excavation and ever since." National Geographic has stated publicly that it believes that the artifacts taken during the joint Yale–National Geographic expeditions were loaned, owned by Peru, and should be returned. Lawyers for Yale and Peru continue to talk.

Campaigns to reclaim countries' "cultural property" really began to gain steam in the 1930s. The Italian fascist dictator Benito Mussolini was a great advocate of Italian culture and art. An avid reader of the great Italian poet Dante, Mussolini began his mornings dipping into cantos of the famous author. Seeking to glorify all the country's treasures, the dictator introduced the concept that everything under Italian soil belongs to the government of Italy, that the state was a civil party with paramount rights.

The rules of the antiquities trade were increasingly rewritten in order to define which antiquity trades were "right" and which were "wrong." Yet no one single standard for defining right and wrong emerged. Right was usually only in the eyes of the beholder. The originating countries felt they had been cheated when goods were taken out of their countries, and that sense of grievance was only aggravated when they saw museums and other institutions in the West drawing customers by the thousands, with lines of people often waiting to get in, the museums making money from blockbuster shows of objects the countries considered their patrimony. If nothing else, these nations wanted a larger share of the pie.

All over the world the originating countries started to clamor for what had become enormously valuable in the hands of others. These treasures were sometimes held by wealthy private individuals, but in most cases they were located in major institutions with public budgets or endowments such as universities or museums. Ironically, these institutions had over the years created the market for valuable antiquities, because the objects had value *to them*.

A major reason for the growth in value was the museums'

increasing popularity—whether in New York, London, or Paris, crowds gathered to view the works that came from the countries where ancient civilizations had flourished, including Israel, Turkey, Greece, Italy, Peru, and perhaps above all, Egypt. The museums and other public institutions in the West became victims of their own success. What was at stake was not only who controlled the flow of antiquities but also who gained the profits from the exhibits that drew massive crowds in America and other Western countries. The increasing moralism concerning the antiquities morass reminds one of Samuel Johnson's quip, "Patriotism is the last refuge of a scoundrel."

Questions about the antiquity trade swirl within a maelstrom of often contradictory modern assertions concerning the rights of states, cultural patrimony, the patrimony of humankind, and good old-fashioned private property. Do the artifacts of ancient Rome belong only to Italians, or to the government of Italy, or to anyone? What about objects from predominantly Greek or Hellenic culture in places where Rome once ruled? Does the Italian state that is the descendant of Rome, or the Greek state as the inheritor and propagator of Greek and Hellenic culture, better deserve these prized artifacts? Or do they belong to whatever private individual, often from abroad, who excavated that territory many years ago and then sold or donated his object of antiquity to a major cultural institution in his home country?

Are the Arab Muslims who conquered Egypt in the seventh century and who dominate the Egyptian state today the proper inheritors of objects created during the days of the ancient pharaohs? Should the Copts, the direct descendants of the Egyptians from pharaonic times, also have a claim? And if so, to what? What of individuals who find things in their backyard or whose families have held objects of antiquity for generations?

These are complicated questions. The antiquities dealers who were negotiating between buyers and sellers in an increasingly delegitimized trade were the easy targets in this looming conflict. If they could be accused of dealing in fakes, or of selling or buying forgeries, the entire trade could be discredited.

In a much heralded recent case in Italy, Italian authorities have challenged the J. Paul Getty Museum in Los Angeles by initiating a suit against Dr. Marion True, the museum's curator for antiquities who followed in the footsteps of the controversial Jiri Frel. The Italians let it be known that if they were successful in the case against the Harvard-educated True for illegal trading in antiquities, they would initiate further steps against other museums and collectors, and they cited a few of the institutions on their target list, among them the Cleveland Museum of Art in Ohio and certain wealthy collectors in the United States. At the same time, the Italians initiated negotiations with the Metropolitan Museum in New York, one of their targets, hoping to work out a deal that would avoid lawsuits but assure Italian control of the objects.

"We want this case to be a big deterrent," declared Capt. Massimiliano Quagliarella, of Italy's Carabinieri unit for prosecuting archaeological theft, as quoted in the *Los Angeles Times*. "It is important to stop the phenomenon of illegal excavations and illegal exportation by eliminating the demand and thus eliminating the offer."

Restrictive laws have been passed that delegitimize the antiquities trade in numerous countries and forbid the trading of artifacts beyond national borders. The new antiquities strictures stood Anglo-Saxon law on its head. In order to be sold, the object's "innocence" had to be proven by the buyer in a court of law or, just as important, the court of public opinion. By the standards that were beginning to be applied, many objects in Western museums would have to be returned to the country of origin. A truly strict interpretation would probably empty a fair portion of the items on display in museums in St. Petersburg, Berlin, Paris, London, Madrid, and throughout the United States. Indeed, as Egyptologist Bianchi noted, "many objects in the museums of the world are paperless." Different laws applied back then.

By the beginning of the twenty-first century, the worldwide trade of artifacts was getting tighter. According to one estimate, the illegal trade in classical Egyptian and Near Eastern antiquities alone amounted to some $200 to $300 million annually. The volume of trade had clearly declined as the screws began to be applied by the originating countries, although the pressure also made individual objects more valuable, especially if they could claim to have some kind of provenance.

No country has been more masterful at propounding what it considers its "rights" than Egypt, and no country more aggressive in attempting to squeeze a dollar out of a foreign visitor or a foreign exhibit.

Egypt had a thriving and fully legitimate antiquities market throughout the 1940s. Egyptian papyri and objets d'art were on display in museums throughout the Western world. The busy trade had an attractive by-product. It helped turn Egypt into a major destination for tourists from the West. In the early twenty-first century, an estimated 10 million Egyptians work in the tourism field, and tourism is the country's major foreign-currency earner, with $4.5 billion in revenues recorded in 2001. Tourism jumped from 1 million people in 1982 to 2.5 million in 1993 and 5.5 million in 2001, and it exceeded 7 million visitors in 2005.

Zahi Hawass, Egypt's director of antiquities, in an article in *Al Ahram Weekly,* defined how Egyptian law was changing. In some ways he was defining what legalities may have surrounded the removal of the Gospel of Judas from Egyptian soil.

"The government issued a law in 1951 that regulated excavation and the transport of artifacts to museums around the world," Hawass wrote. "Under this law the buying and selling of antiquities was still permitted and artifacts continued to be bartered and shipped all over the world. More laws followed. Two decrees in March 1952 established a system for the sale of antiquities and also enumerated the necessary steps for their export.

"It wasn't until 1983 that a law was established to stop the selling and export of antiquities," Hawass went on. "The law gave antiquities dealers six months to register the monuments [i.e., objects] in their possession but it clearly stated that no antiquities could be sold or exported.

"Still," Hawass conceded in this article, "we cannot do anything about the sale of antiquities in the United States or Europe unless we can prove that the statues, reliefs, and other antiquities were taken illegally from a tomb or storeroom. If we have this proof, then we can stop the sale."

A writer for *Al Ahram Weekly,* Nevine El Aref, noted that the Egyptian government had itself been a seller of antiquities several decades before.

> After the completion of the Nubia temples salvage operation, the Egyptian government offered a large number of monuments to foreign countries in compensation of their efforts. The Dabur Temple, for example, was given to the Spanish government, which reconstructed it on a hill in the Madrid Museum, while in 1974 the small Dendara Temple was given to the American president

Richard Nixon. The Egyptian government continued to offer items of its heritage or sold them on the international market until Law 117/1983 was issued, prohibiting all such activities. According to this law, all antiquities in Egypt are the property of the state and their unlawful removal from the country subsequent to that date is theft.

Hawass set up a department for retrieving "stolen" artifacts, and it has been trying to trace what the Egyptians consider state property. In fact, the new laws resulted in a flow of Egyptian-originated artifacts back to Egypt, especially since U.S. courts have tended to recognize the legitimacy of Egyptian claims.

The Egyptian law was directed at outsiders, but it also targeted Egyptians, who were the persons first and foremost involved in the trade in Egypt. All antiquities belong to the state, the new law states, and all antiquities must be reported to the authorities.

A number of rich Egyptian families have tended to keep some of their personal riches in objects of antiquity, the possession and ownership of which often goes back decades if not centuries. It will be interesting to see how laws are applied to artifacts that have been held in a family for generations, and whether these riches will have to be turned over to the state. From the standpoint of those families who may be forced to relinquish or hide such artifacts from the authorities, this could be seen as another example of plunder.

Amid the changes in the antiquities business, dealers such as Hanna Asabil had good reason to be secretive. With standards constantly shifting, longtime veterans of the trade could easily run afoul of a government official. Yet in the end, Hanna would not be responsible for the papyrus codex leaving Egypt. The way it was "exported" was illegal in any court of law in the world, and it would be up to Hanna to recover his property.

The antiquities trade is a specialized field. The dealers who are expert enough to know what to buy are relatively few, numbering only a few dozen worldwide. In the 1980s it was not an industry but a boutique. The clients were more numerous than the dealers, of course, and included the world's great museums, some major universities, and a number of private individuals. Yet even these numbers were extremely limited, at least when it came to the purchase of high-priced pieces. "It would be excessive to say that there are more than a thousand buyers for the really great items," said one of those involved in the selling. "Add it up. The museums. The individuals. I can almost make a list of buyers from memory."

One of the dealers who dealt with Nicolas Koutoulakis during the 1980s was Peter Sharrer, an expert in Egyptian art. An American dealer resident in northern New Jersey, he was an active traveler and trader in the markets of Europe and the Middle East. Many times, after the annual Basel Art Fair in Switzerland, he would rent a car with a gem specialist, Jack Ogden of London, and they would together motor down the Swiss superhighways to Geneva.

The Koutoulakis villa is located in the rue de Florissant, in one of the better sections of Geneva. The grounds covered more than an acre, and the house was characterized by Sharrer as "Swiss with a slightly Mediterranean flair, surrounded by wonderful gardens."

"Koutoulakis was an amazing man," Sharrer said. "He was of farmer stock with a flair with women and antiquities. He handled some of the greatest pieces of our time."

Sharrer recalled that the entrance into the Koutoulakis villa was very impressive. The entrance hall had ceilings twelve feet high. The kitchen opened off to the right, while on the left was a combination sitting room and office, studded with valuable objects. A window in the office looked out on the gardens in the back. "Visitors like myself were only allowed into certain parts of the house," Sharrer remembered.

"No matter who you were, he would assess you," Sharrer continued. "He only had that one eye, and he wanted to know who you are, what kind of person you are, what kind of client you might be. Frankly, it was always interesting. His face was very animated, with lots of different expressions."

Sharrer always sought an object at a price that fit his budget. Still, there was often a game of bluff and deception at the beginning of any encounter. "I always believed he owned a great number of fakes. What you had to learn to do was persevere. You'd say, 'Not for me.' You'd say it again. You wanted to be patient." Koutoulakis was really, in Sharrer's words, testing the visitor.

This prologue eventually ended, to be followed by a recess in which Koutoulakis would bring in thick Greek coffee—far denser than Italian espresso—to be drunk together with his guest. The arrival of coffee marked the end of what Sharrer calls the "bad pieces phase."

The real discussions began only after the break. Koutoulakis would dig into his repertoire. As Sharrer described it: "The fabulous pieces came then, as he began to bring out one or two of the better pieces. I visited him maybe ten or fifteen times through the years. In the years I knew him, I bought only three or four outstanding objects. When the first really great one came my way I pounced on it. That improved the output, what I got to see.

"He would size you up. What could you afford to buy. How good was your taste? Eventually I persevered—and I'd buy, not for a vast amount. Maybe $40,000 or $50,000. At that time that was a substantial sum."

In one meeting, Koutoulakis showed Sharrer an artifact that he pounced on immediately. It was a beautiful gold statuette of the primary Egyptian goddess, Isis, suckling her child Horus. Isis wore a close-fitting garment and her wig was surmounted by a horned disc. A hoop for suspension was fixed behind her head. The statuette featured refined and precise workmanship. This was not a fake; it was a dramatic find. In Sharrer's words, "This was one of the best pieces ever."

When Sharrer offered to buy the Isis statuette, Koutoulakis began to waver. Though he had brought out the piece, he hemmed and hawed. He seemed to be undecided whether to sell or not. Sharrer felt that the Greek was testing him. Koutoulakis finally said, "Okay, I'll think about it."

Sharrer remembered that Koutoulakis finally acknowledged that "he would consider me as the buyer of this piece." It was a kind of promise, and Sharrer hit paydirt nine months later. "Koutoulakis called and said, 'Come and see me.'"

Sharrer paid $50,000 for the piece. It was a considerable price at the time, but a fair one. The sale was made, Sharrer recalled, sometime in 1985.

As it turns out, the golden Isis bought by Peter Sharrer was an essential link in the story of the Gospel of Judas. It had previously been in Hanna Asabil's collection—and was one of the items stolen from his collection in a heist that also included the Gospel of Judas. The codex was gaining notoriety, but not of the sort that would befit an invaluable artifact in the history of Christianity. Instead it was a pawn in one of the antiquities trade's most heinous robberies.

CHAPTER FIVE

# THE ROBBERY

ITEMS APPEARING ON THE MARKET,
BELIEVED TO BE FROM EGYPT:
*Gold necklace*
*Middle Kingdom statuette in black granite*
*Golden statuette of Isis suckling Horus*
*Papyrus manuscript*

Nothing can survive for centuries totally intact. The manuscripts from the Jebel Qarara tomb were deteriorating. These papyri were now in Cairo, in the hands of a dealer who did not know what they said. Someone told him they might be written in ancient Hebrew. There were certainly some Greek words in what could be glimpsed, but Hanna Asabil did not read Greek nor could he decipher Coptic. All he knew was that the papyri were neither written in Arabic nor in a form of hieroglyphics that would date the manuscripts back to the time of the pharaohs.

Hanna knew enough not to touch the papyrus folios or try to pry them open, fearing that by doing so he might tear pieces that would affect their worth. But he knew nothing about modern air conditioning or controlled environmental conditions that could help in the preservation of what he knew to be valuable materials.

Whatever the papyrus book said, Hanna felt no urgency to read it. After all, the contents could always turn out to be a severe disappointment. In a way, it was better not to know what the manuscripts said.

But in any case, he wouldn't have time to find out before they were stolen from him.

The robbery of Hanna's most valuable treasures suggests careful planning. None of the perpetrators have been caught, and since the theft took place more than a quarter of a century ago, it is likely that none of them ever will be. The robbery has never been tried in a court of law, and the statute of limitations has by now run out. For those involved in the affair, memories have dimmed.

Still, whatever the details, the papyrus manuscripts were stolen as part of a cunningly planned and executed burglary. The perpetrators had inside information. They did not just happen upon an obscure apartment in the Heliopolis area of Cairo. They not only had to steal the objects, but they had to have a way of getting the goods out of Egypt without being caught. This inevitably limits the range of suspects. Still, the evidence about much of what happened is circumstantial. Sources are wary of exposure and investigation, so the robbery must be pieced together from versions of events as related by people who are knowledgeable about what happened. The whole truth will probably never be known.

For all that, the sources are in substantial accord as to many facts surrounding the robbery. They can point to a number of the events leading to the robbery. They also know, with considerable clarity, about the aftermath of the robbery and the whole process of restoration, when one of the great antiquities dealers of the twentieth century, Nicolas Koutoulakis, personally intervened to make the restitution a reality. The sources agree on the deals and sacrifices required to recover the ancient papyrus documents and return them to their original owner. What they may not agree upon is who did it, and what was the motivation. The robbery that took place a generation ago was either a simple act of greed, designed to enrich the perpetrators, who had become dazzled by the glint of gold and vast wealth that lay before them; or it was an inside act by someone known to Hanna, possibly from his own family, who was prepared to steal from a relative in order either to get even or to get rich. The possibility also exists that it was carried out not simply for profit but also as an attempt at revenge. As an effort to regain lost honor, it was aimed at depriving the victim of his dignity as well as his treasures.

The well-known Geneva-based dealer Nicolas Koutoulakis often arrived in Cairo accompanied by two women who were his regular traveling companions. One was a red-haired beauty, the second a tall brunette. The redhead was a woman known sometimes as Mia, at other times as Effie, and she was known by some Egyptians as Fifi. She and Koutoulakis were understood to have an extremely close relationship. Koutoulakis' son Manolis says that, though Greek, Mia hailed originally from Cairo. Her Arabic was fluent, and Koutoulakis used her as a translator in his dealings with Hanna and other Egyptians. According to those who remember them, the two women were great friends, and they would fly down from Athens to Cairo to meet Koutoulakis. Fellow dealers suspected as well that Koutoulakis used the women to carry the occasional item in their suitcases back to Greece, Geneva, or wherever they might be destined. "Koutoulakis was combining what was pleasurable with what was useful," one of them said.

On one such trip that is understood to have occurred sometime in the months before the robbery, without the Greek dealer's knowledge, Hanna took Mia aside. Speaking to her in Arabic, he asked her to help him sell his wares, including the papyrus manuscripts, and offered her a good commission if she would bring him clients. Hanna probably assured her that Koutoulakis would not find out about their arrangement.

According to Boutros, the colleague of one of Hanna's relatives, Hanna was contacted by Mia a few days after he approached her. She told him that she had a rich client who had come to Egypt, with a yacht waiting in Alexandria.

Hanna asked which type of objects interested this potential buyer. She answered that he was interested in a wide range of artifacts: coins, sculpture, glass, or manuscripts. In effect, she said, "We're interested in looking at whatever you want to sell."

An appointment was arranged. Excited by the possibility of a big sale, Hanna gathered his inventory from the various apartments belonging to relatives and friends in the Cairo area. On that night in March 1980, his entire inventory was on display in an apartment in Heliopolis for the first time.

At the arranged time, the prospective purchasers, including Mia, came to the apartment. They indicated they had plenty of money and were keen to buy whatever Hanna had. He showed them everything. They examined Hanna's inventory: gold pieces, a number of statues, some textiles, jewelry, and other assorted goods. Among the objects were numerous earthenware faience amulets, glass inlays from the Ptolemaic period, statues, textiles, and expensive gold and silver coins of Greek, Roman, and Byzantine origin.

Standing out among the objects were two particularly stunning pieces. One was a small statue in solid gold of Isis suckling the child Horus, about five centimeters high—the same statuette Peter Sharrer would purchase from Koutoulakis five years later. The statuette had what was described as a "terrible knock" on its back. It was completely bent, so that the upper part of the figure was leaning backward, "as if a stone fell on the amulet from the ceiling of a collapsing tomb."

The second object was a torque with Roman coins of gold mounted as pendants.

Also on display were the papyrus manuscripts containing the still untranslated and unknown Gospel of Judas.

"I showed the man an item, and told him the price," Hanna told a fellow dealer. "He nodded his head and said yes. He kept on saying yes for everything I showed him. Otherwise, he didn't open his mouth. He didn't say a word more. He didn't bargain."

Boutros reported exactly the same, as did another person close to Hanna. The prices were fantastic, the dream of any Cairo dealer, although the prices as quoted by Boutros were clearly an exaggeration, since they reached tens of millions of dollars.

The visitors kept asking the price of each piece: "How much?" They accepted the price that Hanna offered for each piece. They wrote it all down, itemizing Hanna's entire inventory. Finally, it was agreed. Hanna would sell them everything.

The price reached an astronomical figure.

"Okay," Hanna said, unable to believe his good fortune, "at that price I will sell."

The money, they said, was being kept on the yacht in Alexandria. "We'll go immediately to Alexandria," they told Hanna, "and return with the money."

Sometime the next day, as Hanna remembers it and related to a colleague, the apartment was burglarized. On the evening of the robbery, shortly after it occurred, a neighbor, who was also a relative, found the door wide open. All the treasures within were gone. Hanna's small safe—with his personal gold, the highly prized gold necklace with ornamental gold settings, and the papyrus manuscripts—was taken whole. Because Hanna had violated his usual practice of squirreling away items in different locations, in the hope of a major sale, he lost everything.

The indications are that whoever broke in knew a lot about the apartment. One account indicates that the robbers had keys or some other means of accessing the apartment, because the police found no signs of forcible entry. The apartment itself was not damaged in any way. The police later found the safe abandoned on a Cairo street, lying open and empty. The account of another person close to Hanna contradicts this. According to this person, the lock on the apartment door was broken.

The robbers, say people familiar with the Egyptian scene, could not have been exclusively foreigners. They had to have included Egyptians who were familiar with the country and how to transport stolen goods out of Egypt.

In 1993, one of Egypt's better-known antiquities dealers, a man who had been associated with Koutoulakis as a youth, admitted to a colleague that he was one of the central figures in this robbery. He had been waiting downstairs with a car to haul the goods away. Whether he was idly bragging, or whether his admission is credible, is uncertain.

Hanna's relatives made a complaint, a *shaqwa* or *mahdar,* to the local Cairo police, according to one account. Yet none of the goods had been registered. There were no bills of sale.

Hanna was distraught. He had lost everything. "He became completely crazy," according to a member of his family. He even retired to a Coptic monastery for six days of retreat to recover his sanity.

Hanna was sure the robbery was an inside job. He had three theories—none of them ever proven. At first he believed the robber was a relative, someone who had access to the apartment. A second theory was that a police officer stationed in Heliopolis, who was one of those who oversaw the investigation of the robbery, was involved. Only a policeman, Hanna reasoned, would have the skills to effectively pull off such a massive heist. Then he remembered that the day before the robbery the Greek Arabic-speaking woman named Mia, or Effie, along with a male foreigner also believed to have been Greek or at least Greek-speaking, viewed the goods in the apartment.

For weeks, Hanna went around crying on people's shoulders, as forlorn a man as ever walked the streets of Cairo. He would have revenge, he cried. He took to carrying a small pistol stashed inside his jacket, occasionally offering those he knew a peek at it. He did not know who was involved in this disastrous robbery, but the presence of a pistol indicated his intentions as to what he would do with that person if he ever found him.

His raving, however, did not help Hanna recover what had been stolen. One of those who remembers him from that period is Manolis Koutoulakis. "Hanna was completely down. He was five hundred meters below earth level because of that robbery. He was a nice man. We always got along with him. We wanted to help him."

Hanna spent two years in agony. As days and weeks passed, he hoped that by some miracle his life's fortune would be returned to him. He needed help and sought it from within his Coptic community. He spent money wildly on fortune-tellers and street magicians and went to Coptic priests seeking magic cures.

The priests and fortune-tellers and magicians offered numerous spells and incantations. These spells have been handed down through the ages and are documented in the book *Ancient Christian Magic: Coptic Texts of Ritual Power*. Many have the haunting ring of the magic chants recorded in the ancient Egyptian Book of the Dead. "Flee, hateful spirit, Christ pursues you, the Son of God and the Holy Spirit have overtaken you," goes one such incantation. These ritual practices are still a part of Coptic life in Egypt, and Hanna was groping for any possible solution to restoring what he believed was rightfully his.

In later years Hanna became more resigned to his fate. He was a religious man and also, in his own eyes, a strong person. He told a friend, years after the robbery, that "it was God's will," and God was with him.

Along with the other antiquities, the papyrus manuscripts had disappeared in the brazen robbery. They had taken one further step from their dry, stable grave toward a clouded future. Still no one had read them. No one realized their incalculable value.

Hanna soon settled on Mia, the Greek woman who frequently accompanied Koutoulakis, as a prime suspect in the robbery. He referred to her later as *el mara el uescha*, the "dirty bitch." As he recovered his emotional balance, he decided to take practical steps to recover his losses. Hanna thought Mia was among those responsible for the robbery. This assessment proved to be almost certainly correct since, according to Manolis, Hanna's missing items were later retrieved indirectly from her.

If you ask Hanna's family, they will also tell you that there were bad feelings between Hanna and Koutoulakis at the time.

These were linked to a statue of Amenemhat IV, a pharaoh of the Middle Kingdom, the son of Sesostris I and ruler of Egypt for thirty-eight years. Hanna sold it to Nicolas Koutoulakis, who probably paid a substantial sum for it. According to one of Hanna's partners, the statue had been estimated by someone they had consulted as worth 500,000 Egyptian pounds, more than $150,000 at the time and a fortune by any Egyptian's standard. After consultation, and what might have been a complaint from Koutoulakis, the possibility arose that the statue might be a fake. If one witness is to be believed, Koutoulakis concluded it was a fake. He returned to Hanna, demanding that Hanna refund his money. Hanna of course refused, continuing to believe that the statue was genuine.

Manolis Koutoulakis, the dealer's son, who sometimes went with him on his trips throughout the Middle East, says that his father did indeed know about the statue and later had it in his possession, though not in a deal that was concluded in Egypt. Koutoulakis checked the statue's authenticity with his usual adviser, Dietrich Wildung, who was a curator for antiquities at the museum in Munich, and then later moved on to Berlin as director of the Egyptian Museum in Germany's capital city. Wildung stated that at the time he believed this was an authentic piece. Manolis Koutoulakis adds that there were no known fakes coming out of Egypt in this period. If it were a fake, he pointed out, the most likely source of its creation was either Syria or Lebanon, and there was no reason at all for a fake to be shipped into Egypt to Hanna, and then to be exported.

Whatever the case, Egyptian dealers do not usually take their fakes back. The dealer who buys an ancient artifact assumes the risk. There is no such thing as store credit in their trade. Normally, the buyer "eats" the fake, keeping the knowledge to himself so as not to tarnish his own reputation as a savvy buyer. He may then go back to the seller, pretending nothing has gone wrong, and buy something of equivalent value. He takes possession of the new piece, saying he will send the money on shortly. Within a suitable amount of time, he announces to the seller that the statue he had previously bought has turned out to be a fake, and he will accept the new piece as compensation.

This form of payback is understood by both sides as correct. A loss has been adjusted, and their trading relationship continues without further recrimination.

This was summed up aptly by Manolis Koutoulakis: "You know, when we buy a fake, we forget about it. That's the way it is in this business. But it's not that it closes the discussion. It may open the door to a new discussion."

Hanna, believing the Amenemhat statue was genuine, was a stubborn man, and he did not want to hear anything about it being a fake. According to a colleague of Hanna, the Egyptian refused to return the money or provide what Koutoulakis considered suitable compensation and, since the statue was probably out of Egypt, there was no question of Koutoulakis physically returning it to him.

Even if the statue were a fake, Koutoulakis did not eat the loss. He later sold the statue onward, a sale confirmed by his son Manolis. The buyer was a well-known wealthy Greek shipowner, Theodore Halkedis, who lived in an elegant Park Avenue apartment in New York City. Halkedis, like Hanna, insisted afterward that the statue—which was of excellent quality, even if it were a modern copy—was not a fake. When one Egyptologist came to Halkedis's New York home and told him it was, Halkedis would not listen and reportedly threw him out. When Halkedis and his wife, Aristea, presented some two hundred objects in a special public exhibition at the Michael C. Carlos Museum at Emory

University in Atlanta between April 2001 and January 2002, the piece was included, the only time it ever has been exhibited.

Hanna then committed what could be interpreted as a second offense against the powerful Greek dealer, as recounted by Hanna to someone with whom he dealt. He approached Mia to trade on his behalf, as told earlier.

Koutoulakis was a dealer who exercised a sizable amount of control over the market. As a colleague commented, "Every dealer at that level wants to make sure that the persons he is dealing with respect him. When one of the smaller dealers gets, or has, an important object, the big dealer wants to make sure it's first offered to him. If there's a problem, he has to teach the smaller dealer a lesson."

If Koutoulakis had actually learned of Hanna's attempt to sidestep him, Koutoulakis must have been seething. Not only was Hanna unwilling to satisfy Koutoulakis's request for compensation for the statue, but now he was adding insult to injury by attempting to use Koutoulakis's companion to enlarge his own circle of clients. A mistake such as this would have been unpardonable, according to the ethics of the trade.

No one, however, can tell Koutoulakis's side of the story at this point. He has died and cannot comment on the possible strains in his relationship with Hanna Asabil at the time. The formidable dealer left no personal account of the events that swirled around Hanna—not that Koutoulakis, a man who preferred verbal agreements to anything written, ever left much of a trail. Despite these tensions, Manolis Koutoulakis denies any involvement by his father, pointing out that the senior Koutoulakis was not in Egypt at the presumed time of the robbery. What is known is that Koutoulakis was a towering figure in the antiquities trade. He was a figure of immense proportions, resembling Zorba the Greek of

Nikos Kazantzakis's creation, who, like Koutoulakis, also hailed from the island of Minoan heroes, Crete. He was a man who was always protective of his reputation as a man of his word.

☥

About a year and a half after the robbery, Hanna turned to a third party for help. Here, the story becomes far more certain in its outlines. Yannis Perdios was a pleasant, smart, cultured man who lived in Athens, but had spent years living in Cairo working in the tourist industry. Perdios enjoyed the search for unusual items, either buying or trading for the occasional antiquity that struck his fancy. Perdios's collecting specialty was artifacts of nineteenth-century life in Greece under Turkish rule. He managed his affairs with discretion, choosing the kind of contacts and arrangements that landed no one, including himself, in trouble. Perdios's native language was Greek, but he also spoke excellent English and fluent French, and during his years in Cairo he became fluent in Arabic.

Perdios still returned to Cairo on a regular basis, partly because the Egyptian government insisted that foreigners renew their residency permits periodically. Perdios wanted to keep his permit active, at least until he managed to sell the apartment he owned in the Zamalek section of Cairo. Hanna sought out Perdios on one of these visits and asked him to help. Perdios could communicate effectively with the wider world, yet he had a reputation for discretion. Most important, Hanna thought he was someone he could trust, and he was also someone on familiar and positive terms with Nicolas Koutoulakis. Upon learning the story of the robbery, Perdios agreed to contact Koutoulakis on behalf of his friend. One of Hanna's colleagues, as well as Manolis Koutoulakis, expressed great respect for the Greek go-between, who was considered a fair player by all parties. As Hanna's colleague related, "He was a gentleman, and he was a friend to both sides."

Back in Athens, Perdios called Geneva to speak to Koutoulakis, as he would know Mia's whereabouts. When Perdios inquired about the robbery, Koutoulakis too suggested that perhaps Mia had pulled off the job. Koutoulakis asserted firmly that he had nothing to do with it. He was totally innocent in this matter.

Perdios cautioned him nonetheless. "It's better to clear the situation with Hanna because you might have problems when you come to Egypt," he said. "Don't leave the problem unsolved. Find the woman."

Perdios added a warning that he thought pertinent: If Koutoulakis did not clear it up, he could be risking his life by going to Egypt. "Don't forget, Hanna goes around with a pistol under his jacket."

Whether or not Koutoulakis believed that this was credible is not known. Whatever he thought of Perdios's warning, he was persuaded, after a number of calls, to meet. Perdios would go to Cairo to meet Hanna and Koutoulakis, who was prevailed upon to bring the woman known as Mia as well.

It is entirely consistent with the known facts, as recounted by different witnesses, that Koutoulakis felt great pity and affection for Hanna, and wanted to do whatever he could to help him. "My father was the one Hanna turned to because Hanna and Perdios believed that my father was the one who could help Hanna get his goods back," Manolis Koutoulakis noted.

Koutoulakis, however he did it, managed to persuade Mia to come with him to the meeting, which took place in Cairo. Strangely, according to an account related by one of the two Egyptians present, Mia brought along her twelve-year-old daughter to the meeting, which was interpreted by the Egyptian side to mean that she was seeking some combination of pity, forgiveness, or reconciliation.

Hanna's position was not a particularly strong one. He knew he had to plead for mercy and restitution himself. He had only a vague threat of violence to sustain his negotiating position.

That first meeting took place at Perdios's tastefully furnished apartment in the Zamalek district. The antagonists were fuming beneath their outwardly calm exteriors as they tried to figure out a way to extricate themselves from a situation fraught with danger for each of them.

The session was fairly short and to the point. Both Koutoulakis and Mia strenuously denied their involvement. "We didn't do it," they stated succinctly, both separately and together.

Yet even while denying they were involved in the robbery, Koutoulakis and Mia both promised to help Hanna regain his goods. Hanna said he wanted not only the prized papyrus manuscripts but also whatever else was stolen.

At one point, while one of the participants and Koutoulakis were out of the room, Mia related to Hanna's colleague who had come to the meeting with him that her second child, a son, was quite ill either with cancer or a tumor in his head. She was nervous and afraid.

The meeting broke up inconclusively.

The next steps played out over the following months and only after a series of telephone calls between Athens and Geneva. Communications with Cairo were held to a minimum.

Different objects from Hanna's collection had begun to show up in the markets of Europe. Some signs indicated that a center of activity was Athens. There was later speculation that the goods might have first transited Switzerland or somehow arrived there first. In order to be returned, the items had to be found, recovered, gathered together, and stored in a central location.

Among those whom Koutoulakis called in his recovery effort was Dr. Jack Ogden, the distinguished London gem specialist who, although only in his mid-thirties, was considered among the world's greatest experts on gold and other precious jewels. Ogden's book *Ancient Jewellery* was just about to be published through the University of California Press and British Museum Press. Ogden at the time had his own gem shop at Duke Street and St. James in central London. With a reputation for honesty, total observance of the law, and the utmost discretion, Ogden would later be named executive director of the International Jewellery Confederation and chief executive of the National Association of Goldsmiths of Great Britain.

"There were a few pieces of gold coming out of Egypt about 1979 that were making their way into the European marketplace. These pieces went to Athens, and then were sent to various places in Europe," Ogden recounted. The exodus of gold from Egypt, according to Ogden, recalled an earlier wave of valuable gold items from Egypt that appeared on world markets in the 1920s and 1930s. At that time, Alexandrian Greeks had been subject to one of the sporadic periods of persecution by governmental authorities, and many sent their most valuable and precious possessions out of the country or left the country altogether.

In 1982, Koutoulakis called Ogden, saying he knew that Ogden had a beautiful gold necklace and a number of other pieces, including a gold statuette of Isis.

Ogden was taken aback because he had received the objects on consignment only several weeks before. Koutoulakis knew Ogden had the objects before he had even had a chance to properly register them, much less display them. "How the hell did Koutoulakis know I had these pieces?" Ogden wondered. "Koutoulakis's call was extraordinary in that I'd only had the pieces for such a brief time. I'd got the necklace from Athens. Koutoulakis knew exactly. He claimed he was worried about me and the potential problems involved for me." Whoever it was that was supplying Koutoulakis with information, it was enough to give him precise knowledge that the artifacts had been sent to Ogden and that Ogden had recently received them and had the two artifacts in his possession at the London shop.

Ogden knew Koutoulakis quite well, having visited him numerous times at the villa in Geneva, both along with Peter Sharrer and alone. "He said that they were stolen from Egypt. He told me I had to hand them over or the police would be involved. Somehow, there was a gun involved. I don't remember the details. It was not an easy situation."

The person who had sent the necklace to Ogden was a redhead named Effie, Ogden said. She had come to London on several occasions to provide him with small items such as earrings or a tiny ring, which Ogden took on consignment. Some of these goods he assumed were bought by Effie in the souks of Cairo.

Was the Effie who visited Ogden the same as the Effie or Mia who was a companion of Koutoulakis? That link makes sense because, according to one source, Effie's full first name was Efthimia. The name means "joy" in Greek. In popular Greek usage, she could be called either Effie—or Mia. In other words, judged only by the name, Effie and Mia could be one and the same person. As recounted by Ogden, Effie was a redhead. Manolis Koutoulakis, twenty-nine years of age at the time, agrees that the Effie his father knew was also a redhead. It is reasonable to conclude, but not absolutely certain, that the woman who provided the goods to Jack Ogden was the same Effie who hailed from Athens and had been Koutoulakis's translator and assistant during his trips to Egypt.

In any case, Ogden remembers being surprised by Koutoulakis's aggressive handling of the situation. Ogden did not want trouble. Though the pieces were on consignment, if they were stolen, he did not want to have anything to do with them. He was ready to return them to whoever the rightful owner was. He does not recall whether he contacted Effie or not, but he does remember that was probably the last he ever heard from her.

In order to recover the necklace and the statuette, Koutoulakis contacted Perdios. Speaking in Greek to his fellow countryman, he instructed Perdios to fly to Paris, pick up Koutoulakis's son Manolis, and then proceed to London together. There, they would meet Ogden.

The visit was brief, because Ogden was more than eager to surrender what he had. Manolis and Perdios told him what he had to know, that the necklace and other objects needed to be recovered and returned to the rightful owner. "We told Jack that they were stolen goods. It was enough for him. Ogden reacted completely normally. My job was to identify the objects that we had seen in Egypt, to say these were the same items we'd seen there," Manolis said.

Ogden, with a sterling reputation to defend, was eager to be rid of the items. He was not told that the origin of the objects was an apartment in Heliopolis. Ogden shortly returned the golden necklace and statuette, objects received on consignment from the woman he knew as Effie, without argument.

"Ogden was scared. He didn't want to have anything to do with it," Perdios recounted to an intermediary. Perdios made a purchase at the same time: a little Roman marble box for funeral ashes for five hundred pounds, Ogden recalled. Perdios declared the piece with Greek customs officials, and the dating on that customs slip was 1982.

Despite the upsetting incident, Ogden remained close to the Koutoulakis family. Ogden's wife is a distinguished scholar of Greek origin and museum curator. Daphne Koutoulakis, Nicolas's daughter, became not only a personal friend, but was godmother to one of Ogden's daughters.

With Perdios as intermediary, Hanna and Koutoulakis were now ready for a final meeting that would conclude the restitution of the papyrus manuscripts to Hanna.

Antiquities dealers are divided into three essential categories: some specialize in ancient art, some in coins, and a relative few like the glamour and allure of old manuscripts, though that is generally considered less lucrative than the other fields.

Koutoulakis was attracted to ancient art. He also had a flair for numismatics, so he occasionally dabbled in coins, but that was a minor passion, since it was not nearly as profitable as ancient art. However, he did not like old manuscripts. Not only was he unfamiliar with papyrus texts, he did not trust them. Their value did not lie in their inherent physical property or in the artwork, qualities that were apparent to the human eye. Rather, it resided in the words that had been written on parchment or papyrus.

A particular problem with ancient manuscripts is their fragility. They can crumble at the touch. Like other antiquities dealers specializing in objects, Koutoulakis must have detested the fact that a match could burn a papyrus or parchment investment. Water could soak papyri and destroy them. He preferred hard objects that could withstand the elements or other adversity.

That next meeting with Hanna occurred in the summer of 1982, although the principals still alive have no precise record of the date. Hanna, despite some trepidation about leaving Egypt and landing on Koutoulakis's home turf in Switzerland, flew to Geneva along with an Egyptian colleague. They met Perdios by agreement at Koutoulakis's villa at the end of rue de Florissant.

Hanna's initial impressions of Koutoulakis and his villa were vivid. The place was huge, he recalled, unlike anything he knew in Cairo with its teeming streets. Only kings and presidents lived like Koutoulakis. He was struck by what he called the "eyes" posted all around—meaning the security cameras placed in strategic spots. In addition, Koutoulakis kept dogs that had to be secured before a visitor could enter the gate.

Koutoulakis did not invite them into his house. Instead he received the Greek and the Copt outside in his garden. Mia was not present. Manolis Koutoulakis says that neither was he.

The meeting was, like the first one, short. The senior Koutoulakis, as cool as ever, did not overplay his hand. He had managed to recover the precious manuscripts, he informed Hanna, volunteering his opinion that the codex was written in ancient Hebrew.

Hanna was nowhere near as refined. He was upset about the robbery, and the conversation quickly became heated. According to one account, he went as far as to threaten Manolis's safety before Perdios intervened. Manolis Koutoulakis disagrees: "I wasn't ever threatened. Hanna was down, he was a little crazy, but he wasn't the kind of man to threaten. He was a peaceful man."

While the Egyptian dealer calmed down, the two Greek speakers discussed the situation in their native tongue.

The account of what happens next comes from the second Egyptian, Hanna's colleague, who was with Hanna at the meeting watching every movement. He recounts that the denouement was swift. He, Perdios, and Hanna drove off in a taxi to collect the papyri from a white-haired gentleman they understood at the time to be one of Koutoulakis's relatives. According to Manolis, that white-haired man was most likely Koutoulakis's customs broker, who was white-haired, and not a relative at all.

Somehow, Koutoulakis had managed to recover the manuscripts. In the words of his son, "My father was the only one who could help Hanna. No one wanted to contact the police. That's why they turned to him. No one else could have done it."

However it happened, Hanna's prize had finally been recovered thanks to Koutoulakis' efforts. Yet it would come at a price. There was a clear understanding between the parties that Koutoulakis would restore Hanna's papyrus manuscripts to him, nothing more. That was a business agreement. Someone else—whoever that might be—would keep the solid objects, including the torque and the gold statuette of Isis suckling Horus, and these would not be restored to Hanna. That was also part of the understanding between the parties. "This cleared the subject," acknowledged Hanna's colleague, a personal eyewitness to the entire process, indicating that with the return of the papyrus manuscripts the matter was settled.

Manolis agrees with this interpretation of events. "For Hanna, the books were the most important thing. We were able to locate the two items in London, but that was part of the deal. My father never stole anything. What he did was specifically agreed with Hanna."

Based on Hanna's evaluation of the worth of the manuscripts at $3 million, the necklace and the statuette, worth about $50,000 each, could be regarded as a commission for undertaking the restitution of property to Hanna.

"We are people of our word," Manolis says. "My father tried to be honest with Hanna and deal with him honestly. Whatever he did he got because of a business deal, because of money that was paid. It was part of the price of the deal."

He contends that his "father was a legend in the trade—not because of his wealth, and we don't have as much as people allege—but because of his knowledge, his sense of commerce, and his daring—and most of all, because he was a man of his word."

Koutoulakis had fulfilled his obligation as he saw it: to return the precious papyri to their rightful owner. He had made Hanna "whole."

According to Manolis, his father broke off relations with Effie directly after these events. When Koutoulakis died in January 1996, Effie called to offer her condolences. Manolis said there had been little or no contact between the Koutoulakis family and Effie in the intervening years, and none since his father's death. Effie's precise whereabouts are unknown, and efforts to contact her were unsuccessful.

When the meeting ended, Hanna, Perdios, and the second Egyptian left for downtown Geneva with the papyrus manuscripts in hand. Hanna had recovered "the book." At Perdios's suggestion, they proceeded to what they considered the most secure location possible: a vault in a Swiss bank. Perdios helped Hanna understand the forms and fill them out as necessary. Perdios opened the account in Hanna's name with Hanna as signatory. The codex was then deposited in the vault—the first but not only time that the Gospel of Judas would be stored in a safe-deposit box.

Perdios gave Hanna the keys to the vault and they separated. While Hanna flew back to Cairo, Perdios made another stop in Switzerland before he returned to Greece, visiting Frieda Tchacos Nussberger at her gallery in Zurich. He did not tell her what had just occurred, nor did he describe the nature of the papyrus manuscripts that had just been returned to their owner. Perdios merely asked if Frieda possibly had a client for some valuable texts, giving her some photographs that had been taken previously. That was Frieda's introduction to the texts.

Frieda made several inquiries, but with only photographs to show potential clients, nothing came of it. She soon let the matter drop.

A few years later, Sharrer visited Koutoulakis in his Geneva mansion and was shown the golden Isis statuette. As described earlier, the Greek was wary and, though he was ready to let Sharrer see it, he was not yet ready to sell. One explanation for his behavior is that he wanted to make certain there were no Interpol alerts on the item. Some nine months later, Sharrer was permitted to buy the treasured piece.

As for the papyrus manuscripts, they had left Egypt for good. Hanna could now continue to try selling his merchandise, but from now on his customers would become more rarefied. To help substantiate his $3 million price tag, he would need to invite scholars to examine, albeit briefly, the manuscripts. For the first time, the codex would be seen by experts who could read the text and decipher its meaning.

# CHAPTER SIX

# UNDER A MAGNIFYING GLASS

*My impression of this man was that he was very ignorant
and only interested in money. From his point of view,
it should have been enough that he opened the shoebox and said,
"Ah, yes, that's papyrus, now let's talk price."*
—STEPHEN EMMEL

Yannis Perdios and Hanna Asabil needed to interest people in
buying the precious manuscripts, and one of the first persons to
come to mind was the famous "Koenig"—Ludwig Koenen—the
so-called king of papyrus scholarship whose interest in the subject
had frequently helped Cairene dealers appreciate the worth of
ancient papyrus fragments and texts. Perdios contacted him in late
1982 and, following up, sent a set of photographs similar to those
he had given to Frieda Tchacos Nussberger.

Koenen distributed the blurry photographs to a few select scholars. The first identification was made by a scholar of ancient scripture at Brigham Young University, S. Kent Brown, who recognized
a few indistinct words of text as coming from the First Apocalypse

of James. From that moment on, the small band of scholars linked to Koenen believed that the documents were not only authentic but a rare scholarly find, possibly linked to the Nag Hammadi codices. Koenen, who had met Hanna in Cairo and considered him a credible dealer, now assembled a team to further assess the authenticity, age, and content of the papyri.

☥

Koenen's team gathered in Geneva on the morning of May 15, 1983. The group of academics featured several of the most distinguished scholars in their fields. They came ready to inspect what they hoped was a great new find and, if so, to purchase it.

Three of the four were from the University of Michigan in Ann Arbor, whose library holds what is generally considered the most outstanding papyrus collection in the United States. The leader was Koenen, whose expertise was as a papyrologist. Born in Germany, with a Ph.D. from the University of Cologne, he had become a full professor at the University of Michigan in 1975 and was ambitiously trying to expand Michigan's superb collection of papyri.

With him was a colleague, Professor David Noel Freedman, an enormously respected figure on his way to becoming, in the words of one of his students, "the grand old man of American Bible studies." Among his credits, Freedman was the general editor of the enormously respected *Anchor Bible Dictionary*. His specialty was the Old Testament.

Accompanying Freedman was one of his graduate assistants, Astrid Beck, a young woman completing her Ph.D. at Ann Arbor. A medievalist by profession, she taught comparative religion and comparative literature and would later become managing editor of

*The Anchor Bible Dictionary* under Freedman and of the *Eerdmans Dictionary of the Bible.*

A fourth member of the team was needed to provide expertise in Coptic. Koenen contacted James M. Robinson, who had gained prominence in the field because of his work as general editor of the Nag Hammadi library and secretary of the entire Nag Hammadi project. Robinson, based on information provided him by Koenen, also believed that the find was genuine.

The Nag Hammadi library consisted of material from thirteen codices—bound manuscript volumes, as opposed to the more common scrolls of the day. The Coptic scholars involved in the Nag Hammadi project believed that clues abounded in the scholarly work that at least one and possibly more additional manuscripts existed. A few Coptic scholars working with Robinson suspected there might be another codex that was part of the Nag Hammadi library, though it had somehow been separated out from the initial find and was still unknown. Robinson hoped the new papyri would solve the remaining Nag Hammadi mysteries, amplifying the body of literature and providing another impressive achievement to his long course of scholarship.

As his emissary, Robinson chose a young scholar, Stephen Emmel. Born in Rochester, New York, Emmel was soon to receive his doctorate from Yale University. He was currently working in Rome with Italy's most renowned Coptologist, Tito Orlandi, researching a fifth-century Coptic abbot, Shenoute, and the White Monastery where he lived, the subject of Emmel's now heralded Ph.D. thesis. Emmel had worked on the papyri texts of Nag Hammadi during the 1970s in Cairo and was close to Robinson.

That rounded out the team.

☥

Astrid Beck had begun her journey to Europe in Ann Arbor, flying to Newark International Airport where she met up with Dr. Freedman, who had come from Nantucket. They then flew together to Geneva. Waiting at the Geneva airport to greet them on arrival were Koenen and his wife. "Freedman and Koenen had an excellent professional and personal friendship," Astrid recalled about the Geneva weekend. "Ludwig was very excited about the possibility of acquiring these valuable manuscripts."

Freedman, less experienced in the acquisition of papyrus manuscripts, but eager to examine any biblical texts that might be in the collection, was more reserved. "My part in the venture was in association with Dr. Koenen," Freedman notes. "We represented the University of Michigan."

The Koenens and their jet-lagged passengers drove in the Koenens' rental car through the morning damp from the airport to downtown Geneva. Their destination was the Hôtel de l'Union off rue de la Servette.

The Geneva meeting had taken Koenen a number of months to arrange. When Perdios had finally found Koenen's telephone number and address and contacted him from Athens, he told Koenen that he believed the ancient manuscripts had historical significance. "It would have taken that [kind of suggestion], and probably a bit more, to get me out of my study," Koenen commented later. Koenen knew Hanna, and from what he had learned about the photographs, he believed the find was authentic, though the price and full scholarly value of the manuscripts remained in question.

Most scholars are not museum curators, accustomed to purchasing art and artifacts, nor are they necessarily capable negotiators. Like Koenen, they might want to augment the collections at their respective universities, but they often lack financial resources to do so. More often, they recommend valuable artifacts to others, serving as consultants to museums or private collectors.

According to Freedman, the funds that the scholars had been able to hastily arrange were limited. Koenen "was prepared to offer somewhere between $50,000 and $100,000," he said, while he himself "had been promised up to about $50,000 for any biblical manuscripts that might be in the collection." Thus, the total war chest from the University of Michigan for purchase of the manuscripts was about $150,000.

The Michigan team's primary backer was the Dorot Foundation, one of the principal financial supporters of the Israel Museum and its showcase Shrine of the Book in Jerusalem, which houses the famous Dead Sea Scrolls. The leading force behind the Dorot Foundation was Joy Ungerleider, later Joy Ungerleider Mayerson, a woman whose resources came from her father, Samuel Gottesman. The Gottesman family and its foundation had made some of the twentieth century's most significant philanthropic donations in archaeology and biblical history, but Ungerleider was interested only in biblical texts, not Christian apocrypha. As recalled by Freedman, "it was my impression, if not full understanding, that any manuscript materials that Joy Ungerleider might purchase would end up at the Shrine of the Book.... I had no interest in keeping them at the University of Michigan or anywhere else.... It would have been entirely appropriate for them to be in the Shrine of the Book, which would make them available for inspection or even study by any qualified person."

The Coptology side also had a backer. Robinson turned to one of his longtime associates, Harry Attridge, a professor of New Testament studies at Southern Methodist University (SMU) in Dallas. The Coptologists first needed to assess what the papyrus manuscripts actually were, but Attridge was ready to support the venture and got help from the Bridwell Library of the Perkins School of Theology at SMU—which has a rare books section—in providing a budget for purchase. That sum was $50,000. Robinson felt assured that there would be adequate monies to make the purchase if the papyri were genuine and significant.

The meeting was scheduled to take place shortly after noon on May 15 at the Hôtel de l'Union. In anticipation of the sellers' Arab or Muslim prejudices, the two senior University of Michigan scholars told their junior colleague, the only woman on the team, that she should not attend the meeting. Beck, unable to resist the collective wisdom of her academic seniors, bowed out. "I was very disappointed and angry, to be excluded from the meetings," she remembers, "but I was told that the sellers were Arabs, and that was their custom. And, of course, I didn't want to jinx the negotiations."

As it turned out, neither of the two sellers was Muslim. Hanna was a Christian Copt, and Perdios was a sophisticated Greek man of the world and a collector himself, fluent in a number of languages.

The Egyptian dealer and his Greek interpreter came to the hotel, picked up the scholars, and drove them to a second hotel in Geneva. The rules that were laid out were strict. "We would be allowed to examine the papyri for a few minutes," Emmel recalled. "No photographs would be permitted, and we weren't allowed to write anything. We were also told that we would not be able to take any notes so we had no paper, no writing implements of any sort." He commented sardonically, "Otherwise, there were no restrictions of any sort."

Of the two, Hanna as the owner was the dominant force. He was the one who would not permit photographs or note taking, which the scholars had to do later from memory. Perdios, knowing how distinguished the American group was, wanted to help them make a proper identification and arrive at a price that matched the importance of the find. But for Hanna, according to the team's impression of the man, all that counted was the money.

Though Perdios was fluent in Greek, French, English, and Arabic, Hanna had only a village education. As a result, the meeting was conducted with only the most limited of linguistic exchanges. "The Greek guy spoke Arabic—probably also French," recalled Koenen. "The talks were done in a mixture of English and kitchen Arabic."

The setting for the examination was a room in the hotel. There were three shoebox-like containers lying on the bed. "We were told they contained the papyri," Emmel noted. The Americans were appalled to see how the manuscripts were apparently boxed, transported, and cared for.

Emmel's write-up of the meeting, submitted two weeks later to his colleagues at SMU and to Robinson, does not indicate the full extent of the dismay at the condition of the manuscripts and the way they were handled. "The material was being stored in three cardboard boxes lined with newspaper," Emmel recorded. He did, however, issue a warning about their future state. "There is great danger of further deterioration of the manuscript as long as it is in the hands of the present owner."

A first look at the papyrus manuscripts was enough to convince anyone who saw them that they were genuine. "I myself am completely convinced and was convinced from the first time I saw this manuscript that this is a genuine ancient papyrus codex," Emmel commented. "The question of whether or not someone in modern times could fake an object like this is for me a nonquestion. It's out of the question." He explained why the possibility of a forgery was nonexistent. "One would not only have to have genuine material, papyrus—and not simply any papyrus, but ancient papyrus, old papyrus that is clearly hundreds of years old—one would also have to know how to imitate Coptic script from a very early period. The number of specialists in Coptic that know that in the world is very small. You would also have to be able to compose a text in Coptic that is grammatically correct and convincing. The number of people who could do that is even smaller than the number who could read Coptic."

Later testing would confirm the papyri were indeed real. "They were not in great condition, but it was exciting to see them and to get to touch them." Emmel said.

As to the origins of the manuscripts, Hanna was quite specific in what he told the three academics. "According to the owner, all four of the manuscripts in this collection were found near the village of Beni Masar, about eight kilometers south of Oxyrhynchus (modern Eshnasa)," wrote Emmel. But, he cautioned, "It is difficult to know how seriously to take such information."

The three scholars got to work. One box was put on the bed, the second on a desk, and the third on the bureau in the room. "I was very excited," recalled Emmel later. "I just did not have adequate time to make as thorough an initial inspection as I would have liked."

They were surprised by the diversity of the materials. The collection included both Coptic and Greek manuscripts. The scholars agreed among themselves that Emmel would handle the Coptic language documents, Koenen the Greek.

"A system of numeration and designation was agreed upon with the owner and his intermediary for referring to the four manuscripts," Emmel noted. His report precisely recorded what the experts saw and how the materials were arranged. The portion written in Greek included a biblical manuscript and a metrodological fragment—a mathematical treatise on metrodology, the science of weights and measures. The Coptic included some letters of Paul and what Emmel referred to as a "Coptic apocalyptic codex."

In the limited time they had, the scholars attempted as incisive an analysis as possible. Koenen undertook a hastily written translation of a few pages of the mathematical treatise. The "metrodological tractate" was ten pages long. It was later identified as a document for teaching problem solving through mathematics and offered practical case samples. The document, probably a mathematical essay from the Greek period in Egypt, mainly consisted of geometrical problems that had nothing to do with religion. However, its inclusion in the group indicated that—assuming the group of manuscripts had been found together—whoever had owned the various papyri long ago was a learned man with broad interests.

Studying the Coptic documents, Emmel was able to draw some quick, though tentative, conclusions. "I saw immediately it was probably not a New Testament text—that is, a canonical text. I thought it could be Old Testament, though that wasn't likely. There was a possibility that it was in Greek language as well as in Coptic." He described the Coptic codex as "the gem of the entire collection of four manuscripts...a papyrus codex from the fourth century A.D., approximately thirty cm tall and fifteen cm broad, containing gnostic texts."

Emmel had brought a small pair of tweezers, the kind used by stamp collectors, which he describes as "the best kind of tool for handling papyri when they are brittle." With them, he lifted the top page and peeked below. "Since I didn't want to take anything out of the box for fear of damaging it, I simply used my tweezers to reach in, here and there." What Emmel was trying to do was to "in a sense, peek inside, where I could find pages where I could read some of the text and perhaps recognize what work of literature it was or perhaps find a title. I was looking for page numbers to get some idea if we had the beginning of the book or the middle or the end, how much of it, and so on. But I didn't look at every page and I didn't turn any pages, and I didn't remove anything from the shoebox itself simply because I wanted to protect the material physically as much as I could."

Emmel tallied some fifty-four or fifty-six pages, and he thought some pages might be missing. "At the time that the codex was discovered, it was probably in good condition, with a leather binding and complete leaves with all four margins intact," he wrote later.

> But the codex has been badly handled; only half of the leather binding (probably the front cover) is now preserved and the leaves have suffered some breakage. The absence of half of the binding and the fact that page numbers run only into the 50's leads me to suppose that the back half of the codex may be missing; only closer study can prove or disprove the supposition. The texts are in a non-standard form of Sahidic.

Emmel was hopeful that further study of the surviving bindings, or covers, would provide more information as to its provenance.

One of the essential tools of analysis when examining such papyri is to see how the book was constructed. Emmel initially believed it to be a single-quire codex, but later study showed that it had multiple quires. A quire is a stock of sheets of paper or papyrus containing four pages of text on a folded sheet. The use of quires in early Christian literature constituted a markedly different technology from the scrolls that were, and are still, used in the Jewish religion. Torah scrolls, for example, are rolled out, read, and then rolled back together again. Quires are different—more like a modern book, where one big sheet of paper combines the front and back sections of a section, and are numbered, for example, 1–2 and 15–16. Another sheet is folded in, becoming pages 3–4 and 13–14, and so on.

Within the limited time allotted, Emmel's detective work resulted in a reasonably good analysis. The manuscripts were clearly important. His heart pounded as he discovered elements of what was in front of him. He was crossing through centuries to touch the writings of an unknown scribe of centuries past. Emmel later recalled: "By good luck I happened to look at one point at a page that had a title written on it. And the title in Coptic meant 'The Letter of Peter to Philip.' That's also gnostic literature we know from one of the Nag Hammadi codices. And I also recognized some of the text at the very end. It's a short work.

"I knew the content of the text and it was clear to me that this was another copy of the Letter of Peter to Philip from Nag Hammadi Codex VIII. So we had two known works of gnostic literature, but as I looked further I could read enough to see that there was another work that at least wasn't familiar to me, although the genre—the type of text—was familiar."

In his report he made a more precise identification:

> The codex contains at least three different texts: "The First Apocalypse of James," known already, though in a different version, from Nag Hammadi Codex (NHC) V (2); "The Letter of Peter to Philip" known already from NHC VIII.

Emmel attempted to identify the third part of the codex, which was unknown to him. It is, he wrote, a dialogue between Jesus and his disciples (at least "Judas" is involved, similar in genre to "The Dialogue of the Savior" (NHC III) and "The Wisdom of Jesus Christ" (NHC III and the Berlin gnostic codex PB 8502).

Yet in gnostic texts 'Judas' usually referred to Judas Thomas, Jesus' supposed brother. Emmel's initial speculation therefore focused on the brother, and he missed the dramatic revelation of what lay in the box. "I assumed it was a probably previously unknown gnostic dialogue between Jesus and his disciples. And I assumed Judas was Judas Didymus Thomas, the same character who shows up in the Gospel of Thomas, for example, or the Book of Thomas. It was possible it would be Judas Iscariot, the Betrayer, but that was less likely simply because of what's typical of gnostic literature."

He later regretted the misidentification. He simply had lacked the time, and also the resources in that small hotel, to determine which Judas it actually was.

Besides, the idea that the Judas whose name appeared in the codex could be Judas Iscariot was too radical to consider. No one would write about Judas the Betrayer, it was believed. No one from the early Christian era would have had the nerve to tell Judas's side of the story.

Koenen had been led to believe that Hanna would accept a reasonable offer. "Reasonable" is, of course, a highly subjective term—especially when haggling with Egyptian antiquities dealers. Negotiations in Egypt usually began with a long and very general chat over a glass of hot sweet tea or Turkish coffee,

Koenen knew, the discussion inevitably revolving around the eternal hunt for treasures: Who bought what, who offered what to whom, what the price was, what the latest news about discoveries was, and so forth.

The interminable opening was eventually followed by an often very short negotiation in which the deal was or wasn't made. One dealer summarized the process: "You put the price down by—let's say, if you are courageous—by half, and then you go up, while you give the reasons of your depression about the price."

Right from the beginning, Koenen's team of academics was simply not on the same playing level as the sellers. To open, Hanna bluntly asked for $3 million. The Americans were flabbergasted. They had been expecting an initial selling price in the range of $50,000 to $100,000. The sum of $3 million for such a book was unheard of at the time.

Freedman was outraged: No papyrus could be worth that much. It bore no relationship to the real world. No one had that kind of money.

"How serious [Hanna] was, I do not know. There was certainly no serious counteroffer," Professor Koenen said later.

The American side was thrown off balance. That $3 million price was well beyond the combined budgets of the SMU and Michigan backers.

Freedman took the initiative, even though he had no experience in dealing with Middle Eastern traders. He made a counteroffer on the spot, shaving off a zero and offering $300,000.

Hanna regarded the counteroffer as an insult, clearly meant to end the negotiations. "When Hanna heard what the Americans had to offer against his three million, he got up, disgusted and outraged," Perdios reported. "He said in Arabic, '*Yialla, yialla,* let's go. These people are not serious. They are wasting our time.'"

Perdios advised him to wait. The Greek had been far more patient during the examination and actually asked some questions and showed interest about the content, while Hanna had paced back and forth nervously. According to Emmel, the Greek "seemed to have some interest in what we were finding. But we didn't reveal very much. We didn't want to suggest that the manuscripts were worth more than they already thought they were worth."

Emmel, far younger and less daunted by impossible sums of money when genuine scholarship was at stake, summed up the situation in his report two weeks later:

> The owner asked $3,000,000 for the entire collection. He refused to consider lowering the price to within a reasonable range, claiming he had already come down from $10,000,000 in negotiations with one previous prospective buyer. He also refused to discuss the prices of the four individual items separately. He would like to sell all four manuscripts together, but probably will sell them individually if necessary.

Still, Emmel felt the find had incalculable worth as an artifact of history. His report concluded with a recommendation:

> I strongly urge you to acquire this gnostic codex. It is of the utmost scholarly value, comparable in every way to any one of the Nag Hammadi Codices. Like them as well, it is one of the oldest specimens of a book in codex form; the fact that part of the cover is also preserved is a remarkable stroke of luck.... There is great danger of further deterioration of the manuscript as long as it is in the hands of the present owner. This unique item must be put as quickly as possible into the hands of a library or museum where it can be restored, published, and conserved.

Though he was clearly disappointed, if not disgusted, Hanna did go through the motions required by etiquette to finish matters in good order. Everyone went out to lunch together, and Hanna and Perdios acted as hosts and paid the bill. Notwithstanding the failure to make a deal, they were gracious and hospitable.

During lunch, Emmel slipped off to the men's room, took out a pencil and paper, and scribbled "everything that I had consciously tried to memorize concerning the conditions of the two Coptic manuscripts." He managed to record the approximate dimensions of the pages, the title of the letter of Peter to Philip in Coptic, his impressions of the handwriting and the dialect, and the highest Coptic page number he had seen.

After the luncheon, Hanna put the manuscripts back in the Swiss bank vault and returned to Cairo, and Perdios went home to Athens. Both were now determined to fly to the States, the land of hope and opportunity, where they believed they could sell the manuscript.

As for the academic group, Koenen was sad and frustrated. Freedman was still outraged by the price. "Disappointment reigned ... but people were still cordial," Astrid Beck recalled. "Everyone felt the price was just way out of line for what they had to sell, and there simply wasn't more money to be had. The difference was too great." The group felt there was too great a disparity between the $3 million requested for the manuscripts and the careless manner in which the documents were physically handled, which was appalling to a scholar's eye.

The group split up, each going his or her separate way. Freedman and Beck were off to visit Professor Hans Kueng in

Tübingen, West Germany, because Kueng was going to be a visiting professor of religious thought at the University of Michigan in the fall of 1983, and his term had to be arranged. Beck was to be his assistant. Emmel and the Koenens drove off together towards Italy, Emmel to finish up his doctorate research, the Koenens to attend a papyrology conference in Naples. Beck summed up, "There were other itineraries in association with the meeting in Geneva, which I suppose alleviated some of the disappointment. We didn't go there just to buy scrolls."

Surprisingly, years later, no one in the group knew what had happened to the manuscripts. As far as they were concerned, the papyrus manuscripts, including the still unidentified Gospel of Judas, had disappeared into the obscurity from whence they had emerged. Unknown at the time, the manuscripts were headed to America, where another round of selling would end in failure. By this time, it was apparent that the centuries-old curse of Judas had lost none of its power. The only existing document in which he was able to speak for himself was soon to be consigned to another bank vault, where it would be, literally, left to rot.

# CHAPTER SEVEN

# THE GLORIES OF NAG HAMMADI

*Jesus answered and said, "You will become the thirteenth, and you will be cursed by the other generations—and you will come to rule over them."*
—THE GOSPEL OF JUDAS

Nag Hammadi, like all Upper Egypt cities in the Nile Valley, is located near the edge of the burning desert, where temperatures reach 110 degrees in the rare bits of shade on summer days. Less than fifty miles away are the magnificent pharaonic ruins at Luxor, whose temples and statues and tombs of the New Kingdom dynasties have long been a major attraction for foreign visitors. The Temple of Karnak features towering pylon gates and pillared courtyards, built by successive pharaohs who all wanted to prove themselves worthy to be gods. On the western shore of the Nile lies the famed Valley of the Kings, lined with once magnificent tombs. How magnificent was shown in 1923, when Howard Carter chanced upon the tomb of Tutankhamun, which had somehow been missed by ancient grave robbers. Several of the pharaohs who built the religious center of Thebes were contemporary with the events described in the Bible's Book of Exodus. The papyrus documents found at Nag Hammadi, however, dated from a far later time, from the era of the Roman Empire.

The historic find in 1945 near Nag Hammadi—the manuscripts were buried probably near the monastery of St. Pachomius at Chenoboskion, approximately ten miles from the city and across the river from the site of the ancient Greek-Roman city of Diospolis Parva—dramatically opened up a new field of antiquity to scholars. They greatly expanded what was known of early Christianity and cast new light on several of the new religion's major movements in the second, third, and fourth centuries after the life of Jesus Christ. The Nag Hammadi manuscripts are generally considered among the twentieth century's greatest archaeological discoveries, ranking second in importance only to the famous Dead Sea Scrolls. They were in fact discovered a year and a half before the Dead Sea Scrolls, which were found in the caves of the Judean desert at Qumram.

The Nag Hammadi library consists of thirteen codices, all written in the Coptic language. A codex—a manuscript volume that is a bound book, as opposed to a scroll—is usually a copy of scriptures or a classic text. Early Christians adopted them because they could assemble far more in a codex than on a scroll, and it was easier to use.

Many Nag Hammadi texts are presumed to be translated from the original Greek—the language in which the New Testament was originally written and copied. Scholars are reasonably certain that the Greek originals of the Coptic documents from Nag Hammadi were written sometime during the second century, possibly as early as the late first century. In other words, some of the Greek originals may have been written not so long after the New Testament Gospels themselves.

The Nag Hammadi codices contained texts inspired by the gnostic movement. In *The Gnostic Bible* (2003), Marvin Meyer, chair of New Testament studies at Chapman College in California, described the gnostics as "religious mystics who proclaimed gnosis, knowledge, as the way of salvation. To know oneself truly allowed gnostic men and women to know god directly, without any need for mediation of rabbis, priests, bishops, imams, or other religious officials." In another book, *The Gnostic Discoveries* (2005), Meyer noted that with the discovery of the Nag Hammadi library, "the study of gnostic religion and its impact upon ancient and modern religion has been fundamentally transformed."

Most of the manuscripts were distinctly Christian, in that they were centrally concerned with the life of Jesus and the meaning of his message. Many of them expanded beyond his teachings, though, using mystic symbolism that requires extensive study to understand. The gnostics constructed elaborate views of heaven, Earth, and biblical personalities and events that were often at odds with conventional views expressed in the gathering body of Christian literature or the Old Testament. However, the codices were highly intelligent, clearly the work of sophisticated thinkers. Though the texts spoke of the devils and angels that inhabit the body, they also discussed the inner secrets that abide within the human soul.

Scholars believe the Nag Hammadi codices were among hundreds and possibly thousands of documents circulating in the early Christian era. Relatively few, though, have survived the ravages of time. In some cases, authorities of orthodox Christianity may have ordered these precious texts destroyed, for this early period was rife with religious sects clinging to their own gospels. Nag Hammadi provided a treasure trove of alternative gospels that were never included in the New Testament.

Many of Nag Hammadi's gnostic papyri had not been read since the fourth century. Most were completely unknown to the modern world. Knowledge of the gnostics before the discovery had come principally through their critics, defined by scholar Bart Ehrman as the "proto-orthodox," the people who would eventually emerge victorious among the competing varieties of Christianity and form the established Christian Church—people such as Irenaeus, the bishop of Lyon who wrote *Against Heresies,* castigating the gnostics and what he regarded as their blasphemous beliefs.

Included in the collection were new religious texts whose existence had never before been known. In recording the nuances of their faith, the documents from Nag Hammadi provide a panoramic view of the thoughts, hopes, and dreams of the gnostics. They give us a window into the past—a past that is still in the process of being uncovered.

The Gospel of Judas found in Al Minya, for example, was bound within a codex that contained several gnostic documents already known from Nag Hammadi. In its alternate viewpoint of the meaning of Jesus' time on Earth, the Judas gospel falls within the broad framework of gnostic tradition.

Elaine Pagels, winner of the National Book Award for her groundbreaking *The Gnostic Gospels* (1979), sums up the impact of the Nag Hammadi discoveries this way:

> All the old questions—the original questions, sharply debated at the beginning of Christianity—are being reopened. How is one to understand the resurrection? What about women's participation in priestly and episcopal office? Who was Christ, and how does he relate to the believer? What are the similarities between Christianity and other world religions?

The field of Coptology is a strange bird among academic specialties. It studies not only the dead language of Coptic but also the entire Coptic culture of Egypt, particularly in the first six centuries after Jesus' life. Coptology crosses over a variety of disciplines: political history, archaeology, Christian theology, biblical philology, monasticism, Egyptology, and the study of the Roman Empire. Coptologists, by the nature of the profession, explore realms of antiquity that have been historically marked by a paucity of material. Throughout much of the twentieth century, the study of Copts and their culture had little apparent relevance to the modern world.

Among the leading lights in this academic discipline is James M. Robinson, a professor at the Claremont Graduate University in Southern California. Robinson, known as "Jim" throughout the world of Coptology, is energetic, likable, open-minded, affable, and generous, though occasionally given to outbursts. He became the secretary of the United Nations Educational, Scientific, and Cultural Organization (UNESCO) committee on the Nag Hammadi finds, and no single person is more responsible for the collection and dissemination of the texts. Robinson also became general editor of the Nag Hammadi library in English. Among his assignments, he wrote the introduction to the Nag Hammadi volumes upon their initial publication, and he was committed to writing the story of the discovery of the library.

Robinson entered the field almost by chance in 1966, after attending a conference in Italy. Though his colleagues considered his scholarship good, he was considered more a theologian than Coptologist, and he himself is the first to admit it: "I was not a

Coptic scholar. As I saw it, at the beginning, the field was highly competitive. I transcended that competitiveness."

Robinson entered the world of the Nag Hammadi discoveries in the late 1960s. What he saw was a field of scholarship in disarray. French and German scholars were particularly at odds. As Robinson recalled, "The French and the Germans were in the middle of the Third World War. They were fighting all the time."

Robinson, the practical administrator, became a major player. The clashes were, to some extent, due to personality and culture, and Robinson knew how to mediate the problems. He soon took over all the administrative and organizational work in bringing the Nag Hammadi documents to light. "I was the pragmatist. I was not feared. I was a flunky who could get things done," he says.

When the project foundered on any sort of shoal, Robinson took the initiative to resolve it. Whether it was a matter of academic rivalry or simply lack of money, Robinson was the one who solved the problem. He helped bring together major funding for the Nag Hammadi project, including substantial support and endorsement from UNESCO.

A general plenary committee was formed, along with a subcommittee for assembling and restoring the papyri. Aside from the difficult textual content of the materials, scholars and restorers faced considerable challenges in actually fitting the frayed, faded papyrus fragments together to make them tell a complete story. That subcommittee, the controlling body that did the supervising of the actual work, consisted of four members: Robinson; Martin Krause, an eminent Coptologist from the University of Münster who was at loggerheads with Robinson; another distinguished Coptologist, Rodolphe Kasser; and Søren Giversen, a Dane ("a big timid guy whom we won't speak about further," Kasser wrote later).

Initially, much of the work was done at Cairo's Coptic Museum, where most of the Nag Hammadi texts were held. It was the early 1970s, a few years after the Six Day War of 1967. Egypt and Israel were in the midst of what was known as the "War of Attrition," with artillery shells flying over the Suez Canal in both directions almost daily. Cairo was often blacked out. "When we weren't there, all the fragments were put into hiding because of the war," Robinson recalled.

The work dragged on for several years, a period Robinson remembers with nostalgia. Still, he became impatient with the slow pace of work, the academics coming in and going out, returning to their academic assignments in various countries. Robinson decided to stay straight through for seven months in order to finish the work, along with two graduate students he brought over from Claremont. "We then placed and assembled the fragments. It was very difficult. The horizontal and vertical fibers had to fit."

The woman in charge at the Coptic Museum was Madame Samiha. Access was restricted, and so were the number of hours anyone could work. "Her record of the fragments held there was crucial. Gradually, we won her confidence," Robinson remembered. "She'd usually come in late and leave early. I wanted her to come in earlier and leave later. Could I pay her taxi fare? I asked.

"'No,' said the director, 'but you can put the money in the hands of the taxi driver.' So that's what I did.

"Eventually, a little cleaning girl got the key and we had somewhat freer access."

Robinson personally supervised and participated in the work. By the end of this intensive period, most of the fragments were in place. When he finally left, one of the students stayed on for three years to get the work done. That was Stephen Emmel, then a very young man. "He stayed and did wonderful work," Robinson said.

Robinson occasionally sent $100 notes to supplement money provided by Emmel's parents or earned in lectures. "I said, 'I'll stay until the project's finished or I run out of money,'" Emmel recalled.

Many of the problems faced by Robinson were practical. "UNESCO paid for the trips of the technical subcommittee to go to Cairo four or five times. The Department of Antiquities put us up at Shepherds Hotel whenever the full committee convened. When we were the technical subcommittee alone, we stayed at the Garden City House Hotel. The committee members had to pay for themselves.

"Then the three Europeans wouldn't come unless UNESCO paid their way. So I got a grant from the Smithsonian Institution. This was paid to the American Research Center in Egypt, which paid the project costs."

That was one problem solved. Another was the clear plastic material that framed each page of ancient text. "Krause was frantically copying materials, but the problem was that the spines [of the manuscript pages] began to break." Part of the problem was the inadequate size: "The size of the Plexiglas we [originally] got was the size of one leaf instead of two leaves." Robinson took the initiative and hopped on a plane to Zurich to buy the right frames.

Robinson next embarked on what his friend and long-time colleague Harry Attridge, now dean of the Yale Divinity School, calls "for Jim, a matter of major principle." As he looked around him, he saw the European scholars often obsessively working on private texts for which they claimed exclusive publication rights that he felt belonged to the entire world, not just to those particular scholars. In what could be interpreted as a self-serving stance, Robinson's view was that the text materials in the original language should be published through the UNESCO committee on the project, of which he happened to be secretary. He decided to attack what he considered "academic fiefdoms and monopolies" in order to give all scholars, not just those working on particular sections, the right to inspect and translate the text.

In the world of European scholarship, the scholars who are designated or obtain the right to translate a text usually have the right, within reason, to complete their work and publish. The Europeans either did not know about Robinson's initiative or could not believe he was serious about such a quest.

The inevitable crisis came early in 1972. Robinson was able to obtain proper photographs of the texts and fragments and actually publish a facsimile edition—featuring photographs of the text in Coptic—at the same time as the first English edition of the Nag Hammadi materials.

Robinson, his colleagues, and the publishers threw a publication party in San Francisco in late 1972. "That was a shock to the Europeans. I was not quite as harmless as I seemed," Robinson remarked, adding cryptically, "The *editio princeps* [first edition] is the claim to fame. If you can't do that one, don't bother doing it at all."

Suddenly Coptologists, and the obscure field in which they operated, had risen to the realm of public attention. Coptology was suddenly seen as a key that could open the door to the Christian past. The skills and knowledge embedded in Coptology studies assumed a previously unsuspected importance.

The next task Robinson undertook was to look into how and where the Nag Hammadi documents had actually been found. In doing so, he was challenging the findings of a well-known French scholar, Jean Doresse, who had investigated the area of Nag

Hammadi in January 1950, five years after the discovery was made. Doresse was not, strictly speaking, a Coptologist, but a scholar of Greek papyrology and Egyptology who had served as head of the prestigious research department at France's premier scientific institution, the Centre National de Recherche Scientifique. According to Coptologist Rodolphe Kasser, Doresse "knew the region well, was familiar with its mores and the character of its inhabitants."

Doresse published his conclusions in 1960 in a groundbreaking book, *The Discovery of the Nag Hammadi Texts: A Firsthand Account of the Expedition That Shook the Foundations of Christianity.* Summarizing the objective, Doresse wrote:

> Two main questions were worrying us: what was the exact nature of the place of discovery—was it a tomb, pagan or Christian, the ruins of a house or monastic building and of what age? And then, under what circumstances could these documents have been buried?

Doresse, according to Kasser, searched out a small number of witnesses who knew what had transpired. These witnesses were separated only by five years from the time of discovery, and their testimonies were, in Kasser's words, "certain."

Doresse, like Kasser later, pointed out that for the peasants involved in the discovery, the Nag Hammadi papyrus documents were merchandise. Since they were basically illiterate, they had no ability to read modern, much less ancient languages. Their valuable goods—the papyrus documents—were prone to break in their "callous" hands, and so they wanted to rid themselves of them and make a profit as quickly as possible.

"The peasants who accompanied us and did not know the real

object of our search (we had come here on the pretext of visiting the pharaonic tombs) guided us, of their own initiative, to the southern part of the cemetery and showed us a row of shapeless cavities," Doresse wrote:

> Not long since, they said, some peasants of Hamra-Dum and of Dabba, in search of manure, found here a great *zir*—which means a jar—filled with leaves of papyrus; and these were bound like books. The vase was broken and nothing remains of it; the manuscripts were taken to Cairo and no one knows what then became of them. As to the exact location of the find, opinion differed by some few dozen yards; but everyone was sure that it was just about here. And from the ground itself we shall learn nothing more; it yields nothing but broken bones, fragments of cloth without interest, and some potsherds.

The Nag Hammadi codices had finally arrived in the capital, Cairo, sold to an important antiquity dealer, who sought to resell them for a good price. Egyptian authorities had found out about them and they were seized. Little by little, the scientific world learned of the find.

Doresse summed up:

> We are now assured that it was not in the ruins of a building, either monastic or other, that the famous library was found, but that it was well buried in a tomb very far away from all the monasteries of the locality, in a cemetery which seems to have been no longer in use by the Christians. There is nothing surprising about these writings having been enclosed in a jar. It was in such receptacles, less costly than cupboards and coffers in this country with so little wood, that people usually stored their books and many other things.

Many ancient manuscripts lack full provenance, Doresse concluded:

> So it was well worth the trouble to find out, in a pagan cemetery a few miles from Chenoboskion, the exact site of one of the most voluminous finds of ancient literature; thus to be a little better able to place this library in the frame of history to which it belongs; and to support, with concordant details, the hypotheses that have been made about its antiquity.

Robinson had a low opinion of Doresse's work: "It's bad. He was an adventurer. He would talk to villagers. But he was not useful as a technical scholar." Therefore, Robinson undertook his own investigation, beginning more than two decades later in the early 1970s. His thesis was that the discovery was part of a gnostic library that had come from the monastery of St. Pachomius at Chenoboskion.

Robinson made inquiries with the Egyptian *fellahin* in the area of Nag Hammadi. He found witnesses who would often tell him to come back in a short time and they would reveal the story to him. Robinson would return as requested, ready with the proper incentives. "Whenever I went down, I would bring the villagers a bottle of whiskey and a ten–pound note. That was big money at the time. That was my chore in tracking it down. I am not a field archaeologist. I went from rumor to rumor, village to village."

The narrative developed by Robinson, after a number of visits to Upper Egypt and months of hard work, was full of intrigue, feuds, and even murder.

As summarized by Bart Ehrman in *Lost Christianities* (2003), the modern story of the Nag Hammadi codices began when "seven Bedouin fieldhands were digging for *sabakh,* a nitrate-rich fertilizer, near a cliff." The group's leader was Mohammad Ali. His younger brother "made the find, accidentally striking something hard below the dirt with his mattock." It turned out to be a human skeleton. Along with the skeleton, he discovered a large earthenware jar, about two feet high, with a bowl over the top, sealed with bitumen.

Though at first they were reluctant to open the jar, they eventually smashed into it, no doubt hoping to find gold or something along those lines. Instead, they found a bunch of old leather-bound books.

The plot thickened after the codices were taken from the ground. Mohammad's family and tribe were engaged in a blood feud with a group from a nearby village. Ali's father had shot and killed an intruder and had in turn been murdered by the intruder's family. A brother-in-law of a local priest took the books to Cairo, where they were confiscated by the authorities.

Eventually, though, the seller from Upper Egypt was allowed to sell one of the priceless documents to the Coptic Museum at a moderate price—not enough to make him rich, but enough to keep him quiet.

The narrative that Jim Robinson put together was detailed. It was also colorful, full of action, and bursting with passion and deception—in short, the stuff of a Hollywood thriller.

Robinson prepared to publish his account of the discovery as part of the introduction to *The Facsimile Edition of the Nag Hammadi Codices,* actually that series' final volume, as well as in various other publications. As Robinson began to make his probe known, the two distinguished European scholars on Robinson's own subcommittee almost immediately expressed their opposition. The real difference of views went to the heart and soul of the question of "scientific inquiry"—what is valid, and what is not, when examining the origins of documents that are among mankind's greatest treasures—and was related to Robinson's own apparently principled quest for universal access to rare scholarly documents.

Professors Kasser and Krause, among Europe's most well-known Coptologists, opened a broadside on Robinson's findings, intensifying the conflict that was already brewing between the two Europeans and the American, dating back to the mid-1970s.

"Robinson went down [to the area of Nag Hammadi] in full force, accompanied by Egyptian notables, promising compensation to his informants. For them [the Egyptian fellahin], the windfall was beautiful," Kasser wrote scornfully. He continued:

> At the end of several months, [Robinson] had his history, a true novel, shored up by numerous precise and detailed testimonies (often contradictory, it is true, but one knows how to distinguish the good wheat from the chaff), specifying not only the exact date and place of the discovery, but the names of the peasants (since dead) who found the manuscripts, all the details of their sale and resale (with exact prices), the family quarrels of the clans of protagonists, a story of murder running through this affair, welcome support from documents provided by the local judiciary, the up and downs of the bargaining and various maneuvers in order to escape the suspicions of the police. In brief, following these revelations, which Robinson published little by little, improving them and expanding them each time in various American reviews, he has presented us with an introduction of nearly 500 pages.

Kasser was upset. "Krause and I, who know Egypt well, and the fabricating capabilities of the Egyptian fellahin lured by the prospect of gain, disapproved, asking Robinson to restrict himself to the minimum kind of presentation foreseen by our committee back in 1970. Or, at least ... wouldn't it be more objective to present side by side two hypotheses—the version of the facts provided by Doresse and that of Robinson?"

Robinson's conclusions were far less definitive than he contended, they argued. One could only wonder, noted Kasser, "whether a small event of minimal importance for the local population could be remembered in such detail so many years after the fact." He questioned whether the testimonies gathered by Robinson and his researchers had not been simply responsive to the strong desires of the investigators to establish facts:

> I've worked a long time in the Egyptian countryside, among these generous and honest people, but with a naïve, somewhat childish mentality, and having experienced this psychology, [it's easy to see] the birth of stories of discovery, inspired above all by the desire to please the listener. The public recitals made by your witnesses, their enthusiastic and touching declarations, have only given birth to suspicions among numerous listeners familiar with the Egyptian countryside.

From Robinson's point of view, the Europeans were "the bad guys," words he used in describing them without a hint of deliberate exaggeration in his tone. They were interested in protecting their fiefdoms. Kasser had one of the codices in his possession, belonging to the Jung Foundation in Zurich, and he wanted to translate it. Robinson published his own broadside against Kasser with an article entitled, "The Jung Codex: The Rise and Fall of a Monopoly."

"I know that Kasser hates my guts because of the article on the Jung Codex," Robinson said later.

The academic rivalry spawned by the Nag Hammadi discoveries would not be healed by time. After scholars first became aware that a stunning new cache of papyrus documents had been discovered, the battle would be waged anew. Both Robinson and Kasser would figure in the struggle to achieve scholarly dominance over the Gospel of Judas.

☥

The discoveries at Nag Hammadi in 1945 propelled a fresh wave of books written by scholars of early Christianity, including incisive academic studies such as Bart Erhman's *Lost Christianities,* Marvin Meyer's *Gnostic Discoveries,* and Elaine Pagels's *Beyond Belief* (2003). In an interesting sidelight, it even provided one of the bases for Dan Brown's best-selling thriller *The Da Vinci Code* (2003).

The scholars have a fertile realm of study, for the new body of gnostic literature includes works never before seen: the Gospel of Thomas, the Gospel of Truth, the Secret Book of John, the Gospel of Philip, and the First Apocalypse of James, as well as the Letter of Peter to Philip. The challenge to restore them, assemble them, and then read them and comprehend their meaning is an effort that has spanned decades. Many of these documents were not well preserved and can be read only in a fragmentary translation. Restorers and translators have had to use substantial scholarship to fill in whatever gaps they can.

There is another reason many gnostic documents are so difficult to understand: They did not—despite the word *gospel*—tell a story. Most of them were not like the narratives recorded in either the Old or New Testaments, following a story line such as the last days of Jesus when he was betrayed, crucified, and resurrected. Rather, a number of them consisted of a dialogue, occasionally between the already resurrected Jesus and his disciples. For instance, as Meyer has written:

> The Gospel of Thomas contains almost no narrative. Jesus in Thomas performs no physical miracles, reveals no fulfillment of prophecy, announces no apocalyptic kingdom about to disrupt the world order, dies for no one's sins, and does not rise from the dead on Easter Sunday. His value, rather, lies in his enigmatic sayings, which are pregnant with possibility and power.

It was a wholly different tradition of gospel than the easier-to-understand narratives that would, by the last part of the fourth century, become the accepted "canonical" Gospels of the orthodox church.

To today's Christian, the gnostic doctrines seem radical. For the gnostics, the importance of Jesus' dying on a cross and then rising on the third day was either of very little importance or irrelevant. As Pagels writes in *The Gnostic Gospels:*

> Some gnostics called the literal view of resurrection the "faith of fools." The resurrection, they insisted, was not a unique event in the past: instead it symbolized how Christ's presence could be experienced in the present. What mattered was not literal seeing, but spiritual vision.

The newly discovered gnostic literature also describes a wholly different cosmology. It comprises a complex framework of ancient symbolism that could take an uninitiated newcomer years to learn. The translations, just as the originals, include unique Greek words such as *Pleroma* (fullness of life and being) and *aeons,* representing all kinds of heavenly configurations.

There are a series of code words for prominent persons or semi-divine beings who were thought to inhabit the cosmos—for example, Seth, Harmathoth, Galila, Yobel, or Adonaios, who ruled over what was called the underworld; or angels such as Saklas, Hormos, or Nebro, also known as Yaldabaoth; or luminaries in the heavens with names like Harmozel, Oroiael, Daveithai, and Eleleth; or the great and invisible spirit, Barbelo, also Youel and Plesithea; or a demon such as Nubruel. The jumble of seemingly irrelevant symbols and patterns of thought take considerable expertise to understand. They involve intricate philosophical considerations that could be compared to the complexities of Jewish talmudism.

The Nag Hammadi documents are diverse, treating different subjects in a varied manner. As Ehrman explains:

> Even though they were presumably all used by a community who interpreted them in a Christian way, the texts were produced in a range of circumstances by authors of varying philosophical and theological persuasion. Some of these authors, for example, were not Christian in any sense. It is interesting to note that some of the non-Christian texts give evidence of having been "Christianized" by later editors. In any event, the books of this collection are no monolith. They represent a wide range of religious beliefs and practices gnostic and otherwise.

Among its more intriguing aspects, gnosticism had a feminist component. Women played a prominent role among those early Christians who were gnostics. Pagels has noted that the

Gospel of Philip "attributes to Jesus acts and sayings quite different from those in the New Testament." One passage calls Mary Magdalene the companion of the Savior and says that Christ loved "her more than [all] the disciples, and used to kiss her [often] on [her] mouth." Pagels further points out that the Gospel of Mary (found in Berlin Gnostic Codex 8502, not discovered at Nag Hammadi) "recalls traditions recorded in Mark and John, that Mary Magdalene was the first to see the risen Christ. John says that Mary saw Jesus on the morning of his resurrection, and that he appeared to the other disciples only later, on the evening of the same day."

One of the outstanding luminaries of gnosticism was Sophia. She was the feminine counterpart of Jesus, the divine feminine, whereas Jesus was the divine masculine. Meyer wrote about her:

> Among the aeons and manifestations of the divine is often a figure who represents the divine in this world, fallen from the light above yet present as the light of god with us and in us. In many gnostic texts this is the figure of Sophia or wisdom.

The concept of Sophia as the lost goddess of wisdom derived from the Greek philosophers. They believed in both feminine and masculine gods. The word *philosophy,* which was first used by Pythagoras, means literally, the "lover of Sophia."

If an appreciation of feminism and the holiness of the feminine spirit was one aspect of gnosticism, another was a belief—contrary to both Judaism and "proto-orthodox" Christianity—that there are two aspects of God. Meyer states that gnostic Christians made a distinction "between the transcendent, spiritual deity, who is surrounded by aeons and is all wisdom and light, and the creator of the world, who is at best incompetent and at worst malevolent." That point is underscored by Ehrman, who says of the gnostic Christians:

> Many appear to have believed that the material world we live in is awful at best and evil at worst, that it came about as part of a cosmic catastrophe, and that the spiritual beings who inhabit it (i.e., human spirits) are in fact entrapped or imprisoned here.

Still, the new texts discovered at Nag Hammadi and elsewhere had their positive moments. As Meyer recounts: "In the Gospel of Truth the fruit of knowledge is a discovery bringing joy. It signifies that one finds god in oneself, that the fog of error and terror is gone, and that the nightmare of darkness is exchanged for an eternal heavenly day."

The new texts discovered in Al Minya Province three decades after the Nag Hammadi find and examined so briefly in the Geneva hotel room contained a gospel that told of an entirely new dimension of revelation. It was Coptic in language, gnostic in formulation, and when it was first read, it raised a specter of apprehension. The man later entrusted with their restoration and translation, Rodolphe Kasser, described his feelings at the first encounter: "It was almost unbelievable. We had never dared to hope to find a text that had totally vanished. I was terrified.

"In my profession we know that we know many things and yet we know nothing. We find things, we develop theories and explanations all the time, and then we find a text that completely surpasses the previous blueprints. We have to be receptive to changing our mindset about the manuscript. The manuscript must be in control and master of the situation."

Kasser, from the first timid moment of encounter with the text, found dramatic meaning in the text that pushes the diversity of Christianity a full step beyond what had been discovered at Nag Hammadi. "The importance of this text is that it is not only a new manuscript, but an entirely new kind of document. The gnostic texts are interesting, but are similar to one another and have the same way of presenting their arguments and the same arguments.

"For the first time, we have a known ancient author who scandalized the Christians of his day, and actually have his own *ipsissima verba,* that is, his own words. So we can't simply say that he was wrong or wanted to deceive us. We can analyze his text.

"It is incredible. It is similar to what happened with the discovery of the Nag Hammadi texts. We previously had only what the church forefathers were saying about the gnostics, but rarely the texts the gnostics wrote themselves. Now we can understand the nuances of what the forefathers said by using the gnostic texts. We will no longer be able to simply say, they were wrong, since we now have a more complete picture.

"The gnostics shocked the Catholic Christians because they portrayed the God in the Old Testament as the Devil that was contrary to what was being written in the Bible. Here, in the case of the Gospel of Judas, it is the New Testament which is being contested on an important point by a document from approximately the same period—a bit more recent, but not by that much. Someone has chosen to defend Judas."

For Kasser, it was all a revelation, far more significant professionally than anything he had encountered as a leading member of the core group of scholars doing work on the Nag Hammadi library. "It is as if one is traveling to a strange land," he observed. "A part of the pleasure for people who explore unknown countries is to see lands that no one else has seen before, and to understand things that one cannot understand without first having seen them. Similarly, you experience this with a new text. It becomes a new environment and a new way of thinking."

CHAPTER EIGHT

# PURGATORY

*"That soul that suffers most," explained my Guide, "is Judas Iscariot,*
*he who kicks his legs on the fiery chin and has his head inside."*
—DANTE ALIGHIERI, *The Inferno*

Hanna Asabil came to the United States in 1984 seeking to sell
the ancient codex for a price he felt he deserved. After all,
America is where millions have made their fortunes. Hanna hoped
to make his own stake, too, though he did not speak English and
did not intend to stay in the country for long.

Hanna brought the papyrus documents with him, wrapped in old
Egyptian newspapers in his hand luggage. An Egyptian colleague
accompanied him. At John F. Kennedy International Airport in New
York, Hanna presented his Egyptian passport with its U.S. visa to an
immigration officer, who stamped it and waved him through. Hanna
thus emerged into the home of the free and the brave clutching his
hand luggage, protective of the precious papyri that he believed
would bring him great wealth. The deteriorated ancient codex had
successfully crossed the Atlantic and arrived on yet another continent.

A contact in Cairo had helped Hanna figure out the best ways of making a significant sale in America. He was a local Cairo medical specialist, and a member of the Coptic community. This gentleman had sometimes helped Hanna out by polishing ancient coins or using dental machinery to bend, renovate, and clean items, especially coins, that Hanna had in his inventory so they would fetch higher prices.

Hanna's initial plan was to sell the documents through contacts in the Coptic community in the United States. The state of New Jersey is a major center for Copts, numbering approximately 30,000, many of whom came to the United States in a wave of Coptic immigration that began in the 1960s.

Using the contacts and introductions garnered in Cairo, Hanna established connections with the Coptic Orthodox Church of St. Mark, located on West Side Avenue in Jersey City. The priest at St. Mark's was Father Gabriel Abdel Sayed, who was described by one of his parishioners, Josef Labib, as "very distinguished" and a true leader. Father Gabriel's enthusiasm and vigor had helped build up the imposing church building into both a center for prayer and a thriving community center that served the sizable Coptic neighborhood. Later, after Father Gabriel died, the side street next to the church was renamed by Jersey City as Father Gabriel Street in the priest's honor.

As a devout Copt himself, Hanna developed warm relations with his brethren in New Jersey. He was introduced to Father Gabriel, and according to Hanna, the priest was ready to help. The sellers made contact with a number of institutions and persons, among them Brigham Young University and scholar S. Kent Brown, who was then working on the Coptic Encyclopedia project. BYU brought in antiquarian book dealer Bernard Rosenthal of Berkeley, California, to help in an evaluation, which took place in a hotel room in New York.

Like a number of rare book sellers in the United States, Rosenthal was a World War II refugee from Nazi Germany, a group later dubbed by Rosenthal as "the gentle nation." Rosenthal was appalled at the deteriorating condition of the manuscript and suspicious of the sellers, who seemed ignorant and interested only in money.

The price the Egyptians demanded was $3 million—the same as the price in Geneva. "Mr. Rosenthal, later in the day, calculated the worth of the documents to be $250,000," Brown commented. "With $200,000 for a conservator for two years...the effective value for the documents was $50,000. Naturally, that news was not well received."

The Egyptians also set up a meeting with one of the best rare book and manuscript dealers in the United States, H.P. Kraus. Known more informally as "HPK," Kraus was a feisty, amusing, wise, and thoroughly engaging rare book dealer in midtown Manhattan. It would take a fair knowledge of the rare book and manuscript business in the United States to find a man like Kraus. Hanna presumably learned about Kraus not only from the Coptic priest but from Yannis Perdios in Athens, who had been a longtime client of the rare book dealer, primarily interested in building up his own collection of artifacts and manuscripts from nineteenth-century Greece.

Kraus was an Austrian Jew who had already been engaged in the rare book business when Hitler's *Anschluss* transformed Austria into a Nazi state in 1938. Kraus was rounded up along with a number of other Jews, dissidents, and gypsies and spent time in the German concentration camps at Dachau and Buchenwald. Luckily for him, that was before the wholesale genocide of the Jewish people began. "After forty years, I am just beginning to discuss openly my life in those horrible times," Kraus wrote in his autobiography, *A Rare Book Saga* (1978). "Only lately have I realized that I am one of the relatively few survivors of captivity by the Gestapo in two of the most infamous concentration camps...."

That I came through without permanent harm to mind and body is a miracle; that I survived is more than miraculous."

Kraus managed to negotiate his way out of the camps and, once a free man, finagled a visa to the United States, leaving Austria with as many valuables as he could carry. He met his wife, Hani, in the States and received considerable help from her family in getting his new life started. He reestablished himself in the rare book and manuscript business, eventually obtaining and buying warehouse space in Mamaroneck, New York, and also purchasing the building where he made his headquarters, 16 East 46th Street, a five-story building between Fifth Avenue and Madison Avenue in the commercial heart of New York City.

Kraus became known as a brilliant dealer and an energetic and honest man, and his firm gained a reputation as the best rare book and manuscript specialists in the United States. His empire spanned rare books, a major reprint operation, and one of the world's largest photographic archives. He had significant experience with Coptic manuscripts, another reason that both Father Gabriel and Hanna might have heard of him. A number of the Coptic texts that are included in the Yale Papyrus Collection of the Beinecke Rare Book and Manuscript Library were either purchased from Kraus or donated by him, including a series of texts sold or donated in spring 1964 and at least one other in December 1966.

Kraus and Hanna negotiated primarily through the good offices of Father Gabriel, who was fluent in English. The first meeting took place at Kraus's offices in Manhattan. Kraus, reaching the end of his prominent career, was by this time wheelchair bound. At one point, according to Hanna's account, Kraus opened a safe in his office and Hanna saw hundreds of thousands of dollars in currency of various denominations inside.

On the contrary, Kraus's daughter, who usually worked in the back of the shop does not recall seeing the men or being present at the meeting herself and could not locate any records that such a meeting ever took place. Kraus has since died, and he possibly did not share details of the story of the encounter with Hanna and the Coptic priest with family members.

☥

Hanna and Father Gabriel arrived with a group of Coptic men, looking like a Coptic mafia. Hanna's understanding was that the others had been brought along by Father Gabriel in order to ensure the safety of the Coptic treasures. That was a critical mistake. Though the others were stationed outside, Kraus suspected the bodyguards had guns. Hanna, of course, was accustomed to carrying a gun in Cairo, which he normally hid underneath his baggy suit, but Kraus was outraged by the presence of what he took to be armed thugs. He was unwilling to do business under such conditions.

"That would be enough to put off my father from making the acquisition," Maryann speculated. "He wouldn't have any part of it."

The priest said something to Kraus in English, and Kraus replied, also in English. The words that were exchanged were beyond Hanna's very limited understanding. Whatever was said, however, the negotiations were over before they had even begun. Father Gabriel tried to reassure Hanna that the sale was still ongoing, but Hanna was extremely upset by the aborted meeting. He would later blame the priest for killing the deal.

A second meeting was held at nine o'clock on the morning of March 27, 1984. The setting this time was the sixth floor at

Hamilton Hall on the Columbia University campus, the office of a distinguished classicist, Roger Bagnall. The Kraus company was still considering the purchase and sought Bagnall's expertise in determining more precisely what the Coptic manuscripts might contain and what their importance was. Maryann's husband, Roland Folter, attended the meeting, and he was the one who wanted to thoroughly investigate the contents of these new Coptic documents. "The claim had been made to Kraus that these were first-century Coptic manuscripts," Bagnall recalled, "but that was obviously nonsense, because there was no Coptic written language at that time."

The strict new Egyptian antiquities law had just taken effect, but as Bagnall recalled, "I don't think that anyone in the manuscript trade at that point was taking that aspect seriously."

According to Bagnall's records, the principals at the meeting were Folter, on behalf of the Kraus office; a Coptic priest whose name Bagnall recorded as Father Gabriel Abd el-Sayed; and himself. The priest was accompanied by two men to whom Bagnall was never properly introduced. Bagnall thought they were bodyguards, but in fact they were the owners of the property in question, Hanna and his Egyptian partner. They stayed totally silent during the entire meeting. "They were dumb appendages to the priest," was Bagnall's impression. "I didn't feel threatened, and no arms were displayed or referred to. They certainly did not show any knowledge about what they had; quite the contrary. I found the whole group rather sleazy and was glad not to be doing business with them personally!" Bagnall also recalled that he was frankly doubtful whether the priest was a real priest—though he really was.

The men sat around a desk in the middle of the spacious Columbia University office. The Kraus company, including Hans Kraus himself, had already seen the manuscripts, but wanted confirmation as to their authenticity and some insight into what the texts might contain, which would be essential in terms of determining their potential worth and whether a deal was worthwhile. Bagnall had been consulted by the Kraus office previously and knew Folter.

Though put off by the seamy nature of the Coptic visitors, Bagnall was extremely impressed by the texts, which he had only a short amount of time to inspect. "My immediate reaction was, 'My God, this is Nag Hammadi stuff.' I'd seen enough to realize what they looked like. I was involved with fourth-century papyri at the time."

The meeting lasted about an hour. In that brief period, Bagnall managed to identify three of the manuscripts. "I think that I would testify under oath to having seen three of the codices," he later recalled. He believed there were only three manuscripts in the bunch, but added, "I think it's unlikely that they only brought three if they were flogging four."

The asking price for the manuscripts at that point was $1 million. The Kraus office was concerned about the price of the manuscripts, which was still a large amount for papyrus texts in 1984, but was also apprehensive about the potential costs involved in restoration, which could take years and had a way of mounting up. After what was apparently some internal debate on the matter, the Kraus company passed on the proposed deal. As Bagnall recalled, "Kraus was scared off by the price tag."

The failure to sell to Kraus was a major setback for Hanna. No matter where he turned, no one would recognize the value of his papyrus antiquity. Of course, since he himself didn't really have any precise idea what the manuscripts said, his entire selling pos-ture was largely a bluff. A classicist like Bagnall would immediately recognize not only the potential scholarly value of the manuscripts but also the essential ignorance of the person selling them. Hanna was out of his league trying to sell his wares in the sophisticated arenas of Western academia.

For safekeeping, Hanna again chose to put the documents in a bank vault. He decided on a bank not in the Jersey City area, but on the far side of New York City in Hicksville on Long Island, where Father Gabriel had a connection with one of the bank clerks. Hicksville, which has no Coptic associations, is a relatively affluent town located just off the Long Island Expressway.

Accompanied by his colleague, Hanna opened an account at the Hicksville branch of Citibank, located in a strip mall. The manuscripts were placed in safe-deposit box number 395, according to bank records, and it was opened on March 23, 1984, four days before the meeting at Columbia. The address given by Hanna was 437 West Side Avenue, Jersey City, the location of the Coptic Orthodox Church of St. Mark. Hanna and his Egyptian friend personally took the keys to the vault, and shortly they would return with them to Egypt and their home base in Cairo.

A treasure that could open up startling new insights into the history of early Christianity—including a totally new appraisal of one of the apostles, a man reviled in history as the betrayer of the Lord Jesus—had been placed in an obscure bank vault in the heart of suburban Long Island.

In hindsight, the thought that such a valuable contribution to history could be stored away and virtually forgotten is unfathomable—and that it would happen in the heart of Long Island is preposterous. Yet to its owner, the codex was a prized possession not because of what it said but principally because of the price it would bring. It was a text for which he had fought and suffered and for which he prayed. He had been eager to get it back, even at the cost of giving up a valuable gold necklace and a statuette of Isis that was considered one of the best pieces to come out of Egypt. That he didn't know quite what the texts said was a minor matter—though, in fact, it was contributing to the problems that were plaguing him from continent to continent. His price had dropped from perhaps as high as $10 million to $3 million to $1 million, and still the thing wouldn't sell. Maybe it was cursed never to sell.

Hanna was a religious man who believed that God would provide for him. The codex would find a home as God and Fate dictated. As the Muslims say, *"Inshallah."* What will be will be, according to God's will.

Back home in Cairo, Hanna consulted additional fortune-tellers. Though the precious papyrus manuscripts had not sold, the information he received from his favorite soothsayer was suddenly bright with optimism. According to one fortune-teller, the skies were turning clear, and warm, glowing rays of sunshine would soon come into Hanna's life. He was about to marry and have a family. Hanna need no longer feel gloomy. Not only would he spawn a family, the soothsayer told him, but his wife would help him look after his interests.

Hanna, already over fifty years of age, was in the process of a new beginning. Soon he would marry a devout Coptic woman, Viola, in a Coptic orthodox wedding. The marriage would be followed in short order by two children, the first a girl named Maria, and the next year a young son, Mikhail.

Hanna's personal life was on the upswing. The invaluable papyrus manuscripts, however, were in limbo. For sixteen long years, they would disintegrate inside a metal box that was never designed to hold such treasures.

Fiber by fiber the Gospel of Judas was fraying into oblivion.

CHAPTER NINE

# SCHOLARLY PURSUIT

*If we had not been taught how to interpret the story of the Passion,*
*would we have been able to say from their actions alone whether it was*
*the jealous Judas or the cowardly Peter who loved Christ?*
—GRAHAM GREENE, *The End of the Affair*

The brief inspection in Geneva in May 1983, though seemingly
forgotten by the team from the University of Michigan, did
bring action from the Coptic experts involved in the visit to
Geneva. After reading the reports of it, the Nag Hammadi expert
who had been contacted by Ludwig Koenen when Koenen was
preparing his team for the Geneva trip would become very interested in purchasing the papyrus codex. He was not a dealer. He
was a professor in California.

Jim Robinson had studied the reports submitted by his
associate Stephen Emmel with great interest. Robinson wanted
the manuscripts for scholarly purposes. With them he could
extend the monumental work he had already done with gnostic gospels.

The small town of Claremont, California, is the home base of the Claremont Colleges, a group of prominent undergraduate schools scattered throughout the area: Pomona, Scripps, Harvey Mudd, Keck, Claremont McKenna, and Pitzer. The academic buildings of the well-known Claremont Graduate University, one of the best educational institutions in a state known for the quality of its advanced education, are located in Claremont. Rising high above the town is San Antonio Peak, once known as Mount Baldy, in the San Gabriel Mountains, often covered with snow in the winter months. Full of grassy lawns and low-slung California buildings, Claremont is one of the most charming college campuses in the western United States.

Claremont also has one of the better graduate programs in the entire country for the study of religion, with a wide range of courses ranging from biblical Hebrew to the history of Christianity. The star professor in Claremont's Department of Religion for many years was early Christian scholar Robinson, now the Arthur J. Letts Professor Emeritus of Religion. Robinson is one of the world's leading scholars on the New Testament and, in addition to his duties on the Nag Hammadi codices, was founder and director of the Institute for Antiquity and Early Christianity at Claremont.

Professor Robinson finished the initial publication of the Nag Hammadi library in 1984, culminating with his introduction and its detailed—though disputed—account of how those documents were found. He was now keen to obtain the new Coptic codices that Emmel had seen in Geneva. Though he had not gone to Geneva personally, Robinson gathered from Emmel's detailed report that what these texts contained had great value for purposes of historical and theological research, and he believed (wrongly) that that inspection meeting had been the first and only Western encounter with the valuable manuscripts. Understandably from his point of view, Robinson felt a proprietary interest in the matter.

Some of that feeling related to his primary role in assembling and editing the Nag Hammadi materials, a field he surveyed as the generally acknowledged "master and commander" among American scholars. That, after all, was why Koenen had approached him in the first place concerning the inspection to be made in Geneva, believing that Robinson with his considerable reputation and expertise could add not only scholarship but also financial muscle to the possible purchase of the papyri.

His sense that he owned the field would later exasperate some of his rivals, not least Rodolphe Kasser, who shrugged his shoulders and said, "Robinson believes it all belongs to him. *Qu'est-ce qu'on peut faire?* What can one do?"

Nor was it a stance that was particularly appealing to a figure like Roger Bagnall, a noted scholar of fourth-century Egyptian papyri, whose book *Egypt in Late Antiquity* is considered a classic in the field. "Robinson came to feel that he owns the domain related to Nag Hammadi, and became proprietorial about fourth-century manuscript finds in Egypt," Bagnall commented. Robinson, of course, had no idea that a Columbia University professor had already inspected the codex in May 1984 and was fully aware of its existence.

Robinson could not be sure of the contents of the new papyrus manuscripts. However, he reasoned that if two parts of the codex consisted of the James and Peter-to-Philip letters and were duplicates or close copies of material already seen at Nag Hammadi, the third, not yet fully identified one that had the word "Judas" in it must include material that was in the Nag Hammadi texts as well.

☥

Robinson began an active pursuit of the codex. The Coptic materials had appeared out of nowhere—and then disappeared mysteriously into the dark Swiss night. They had to show up again somewhere, and Robinson wanted to locate them and obtain them before anyone else did. He wanted that *editio princeps,* which he maintains is the principal scholarly achievement worth pursuing when it comes to ancient manuscripts, and the prestige that it would bring.

He decided to release news of the new find, in a carefully controlled manner, to the world of Coptic scholarship to see if that would stir up any clues as to the whereabouts of the codex. As he wrote later, "I first mentioned the discovery in print in 1984, in an obscure publication (from the viewpoint of the sellers), and somewhat gingerly, in view of the confidentiality imposed by the hope of subsequent acquisition." Robinson provided information to Hans-Gebhard Bethge, who was writing a dissertation at Humboldt University in Berlin on the Letter of Peter to Philip. Bethge noted in this dissertation that "the parallel version" of the epistle "is so far not yet available for scholarly evaluation." Robinson also made an announcement about the new codex at the Third International Congress of Coptic Studies in Warsaw in August 1984. These subtle pronouncements failed to provoke a response, however, and the manuscripts' location remained hidden from Robinson's purview for years.

Moreover, he remained unsure of their precise contents. All Robinson had to go on was Emmel's report and the "almost completely illegible photographs" he had been given by Koenen prior to the 1983 inspection. A number of years later, one of Robinson's associates, Marvin Meyer, a Coptologist who did his graduate studies at Claremont under Robinson and later became his friend and collaborator in various projects, wrote in an introduction to

"The Letter of Peter to Philip" for the volume *The Nag Hammadi Library in English:* "According to the reports of James M. Robinson and Stephen Emmel, another Coptic text of The Letter of Peter to Philip is to be found in a papyrus codex which, at the present time, is neither published nor available for study."

Much about the manuscripts' trail remained elusive and mysterious. Robinson claimed that the codex's owner's "full name was never divulged to me, no doubt lest he be charged by the Egyptian government." Yet that information was clearly available through Professor Koenen at the University of Michigan, since he was the person whom Hanna Asabil, through Perdios, had contacted in the first place concerning the codices. Koenen, who had been in contact with Hanna throughout his early years in Cairo, apparently did not relay specific information about Hanna to Robinson, and Robinson never asked him about it. Hanna was known in Cairo as a reputable dealer, notwithstanding Robinson's insinuations.

No progress was made on locating the codex for several years—as the book rested quietly if not safely in the bank vault in New York—but at some point, Robinson learned of Yannis Perdios's connection to the manuscripts. His name had not been included Emmel's report, but was listed on a summary of the May 1983 meeting written by Koenen. In 1990, Robinson finally managed to track Perdios down in Athens, and a meeting was arranged.

Perdios, who lives in the tony Paleo Psychiko section of the city, has a large private home with a flower-filled front yard. The house is filled with artifacts from his private collection, illustrating the Greek period under Turkish rule. The sophisticated Greek collector welcomed Robinson, also hopeful that a deal for the mysterious codex could be initiated. Perdios took care to protect his own anonymity, however. It was understood that his name would be withheld from any subsequent correspondence or publication.

Robinson noted Perdios's elegant home and hospitality. As the two men talked, the outlines of a possible deal began to emerge.

Meanwhile, Robinson had found a possible backer, Martin Schoyen. The Norwegian Schoyen is a highly cultivated individual who has a reputation for being both enormously rich and tough-minded. He owns arguably the largest collection of manuscripts to have been assembled in the twentieth century. Among his 13,500 items spanning more than five thousand years are fragments from the Dead Sea Scrolls and famous Buddhist manuscripts. He intended to fulfill a lifetime ambition by creating a museum of ancient artifacts in Norway that would serve as a focus of ancient history for the Scandinavian world and all of Europe.

Schoyen agreed to provide some or all of the money to buy the codex and the associated manuscripts, assuming the price was within reason. Robinson arranged a meeting between Robinson, Perdios, and the potential Norwegian sponsor. Perdios suggested New York as the venue.

Robinson related that he had asked Perdios why the Greek proposed New York for the meeting. Perdios answered that he wanted to visit his brother who lived in New York. "I assume that the real reason was that the codices were there," Robinson said, "for he would have known that we would want to see them before committing ourselves and would then want to take possession of them if the negotiations succeeded."

What Robinson didn't know was that Perdios was himself, by then, only tenuously associated with Hanna. Perdios did not have a key to the bank vault in Hicksville; only Hanna and his Egyptian partner had keys and the signatory power to open the safe-deposit box. In addition, Hanna and Perdios had since had a falling out. Perdios had learned of Hanna's independent approach to Hans P. Kraus in New York trying to sell the papyri, and he was furious because he had not been kept involved. Nevertheless, business was business, and Perdios would contact Hanna to get him to meet with the potential buyers.

Robinson, with high hopes for the upcoming meeting, sought out additional backers. One possibility was Canadian sponsorship. He was in close contact with the team of scholars at Laval University in Quebec City that was responsible for publishing the French edition of the Nag Hammadi codices. The excellent Faculty of Theology at the French-speaking university included some of the stars of modern Coptology and theology, most notably a scholar widely respected in the field by both Europeans and Americans, Wolfgang-Peter Funk, who had managed to escape from East Germany to a better life in the West. Robinson thought that one of the Canadian university's main sponsors, the Bombardier Foundation, would help fund the acquisition of materials. The Bombardier family had a manufacturing company in Canada that started out making snowmobiles and progressed to making high-speed trains and jet airplanes that were sold not only in Canada but throughout the world. The project seemed too speculative for the Canadian foundation, however, and the prospect of support from Bombardier fizzled.

More frustration was ahead as the fate of the Gospel of Judas became intertwined with cataclysmic modern events. "Schoyen agreed to attend the meeting on a date in January 1991 agreeable to the sellers," Robinson reported. "I had gone so far in making actual plans as to check out New York hotels! Thus late in 1990 we were actively making preparations for the meeting, at which time President Bush announced he would begin bombarding Baghdad in January."

While President George H. W. Bush never actually made such an announcement, preferring to keep President Saddam Hussein of Iraq in the dark about operational plans, the clouds of war were indeed gathering over the Middle East. American diplomats were hard at work forging the international coalition that would fight the first Gulf War. Much of the world was alarmed, and pessimists foresaw the start of a larger conflagration that might ignite a global war.

According to Robinson's recollection, Perdios and Hanna were among those pessimists. He "received word from Athens that the Copt was not willing to abandon his family at the beginning of World War III, so the trip had to be called off." Hanna did not want to embark on any journeys just then. He was a homebody who was most comfortable on native soil in Egypt. He spoke only Arabic and did not like to travel alone.

During a trip to Geneva in 1992, Robinson tried to set up another meeting. "My Greek middleman said he would contact his Coptic friend and let me know, which he never did."

Robinson renewed his futile quest several times throughout the 1990s. By then his chief contact was Martin Schoyen. The Norwegian visited Claremont at the end of March 1994, and in August Robinson and his wife were Schoyen's guests in Norway, where he was shown what Robinson said was a "magnificent" collection of manuscripts.

The visits were mutually productive. Schoyen later bought

some Dead Sea Scroll fragments that were housed at Claremont for a sum that Robinson remembers as $50,000. "There were ten fragments. Each of them contained one letter," Robinson said. "That means those fragments were worth $5,000 a letter; that's what I used to tell my students."

Robinson then served as a personal courier for Schoyen so that the materials could be safely delivered without interference from outside parties. The respected California professor carried the fragments in a pouch around his neck in order to avoid any involvement from either U.S. or Norwegian Customs, and he personally delivered Claremont's Dead Sea Scroll fragments to Schoyen.

The bold nature of this exporting activity was not new in the world of antiquities dealers, of course. Schoyen himself has been mentioned in several recent news reports regarding collecting activities. According to *The Times* of London, in April 2005 University College London set up a committee of inquiry to investigate the exportation history of 650 Aramaic incantation bowls dating from the fifth century—loaned to the university by Schoyen in 1996. Also reported in the same month was his generous return of priceless Buddhist artifacts that he had bought on the international market but which had later been discovered to have been illegally taken from Pakistan's Gilgit region.

In 1997, Robinson taught a late-April-to-August semester at the University of Bamberg in Germany. While in Europe, he again contacted Perdios to propose another meeting with Schoyen, Perdios, and the owner of the papyri. Perdios checked with Hanna, and the Egyptian told him he was willing to sell. Perdios relayed the information to Robinson.

Excited, Robinson proposed windows for meeting dates: sometime August 11–31, September 8–19, or October 3–24, if the meeting was to be held in the United States, or May 16–25 or July

16–26, if the meeting was to be in Europe. Unfortunately for the Californian, a meeting was never arranged.

Unbeknownst to Robinson, Schoyen maintained direct contact with the people involved with the papyrus manuscripts. When the manuscripts surfaced a few years later on the antiquities market in the United States, the Norwegian did manage to buy certain leaves from the biblical text offered with the Coptic codex, and they would be published in his collection in Norway in the early 2000s. Unlike Robinson—a distinguished scholar, but inexperienced in the Byzantine world of antiquities collecting—Schoyen was a master.

Neither Frieda Tchacos Nussberger nor Jim Robinson had ever heard of each other. Robinson had no idea there was a Swiss dealer who was a friend of Perdios, an acquaintance of Hanna, and someone prominently associated with a number of the world's most prestigious museums. Though highly respected by many of his American colleagues for his organizational abilities and his talents as a theologian, Robinson was an outsider to the world of commerce in ancient art. As committed as he was to finding the elusive Coptic manuscript, he was not familiar with any of the key players. Nor was Robinson intimately familiar with Egyptian society or Egyptian law, and he spoke only limited Arabic, although he had spent considerable time in that country after the discovery of the Nag Hammadi documents.

All of these qualities were possessed by Frieda Nussberger. She was an experienced dealer. She spoke fluent Arabic. She knew Egypt—in fact, had been born there. And she had never forgotten the photographs she had been shown after Perdios had recovered the manuscripts through Nicolas Koutoulakis. Soon she would make inquiries again, and her potential for gathering information was far better than Robinson's. She knew Hanna well, and she would persist in her attempts to rouse him from his new happily married roost. At long last, the Gospel of Judas would be rescued from its Long Island prison. Yet the bad luck that had dogged it ever since its discovery would not magically fade away. In a journey filled with desecration, it was about to face its most dangerous handling of all.

CHAPTER TEN

# JUDAS IN AMERICA

*I had a mission. Judas was asking me to do something for him.*
*It's more than a mission, now that I think of it.*
*I think I was chosen by Judas to rehabilitate him.*
—FRIEDA TCHACOS NUSSBERGER

The words of Judas lay moldering, unknown and undiscovered, in one of hundreds of safe-deposit boxes within an undistinguished Citibank branch occupying a one-story box building of the kind that dot thousands of U.S. suburban malls. Cars whizzed by on the nearby Long Island Expressway. The papyrus manuscript was as entombed as it had been in the Egyptian catacomb where it had lain dormant for centuries—with one vital difference. The air in the desert is dry. The humidity on Long Island, even in an air-conditioned building, can be brutal. For sixteen years, isolated and untouched, the codex underwent a catastrophic process of disintegration.

Its rescuer would be Frieda Tchacos Nussberger.

Her first brush with the Gospel of Judas had come not long after the codex had been stolen from Hanna Asabil in Cairo in

1980. Frieda had known Hanna for some twenty years at that point, and he had aired his grievances with her about the cruel robbery. Hanna had given her a fair description of the stolen objects, including the bundle of manuscripts, in the hope that she might help retrieve them. Frieda was a sympathetic listener. She knew Nicolas Koutoulakis, and she was friendly with Koutoulakis's daughter, Daphne, who would take over her father's business after his death. Unfortunately, Frieda had been unable to help Hanna at that time.

After the negotiations between Hanna and Koutoulakis in Geneva in 1982 led to the return of the papyri to Hanna, Yannis Perdios visited Frieda unexpectedly in her gallery in Zurich. Frieda was well acquainted with Perdios, who, she told a friend, had been involved in a relationship with one of her good friends in Paris back in the 1960s. His apartment in Zamalek also was an essential stop-off point for visitors to Cairo in the early 1970s. Perdios gave her some large color photographs of the manuscripts that were once more in Hanna's possession and asked whether she could be helpful in finding a buyer. These photographs were of middling quality, but they would later offer an indication of the state that the manuscripts were in during the early 1980s.

The focus of Frieda's business was artifacts, not manuscripts, and she had no special expertise in papyri, but she said she would ask around as a favor to Perdios and Hanna. In Europe, she contacted the Berlin museum and several other institutions, with inconclusive results. In the United States, she called an acquaintance, Jiri Frel, the curator for antiquities at the J. Paul Getty Museum in California, who advised her to get in touch with Roy Kotansky, a young Greek classics scholar studying for a Ph.D. at the University of Chicago Divinity School. She then sent

WHEN THE CODEX (or book) containing the Gospel of Judas finally reached conservators in 2001, it was falling to pieces. It took five painstaking years to reassemble the manuscript so that scholars could unlock its meaning.

THROUGHOUT HISTORY, *Judas Iscariot has been hated and reviled as the ultimate villain, the close friend and trusted disciple who betrayed Jesus Christ with a kiss (opposite).*

THE NEW TESTAMENT *presents Judas as the trusted ally who brought about Jesus's arrest in the Garden of Gethsemane (above). He is the disciple who sets in motion the events that lead to the Crucifixion and death of Christ.*

FOLLOWING PAGES: *In the Gospels, Jesus bore a cross to his Crucifixion, reenacted at Jerusalem's Church of the Holy Sepulchre. In the newly found Gospel of Judas, Jesus asks Judas to betray him.*

WHEN COPTIC SCHOLARS *had their first glimpse of the papyrus,*
*they were startled to read the title, "The Gospel of Judas."*
*Condemned by the early Christian Church,*
*its message contained a radical reinterpretation of Judas.*

*THE DRY DESERT CLIMATE had helped preserve the papyrus pages of the Gospel of Judas for 1600 years. From its accidental discovery in the mid- to late 1970s to 2001 when conservators finally began restoration, the ancient document had deteriorated significantly.*

AFTER CHRIST'S DEATH, *news of his life and teachings spread throughout the near east, giving rise to some of Christianity's first religious communities and churches. One of the oldest Christian churches in the world is St. Catherine's Monastery, located in the Sinai (above). Codex Sinaiticus (top right), a Greek Bible from around 350 CE, contains one of the earliest full New Testaments.*

NO ONE KNOWS HOW MANY *ancient texts were lost or perished over the centuries. But the Codex Syriacus suffered a different fate. A parchment book of Gospels created in the fifth century (bottom right), it was erased in the eighth century and its pages re-inked with a religious text.*

WHEN RODOLPHE KASSER, *a Swiss expert in Coptic texts, first saw the Gospel of Judas, he says he had never seen a text in worse shape. "The manuscript was so brittle that it would crumble at the slightest touch."*

CONSERVATOR FLORENCE DARBRE *cuts a sample from the codex as Tim Jull, of the University of Arizona, looks on. Jull is the scientist who performed the carbon-14 dating tests on the manuscript. Left to right: Frieda Tchacos Nussberger, Rodolphe Kasser, Florence Darbre, and Gregor Wurst.*

PRECEDING PAGES: *PERCHED ON MOUNT SINAI, pilgrims worship where the Bible says God spoke to Moses. The Christianity that ultimately reached the ends of the Earth was orthodox, not Gnostic. The Gospel of Judas was hidden away along with its upside down view of Jesus's betrayer and its profoundly different view of salvation.*

THE HANGING CHURCH IN OLD CAIRO *is an early Coptic Church that was built over what was the largest Roman fort in Egypt (above); next to it in the upper left of the frame is the Coptic Museum where the Gospel of Judas will be housed.*

the photographs to Kotansky in the hope that he would be able to identify what the manuscripts were. Kotansky managed to give a general description of the two documents written in Greek and made preliminary transcriptions of all texts that could be read from the photographs. He was confident that a few passages came from the Book of Exodus, containing portions of the LXX (the Septuagint, the oldest known Greek translation of the Bible). His conclusion concerning the mathematical treatise was more tentative: "The larger codex written with a later, Greek cursive looks to be a set of prescriptions, but as I say, this is just an off-hand guess for now."

Kotansky wrote that he would like to examine the rest of the manuscripts, but noted that "the documents cannot be read until unrolled and collated." That, of course, was impossible working from photographs. He was able to ascertain that the smaller codex ("cut through the middle," he noted) is "written in Coptic (Egyptian) which I do not read." He said he had no real idea about the academic value of the odd collection.

Kotansky wrote Frieda that he had sent the photos to Frel "in case he might be interested." Originally from Czechoslovakia, a refugee after the 1968 Czech revolt, Frel was a controversial figure who was accused later of being an unscrupulous, if successful, purchaser of ancient objects. In the mid 1980s, Frel was forced out of his position as curator at the Getty Museum for appraisal irregularities related to items donated to the museum.

Regretfully, that was the last that Frieda saw of the photographs for twenty-three years and the end of her involvement with the codex for almost as long.

☥

In 1999, Frieda received a strange telephone call. Speaking in Greek with a rough village accent, the caller said he had access to an ancient manuscript and photos of it. Intrigued, she asked him to send her the photographs. As she recalls, "I sent the photos to Robert Babcock, a curator I knew at the Beinecke Library at Yale University. He looked at them and immediately called me back. He said they were important. He said these must be part of the Coptic manuscripts some American scholars had examined 20 years ago."

A close examination of the photographs showed a curious and puzzling clue. The manuscripts had been photographed against the background of Greek newspapers. Legible in one of the newspapers was a notice for an upcoming examination open to students at the University of Athens—the date of which was October 21, 1982. That was seventeen years earlier. These pages of the manuscript had most likely been somewhere in Greece during the fall of 1982 and were almost unquestionably photographed at that time.

Good dealers have excellent memories, and Frieda is no exception. She immediately thought of Hanna's manuscripts, the ones that Perdios had spoken to her about in 1982. She decided to pursue the deal with the mysterious Greek. A meeting was arranged at a European location.

The intermediary brought along a colleague whose name she understood to be Lyosis, a dark, swarthy man. The common language was Greek. Frieda remembers that she did not trust or like the people with whom she was dealing.

The Greeks wanted $100,000 for the small manuscript. "Far too much," Frieda told him. "I'm not that interested to begin with."

Frieda felt that this asking price was beyond reason for a scant few pages of ancient text whose content was uncertain. Still, she felt that cash could conclude a deal, and she let them know that she had money in her purse. Frieda countered with a $20,000 offer, to be paid immediately. "I knew that if they saw cash, the deal could be wrapped up."

The men wavered, and Frieda raised her bid to $25,000. "Take it or leave it," she told them.

The men took it. The deal was done.

Frieda had purchased what turned out to be missing sheets taken from the long-lost manuscripts of Jebel Qarara. She placed the leaves in a vault where they could be examined and preserved.

Frieda, with her dealer's instincts, soon began to work out the mystery of her newly acquired papyri. The source of the pages of Coptic manuscript, she determined, could have come only from one of two sources, although additional intermediaries might have somehow become involved in the chain of sale. Those primary sources were Perdios, still representing Hanna, and the elusive Mia—or Fifi or Effie—who could still be holding pieces from the robbery of twenty years before.

Frieda quickly discarded the first possibility. "Perdios is too straightforward and honest to have stolen anything from Hanna," she concluded. That left Mia.

Through Greek sources she will not name, Frieda received information indicating that Lyosis was in fact Mia's boyfriend. This was a major breakthrough, at least as viewed by Frieda. Mia, however, had already disappeared somewhere in the Greek hinterland. She was nowhere to be found.

Finding the detached leaves provided what Frieda called "the kick" for continued spadework. What had happened to Hanna's manuscripts themselves? In recalling the course of events, she remembers, "Everyone knew about the books. There were clients. The problem was the money that Hanna was asking."

Frieda recounts what happened next: "Seven or eight months later, it was the millennium, and we visited Egypt to celebrate the event there. I had an idea, to give Hanna a call. I managed to find him, he was living in a new apartment in Heliopolis. I knew the manuscripts had long since departed Egypt. I asked if he had still had the manuscripts. Or had they already been sold?"

Hanna smiled slyly. "I have the key to the vault," he told her, meaning the vault in New York.

Frieda told him that she would not pay $3 million. "I won't pursue it at that price," she said.

"Do you have a client for me?" Hanna asked.

"I don't know," replied Frieda.

She believes that the crack in Hanna's resolution about price came at that time. He was getting older. He already had a family. He wanted to rid himself of the burden of impossible dreams. From Hanna's point of view, the prospects of a deal to sell what he was sure was his most valuable possession were languishing. Year after year had gone by and there were still no results. As Frieda recalled, "He was a broken man when I got to him."

Frieda and Hanna had known each other by this time for three decades. They could speak Arabic to each other and find enough common understanding to make a deal. Finally, Frieda made a tentative offer. She won't say exactly what that offer was, but she admits it was in the hundreds of thousands, not millions, of dollars.

They came to an understanding that the price could be finalized once Frieda was certain the manuscript truly existed and there was something to read in it. Frieda was assured that the price would be within the realm of reason.

Hanna had not been to the United States in the intervening

sixteen years, so the next step was convincing him to go. That turned out to be an enormous challenge. Hanna hated to fly. He did not speak English, and he could not bear to leave his homeland, Egypt, where he felt comfortable. Despite the money that awaited him at the end of the trip, he continued to drag his feet.

Finally, Frieda had an inspiration. She telephoned Cairo early one evening when Hanna was likely playing *trik-trak* in a nearby café. She was right. He was out, and his wife, Viola, answered the phone.

Frieda spoke to her woman to woman. "Viola, your husband is an old man and you are young and have two young children. Believe me, if you don't push him to come to New York now, every year will be more difficult. A time will come when he will be unable to undertake such a trip. I will be in New York the first days of April. See that he organizes himself to meet me at that time. It is his last chance and you have a strong interest in making him go."

Two weeks passed. One evening on her way home from her gallery in Zurich, her mobile phone rang. "I am ready," Hanna announced. "I have my visa, come and fetch me from Cairo, so that we can fly together to New York."

Frieda was excited, but balked at flying all the way to Egypt for no reason. "No way, Hanna. I am not coming to Cairo to fetch you. Take a plane and come to Zurich. We can then fly together."

"I cannot take a plane alone," Hanna complained. "I don't speak any other language. I will get lost."

Frieda remained firm, but without her, Hanna didn't want to move. In early April 2000, Frieda was going to be in New York for the opening of the New Cypriot Galleries at the Metropolitan Museum of Art in Manhattan with a splashy exhibit on Cypriot antiquity. There would be no better time to conclude the deal with Hanna, but he was difficult to convince.

"I can't do it," Hanna said. "Can you come to Cairo to fetch me?" he repeated. Frieda pressed him: "You've been asking $3 million and you can't even come to New York? I'm not helping you. Don't be an ass," she said—or the Arabic equivalent.

Hanna still resisted, and Frieda lost her temper and yelled at him.

Abashed, Hanna finally decided to come. He was now ready to make the sale.

☥

Frieda asked her wide-flung family for help in organizing the visit with Hanna. The first call was to her sister Deda and her husband, Alec, who lived in Montreal. Deda was formerly an immigration and Canadian Customs officer at the city's Duval Airport. Alec, an engineer, had established the Olympic Airways office in Montreal.

Hanna did not know the couple, and they had never seen him. Yet their assignment was to greet Hanna on his arrival in New York. They agreed on the green Egyptian flag as their recognition signal. Hanna would wear a brown suit, but as expensive as the suit was, it was baggy and ill fitting, just like all his other suits in Cairo.

As it turned out, Alec and Deda could not find a proper Egyptian flag and had to fasten a green scarf to the top of a broomstick.

When the EgyptAir plane landed at John F. Kennedy International Airport early on April 3, 2000, Alec and Deda were there to meet him. The signals worked, although the broomstick-flag turned out to be extraneous because Hanna immediately recognized Deda: "You are Frieda's sister."

Frieda waited nervously at the Stanhope Hotel on Fifth Avenue. She finally got the call that Hanna had arrived.

The couple drove Hanna from the airport to a hotel on Chambers Street in downtown Manhattan. The next step, after a brief rest, was to head to the bank and recover the codex from its resting place. While Frieda stayed in New York, the others stopped to pick up the couple's daughter, Sybil, who was married and lived in Brooklyn. Deda stayed behind, while Alec and Sybil stuffed a large cardboard box into the car with Hanna to collect the precious manuscript.

There was only one problem: No one except Hanna had ever been to the bank, and he did not have a precise address. He did, however, have his receipt for the bank vault box, saved through more than sixteen years of waiting. Using that, though a precise address was not listed, Sybil made some telephone calls and managed to identify where the bank was located.

It was a good half-hour's drive out the Long Island Expressway from New York City to Hicksville. "We didn't know if the bank existed, or what would be inside the vault if it did," Deda recalled.

The entire assignment struck Sybil as bizarre, and she recalls thinking, "It was particularly odd that Hanna had chosen a bank so far from downtown. I am not sure what the reason was, I think it had to do with a relative or friend who helped him before."

With Hanna nervously smoking cigarette after cigarette, he and Alec proceeded inside to open the safe-deposit box. Sybil waited outside in the suburban mall parking lot. "I remember that it took a very long time," Sybil recalled. "I don't know whether the bank had relocated since his last visit. I think not, as Hanna did not seem surprised by its looks. I do think they had changed the keys on the safety deposit boxes."

That was in fact the problem. The key given to Hanna sixteen years before no longer fit the lock. The bank clerk asked the group to come back in a few days, but Alec and Hanna both protested vigorously. They wanted to retrieve the manuscript immediately. Alec explained that the gentleman who did not speak English had come thousands of miles to take his goods out of the safe. Finally, after some discussion, the bank called in a locksmith. Deda recalls that they paid something in excess of $100 to open the safe-deposit box.

When they finally did, Hanna's face turned pale with shock. The stale air was filled with the odor of rotting papyrus. The manuscript had deteriorated significantly in the bank vault. As bad a state as the manuscript had been in previously, it was in miserable condition now.

Alec put the desiccated papyrus manuscripts into the cartons he had brought with him. Deda recalled him saying, "Good thing I was organized. Thank God we brought boxes."

Hanna looked mournful. The group could hardly speak to each other, and they drove back in silence.

Once back at Sybil's home, Hanna went to take a nap. The long flight from Egypt had caught up with him.

What Sybil remembers most about Hanna is how much he smoked. Cigarette butts piled up in the ashtrays of her living room and the bedroom where Hanna rested. The smell of stale cigarettes was everywhere. She also remembers how discouraged she was by the adventure: "It upset me to see the manuscript's terrible condition, and I was saddened to know that it had been in reasonably good shape until then."

Later they called Frieda, who was relieved to hear that the manuscript still existed, but was also unhappy to hear about its condition.

Frieda came to see Hanna and the codex the next morning. The two signed a sales document, dated April 4, 2000. It stated the price, plus the fact that Frieda would wire the money within days to the account of Hanna Asabil at the American Express Bank in Cairo. For his part, Hanna affirmed that he had reacquired the papyrus manuscripts through Nicolas Koutoulakis in Geneva.

Hanna then asked Frieda for some ready cash, saying he wanted to go shopping for his two children. She gave him a few hundred dollars. He made a reservation to return to Cairo that same evening.

His second visit to America had lasted only one night, and, while he had obtained a substantial sum of money, it was far less than his original asking price.

Soon Hanna was back in Cairo, where he felt at home, and he accompanied his wife, Viola, as he always did, to the Coptic Orthodox church in the neighborhood, where the family prayed. Though troubled by the events of his past few days in America, Hanna could feel content. His dreams of enormous wealth had not been realized, but he had sold the troublesome artifact. His venture was not a total waste of effort. It was off his back at last.

The papyrus documents had turned into brittle fragments that could easily become no more valuable than dust on a windowsill if efforts weren't made to restore them quickly. During the time of Hanna's ownership, the deteriorating papyrus had become almost a total loss.

From the moment she saw the papyrus texts, Frieda felt she had a mission. "I had the opportunity to take them away from people who didn't know what they were and how to handle them. I wanted to protect them and to give them to people who could read them and conserve them. I wanted to save them. It came slowly to me that there was something that was pushing me. Looking back, I made mistakes, but ... ," she took a deep breath, "I was guided by Providence."

Once the ancient codex was in her legal possession, Frieda took a private car and driver and headed up the Merritt Parkway to New Haven, Connecticut, the home of Yale University and the prestigious Beinecke Rare Book and Manuscript Library. The Beinecke Library houses some of the world's most ancient and most important documents, including a significant collection of Coptic papyri, some of them acquired through H. P. Kraus, the New York manuscripts dealer.

At Yale, Frieda met with Robert Babcock, one of the chief curators—on whose recommendation she had purchased the initial loose pages—and she left the documents with him, suggesting the possibility of a purchase by the library at what she claims was "a very modest price—namely, $500,000."

"I was relieved because I knew that they were the right people, who would really take care of it. And then I left and waited to hear the news: What was written there?"

A few days later, Frieda was about to leave the United States to return home to Switzerland when she received a telephone call from Babcock: "I remember I was in the taxi leaving New York toward Kennedy Airport, and my portable rung. Professor Babcock had an extremely emotional voice, and he said, 'Frieda, this is fantastic! It's fantastic! These are very important documents!' He was very excited. He told me, 'Frieda, this is fantastic! The name Judas is on it. Judas's name ends this codex. It's a great find. There's nothing like it!'"

Babcock told her he thought it was the Gospel of Judas Iscariot. "I did not know what that meant, because I didn't know anything about gospels," Frieda admitted. "But his emotional voice gave me the hint. And that was it, and then I went back to Zurich."

Yale held the codex for the next few months, and the curator applied himself diligently. A second Yale professor entered the picture as well. Bentley Layton, an associate of Babcock's, was a classics scholar considered by many to be America's leading Coptologist. Layton, whose credentials, like Rodolphe Kasser's, include a term as president of the International Coptic Studies Association, made the initial identification of the back part of the codex, which his former student, Stephen Emmel, had not had the time to do.

Harry Attridge, by then a professor at Yale who within two years was to become the dean of Yale Divinity School, also examined the texts at the Beinecke Rare Book and Manuscript Library. He was joined during his visit by Babcock and Layton. He was excited to see the texts that, he surmised, were the same ones that he had hoped to sponsor seventeen years earlier when he was a professor at Southern Methodist University.

However, there were questions of provenance that were being discussed by those involved. Yale has been among the most cautious and hesitant of American institutions with regard to issues of provenance, bending over backward to avoid any impropriety, to the point of frustration among potential donors.

The Beinecke Library held the valuable papyrus manuscripts from April to August 2000, but still did not make an offer. Babcock wanted to buy the codex, but the university lawyers and higher administration officials raised questions about its history and ownership. In the end, the Yale administration decided that, in view of the potential legal issues, it was not interested in a purchase.

One of the experts who visited Yale and also had the opportunity to see the manuscripts was Columbia University classicist Roger Bagnall. According to him, "As I understand matters, it was only lack of clear legality that dissuaded Yale from buying."

Frieda received a written report from a Yale professor on August 21, 2000. The document bubbled with understated excitement. It stated that identification of the parts of the extraordinary and unique gnostic codex had finally been made. Of the first two parts, the First Apocalypse of James and the Letter of Peter to Philip, the report said, "The Nag Hammadi codices are defective and the present codex fills some of these gaps ... (so some of the text present here is unique).... The first two were first discovered and published from Nag Hammadi codices (V and VIII, respectively), and the Nag Hammadi manuscript in each case is the only one known till now."

Further on, the report commented on the long-lost Gospel of Judas. This text, it read, "is totally unknown to the modern world. The portion that could be read (from the very end of the work) suggests that the whole text is a dialogue between Jesus and Judas Iscariot, ending with a report of Judas' betrayal."

The report's summation was unequivocal: "This is unquestionably ... important ... equivalent in importance to the Nag Hammadi books." However, a general caution about the state of the papyrus manuscripts was included: "The papyrus is, in general, in brittle condition and desperately needs conservation." This reemphasized what Stephen Emmel had written seventeen years before—only now the situation was far more dire.

Despite the undoubted importance of the codex, Yale chose not to invest in one of the greatest manuscript finds of our time. However prinicpled the Yale decision had been, the practical effect was potentially disastrous for the just-identified historical treasure.

Frieda Nussberger was left holding the papyri. She was out of pocket a substantial sum, probably hundreds of thousands of dollars, and she believed the financial burden was too great for her to bear. She had to sell the document to someone who had the funds to carry out the expensive restoration.

Indeed, she would find a buyer, but the odyssey of the cursed manuscript would take another wrong turn. Things would get still worse for the unique papyrus text before they got better. The ugly underside of the antiquities market was about to be exposed again.

CHAPTER ELEVEN

# THE ENFORCER FROM GAUL

*Jesus said to Judas, "Step away from the others*
*and I shall tell you the mysteries of the kingdom.*
*It is possible for you to reach it, but you will grieve a great deal."*
—THE GOSPEL OF JUDAS

The enforcer arrived from the east to become the Christian bishop in the town of Lugdunum, the "Shining One," named after a Celtic god of the sun. Located on the banks of two rivers, the Rhone and the Saône, the city served as Rome's entry point to Gaul. Today, this region is one of the great wine-growing regions of the world, Burgundy. It is part of a highway of trade and communication, just as it was also once a path to conquest and territorial advance. Lugdunum has become the modern metropolis of Lyon, the second largest city in France.

Irenaeus was most likely born in Smyrna in modern-day Turkey, and he lived from roughly 120 until 202 CE. During the crucial time period of second-century Christianity, he helped define the founding principles and theology of the emerging universal, or

Catholic, Church as much as any single individual in history. He became a priest, a bishop, and finally after his death, a saint, recognized by both Roman Catholics and the Orthodox churches of the East.

Many modern-day readers may be surprised to learn that Christianity could not boast a "definitive" faith or Bible early in its history. Christianity took well over three hundred years to informally acknowledge what has been generally accepted as the canonical "New Testament," recognized as the basic, essential holy literature of the Church. Before the second century, Elaine Pagels writes in *The Gnostic Gospels:*

> numerous gospels circulated among various Christian groups, ranging from those of the New Testament, Matthew, Mark, Luke, and John, to such writings as the *Gospel of Thomas* and the *Gospel of Truth,* as well as many other secret teachings, myths, and poems attributed to Jesus or his disciples.

Marvin Meyer carries the point even further:

> The formation of the New Testament as the Christian Bible was a gradual process that took centuries to complete. Finally, at the Council of Trent in 1545, the Roman Catholic Church acted to recognize its list of biblical, canonical books as final, that is, closed to any additions or subtractions.

In these early times Christians suffered sporadic persecution by Roman authorities. Emperor Marcus Aurelius—born in nearly the same year as Irenaeus and generally considered a great emperor, reigning with the blessings of a "Pax Romana" that regulated the civilized world—occasionally cracked down on what was termed "the obstinacy" of the new Christians and their church, creating martyrs throughout the empire. But the believers in Jesus were hardly a monolithic group.

The world of early Christianity brimmed with turbulence. Circulating in this variegated world, there were not only the four Gospels the Bible now contains, but thirty or more, all proclaiming that they were the truth. The outlines of Jesus' story were generally agreed upon, but the Gospels disagreed on specific historical facts or the sequence of events in the biblical narrative. Some of them contained differing interpretations of faith based on the same specific incidents.

Each of these sects adhered to some variation of Christian belief. Among the questions of debate was the extent of Jesus' divinity: To what extent was he human, to what extent divine? Was there a Trinity? Could Jesus be separate from God, or was he part of God—and if so, how could he experience a human fate such as crucifixion? Did Jesus, as he himself proclaimed, come to fulfill the Jewish law and the prophetic dreams of Isaiah and other biblical visionaries? What was his relationship to the Jews, and the messianic vision first expressed in the Hebrew Bible? The answers to questions like these led not only to bitter schisms within the framework of Christendom but also to extraordinarily complex formulations that would attempt to weave certain doctrines together, while excluding others.

Bart Ehrman has written about the far-out nature of some of these believers. For instance, the so-called Carpocratians invented a theology that justified free sexual relationships "conducted under the guise of religion, where all things were to be held in common among God's people"—including wife-swapping during church services. The professed theory was that, since God had sovereignty over all creation, no single person should own property or another person's body or soul. Ehrman points out that the Carpocratians, on religious grounds, "urged every bodily experience imaginable, all as part of their plan of salvation."

Not all of the sects were as exotic as the Carpocratians, of course. Among the principal ones were the Valentinians, the Marcionites, the Ebionites, and later the Arians. Each of them formed their own leadership group to define how and why Jesus was the Messiah, what kind of messiah he was, and how he was to be worshipped.

The Marcionites, for instance, followed Marcion, a Christian devotee from the Black Sea area. Marcion was an admirer—one might say "disciple"—of the writings of Paul. He emphasized the distinction that Paul described in Galatians between the Law of the Jews and the gospel of Christ. The Marcionites, Ehrman says, believed

> the gospel is the good news of deliverance; it involves love, mercy, grace, forgiveness, reconciliation, redemption and life. The Law, however, is the bad news that makes the gospel necessary in the first place; it involves harsh commandments, guilt, judgment, enmity, punishment and death. The Law is given to the Jews. The gospel is given by Christ.

Marcion decided that one God could not be responsible for both the Old Testament and the New. So he proclaimed that there was not one God, but two gods. The new God of Jesus came to save people from the old, vengeful God of the Jews.

Marcion went on to say that Jesus was not part of the physical world. If he were God, or a part of God, he could not be a human being as well. He only appeared to be human. Gods do not die. They do not suffer.

How could Jesus live on Earth and then be betrayed and die? The answer was clear: He could not.

Another principal group, the Ebionites, were at the opposite end of the spectrum from the Marcionites. They emphasized the Jewish roots of Christianity. They believed, in Ehrman's words, that

> Jesus was the Jewish Messiah sent from the Jewish God to the Jewish people in fulfillment of the Jewish scriptures. They also believed that to belong to the people of God, one needed to be Jewish. As a result, they insisted on observing the Sabbath, keeping kosher, and circumcising all males.

These conflicts were reflected in considerable depth in the New Testament: In debates, for instance, among the apostles—all of whom were Jewish and circumcised—as to whether circumcision was essential in order to be accepted into the community of believers. The apostles decided that faith and belief, rather than any physical sign, were the essential requirements.

The Ebionites disagreed, however. Jesus was the Son of God, they said, "not because of his divine nature or virgin birth," in the words of Ehrman, "but because of his 'adoption' by God to be his son. Jesus' crucifixion was the 'final sacrifice' and now ritual sacrifice, as practiced in the Temple, could be done away with."

The Ebionites' primary text was the Gospel of Matthew, the most Jewish of the four Gospels, believed to have been directed largely at a Jewish audience. The Ebionites did not accept any of the writings of Paul, the man whose extraordinary missionary effort brought the message of the Christian savior not only to Jews but also to the gentiles in the wider world—to a great extent by ridding the religion of the burdensome requirements of circumcision and the Jewish dietary laws, gaining the added benefit of making conversion to the new faith far less cumbersome.

Among the gnostic Christians, a sect called the Cainites took a radical step away from Judaism. They believed that the Old Testament was totally false and that the Old Testament God was a false god. They also believed certain characters in the Old Testament must be reassessed, and they turned conventional judgments about these figures upside down. For example, this group considered Cain the good brother, not Abel, and so the group came to be known as Cainites.

In order to understand how all these groups could have proliferated from the words of a single prophet, it is necessary to look at the years that immediately followed Jesus Christ's death. At first his believers were all Jewish. Jesus' message sprang from Jewish messianic tradition and was considered a fulfillment of it by his disciples and followers. As a result, Jerusalem was inevitably a focus of the new religion that would be called Christianity.

Jesus is believed to have died in what is now calculated as year 30 of the Common (Christian) Era. At first, those who believed he was God were regarded as just another Jewish sect among many. The apostles—as reflected in the canonical Gospels—spoke to each other as Jews who had seen the Messiah and believed in him. Within the framework of the developing Christian religion, ideological struggles were waged between those condemning aspects of Judaism and those supporting it. Partially, the new Christians were rebelling in their own way, not against the powers of pagan Rome but against what they believed was the corruption of Judaism as practiced in that period.

Within a decade after Jesus' death on the cross, a rabbi named Saul of Tarsus, who had been among the fiercest critics of the new belief in Jesus as the Messiah, had a divine revelation while on the road to Damascus. Afterward, he accepted wholeheartedly the vision of Jesus as messiah and, now known as Paul, became a central figure in spreading the Christian message. One of his great contributions was making the new religion more accessible to gentiles, non-Jews.

Paul embarked on his apostolic journeys from the Judean coastal city of Caesarea. The city had become the administrative home of the Roman provincial governors in 6 CE and was the headquarters for the Roman military force stationed in the province, the famed Tenth Legion. A huge pagan temple, dedicated to Augustus Caesar, occupied the high ground overlooking the newly constructed harbor. The city, built at the initiative of King Herod, had public buildings and a palace for the king in the southern part of the city. In this city, one of the first gentile converts, a Roman officer named Cornelius, was baptized (Acts 10:1–5, 25–28).

Later on, Caesarea would be where Christian history was written down and stored from the third century onward, and where a great philosopher and translator, Origen, created the Hexapla version of the Bible. In days of old, Origen, Pamphilus, Eusebius—who was considered the father of church history—and others like them trod the streets of the Roman city, working industriously to explore the intricacies of faith and to create a record that could help convert new adherents to Christianity.

From Caesarea, Paul journeyed to Cyprus, Greece, Turkey, and other parts of the eastern and northern Mediterranean. As a result of his unceasing efforts, the new religion of Christianity soon stood more and more on its own, increasingly disconnected from its Judaic parent. By its own definition, it was open to all humanity—not only to Jews—accepting all those who would accept Jesus as Christ, even if Jesus had said in the Sermon on the Mount that he had come to fulfill and not to repeal the Judaic law. Paul helped create the framework that would make the new religion accessible. The apostles were creating a new fraternity—what the New Testament referred to as the "Israel of God," bound together not only by a belief in Jesus as messiah, but by the Messiah's ability to offer eternal life to those who had faith.

In 60 CE—six years before the outbreak of the Jewish revolt against Rome—Paul was arrested and brought to Caesarea. He requested, as a Roman citizen, that he be tried in Rome. That was either a big mistake or a divinely inspired idea, depending on how one looks at it. When he finally faced trial in Rome, he was sentenced and put to death.

According to most modern scholars, the Gospels had still not been written at that time. Paul's own letters are among the earliest Christian remnants from the period. It is likely that the Gospels, and various apocryphal writing, were in an early period of formation.

Within a few short years, the revolt in Judea and the resulting battle for the Holy Land had led to the fall of Jerusalem. The Jewish rebellion began in 66. The Jews were resentful of Roman rule and especially the attempt to curtail their religious beliefs and substitute Roman gods for their own—even on the grounds of the Holy Temple in Jerusalem. The Romans had to invest considerable effort in crushing the Jews and regaining control, bringing in troops from other parts of the empire.

Judea was the first Roman province ever to seriously rebel against the Romans. Spurred on by their religious faith, the Jews were initially successful. The Romans required four full years to crush the uprising; tens of thousands died amid considerable destruction. The battles were capped by a siege and then the destruction of Jerusalem in 70.

The horrific defeat of the Jews by the Romans would have repercussions on the developing Christian religion and on the way the Jews and others looked at the deeply held beliefs in Jewish messianism. The Jews lost their homeland, and thousands were either killed or expelled. It was interpreted by many as part of God's plan.

A second revolt occurred at roughly the same time. This one also involved Jews and Romans, but took place in Alexandria, Egypt. A large Jewish community thrived in Alexandria because Alexander the Great had provided the Jews a charter over 300 years before guaranteeing them a place of safety and security. In 68, the Romans attempted to impose the same kinds of religious restrictions on their Egyptian province as in Judea. The Jews of Alexandria, like those in Jerusalem, rebelled. According to Coptic tradition, the apostle Mark was killed in this uprising.

The Jewish double defeat by Rome had an impact on the writers of the four biblical Gospels. From the standpoint of many believers in Jesus, the fall of the Temple in Jerusalem was seen as a confirmation of God's divine plan and willingness to punish the Jews for having spurned Jesus' message. Judas, as the betrayer, would soon be viewed as a symbol of this willful refusal to accept Jesus as the Messiah.

The new religion now had many gentiles among the believers. As the word spread far and wide, the figure of Judas became increasingly important. Jesus had been betrayed by Judas. Judas was not only a Jew but also a symbol of Jewish resistance to the spread of the gospel of Jesus.

By this time, many members of the emerging Christian Church felt that the different views had to be pulled together into a single, cohesive religion. In the chaotic second century of competing Christian sects, one man came to the fore in helping to define what would later prove acceptable—and what not—within Christianity: Bishop Irenaeus, who was writing from the far western reaches of the Roman Empire.

Irenaeus's mission was to provide the inchoate Christian groups, not only in Gaul but throughout the world, with a framework of accepted orthodox theology. He made an indelible mark, forging the basis of the doctrines that would be embraced more than 140 years later at the Council of Nicaea in 325, creating the Holy Church.

What we know about this towering religious figure comes mainly from his writings, which are more often than not complex and difficult to understand, though that may be because of the clumsy and even burdensome quality of the translations that have been carried down through the centuries to the modern day. Irenaeus's writings are not believed to have survived in the original language in which they were written. Irenaeus wrote in Greek, which in turn was translated into what some scholars feel is a stiff and awkward Latin. A few of his chapters were translated into Armenian, but, as with the Latin, only the Armenian of those chapters, not the original Greek, survives.

From that outpost of empire in Gaul, Irenaeus observed a Christianity that was chaotic and yet full of energy. It was almost untamable, spreading its influence through much of the known world. A religion was in the process of being formed. Still, it had no organized church to determine, even arbitrarily, what was and was not doctrine. Nor was he alone in trying to impose rules or dogma on the proliferating sects. "By A.D. 200," Elaine Pagels writes:

> the situation had changed. Christianity had become an institution headed by a three-rank hierarchy of bishops, priests, and deacons, who understood themselves to be the guardians of the only "true faith." The majority of churches, among which the church of Rome took a leading role, rejected all other viewpoints as heresy.

It was Irenaeus's destiny to draw the line. He wrote in a letter:

> This then is the order of the rule of our faith, and the foundation of the building, and the stability of our conversation: God, the Father, not made, not material, invisible; one God, the creator of all things: this is the first point of our faith. The second point is: The Word of God, Son of God, Christ Jesus our Lord.... And the third point is: The Holy Spirit, through whom the prophets prophesied, and the fathers learned the things of God, and the righteous were led forth into the way of righteousness; and who in the end of the times was poured out in a new way upon mankind in all the earth, renewing man unto God.

Irenaeus sought to mold Christendom into more of a single body with an agreed-upon literature. He declared that there could not be numerous gospels, but only four. The number had significance: There were four winds, four directions. Irenaeus considered these facts to be of the utmost importance. There should therefore be four gospels. He listed the four acceptable gospels—Matthew,

Mark, Luke, and John—and said they were divinely inspired. These would become the canonical Gospels.

Irenaeus felt himself surrounded by heresy. His most famous work is a five-volume work entitled *Adversus Haereses,* or in translation, *Against Heresies: Refutation and Overthrow of Knowledge Falsely So-Called.* An alternate translation of this title is *On the Detection and Overthrow of the So-Called Gnosis.*

Having roughly defined for himself what heresy is—though not necessarily sharing a precise definition explicitly with others—he pursued those who would commit heresy, that is, what was to *his* mind heresy, with a steady and determined hand.

Irenaeus's bête noir among the dissident Christian groups was the gnostics. Gnosticism was a popular and strong movement throughout the spreading but still persecuted world of Christians. Irenaeus went on the offensive against their blasphemous, in his view, claim to secret knowledge within the soul of individual men. Pagels elaborates:

> Gnostic Christians undoubtedly expressed ideas that the orthodox abhorred. For example, some of these gnostic texts question whether all suffering, labor, and death derive from human sin, which, in the orthodox version, marred an originally perfect creation. Others speak of the feminine element in the divine, celebrating God as Father and Mother. Still others suggest that Christ's resurrection is to be understood symbolically, not literally.

According to Ehrman, "Gnostics are people who are in the know, who are able through their knowledge to escape material existence." He defined the basic tenets shared by most of these sects:

They were Christians who believe that this world in which we live is an evil place, and [some believe that] material existence itself is evil because this world was created by an inferior or an evil deity.

The point of the Gnostic religion was for people to escape from the material trappings in their bodies.

Gnostic influence extended throughout much of Christendom. The gnostics inhabited not only the Nile Valley, its great river coursing for a thousand miles through Egypt, but also the bare hills of Antioch, the seashore cities of Alexandria and Caesarea on the Mediterranean, and even to the upper reaches of empire in Lyon, where Irenaeus was bishop and keeper of the faith. Irenaeus's theology emphasized the unity of God, whereas many gnostics divided God into a series of "aeons," all of them divine and holy, and other beings or spiritual urges that were wicked and unjust.

One sect that was targeted in particular followed the teachings of Valentinus, after whom its adherents were called Valentinians. Marvin Meyer writes:

In Valentinian gnosticism Christ and the word (logos) are eternal beings (aeons), and Jesus is brought forth to bring salvation and enlightenment here below. This recalls the logos made flesh in the Gospel of John. But ... the Valentinians offered a whole new scheme of salvation through knowledge, and an unknowable father in the heavenly realm of light, which is the pleroma or fullness. Traditional Christians were right to suspect otherness in the Valentinians.

The Valentinians were more like a school of intellectuals than a doctrinaire religious movement, tending to use allegory extensively and indulging in a wide range of theological speculation. Valentinus himself was an eloquent leader, who, in the words of Yale professor Bentley Layton in his book *The Gnostic Scriptures,* "aspired to raise Christian theology to the level of pagan philosophical studies." There were Valentinian schools scattered through the Roman Empire, from Gaul to Rome to Egypt and even as far as Mesopotamia. Generally, a scholar held classes in private for qualified students, but the Valentinians kept good relations with local communities by worshipping in ordinary churches and using the same books and prayers as did others. Their purpose was not only spreading of the faith but intellectual inquiry, and they were diverse and sophisticated.

The movement lasted until the seventh century, but from as early as 160, Layton notes, "opponents of the Valentinian school began their attempt to label, alienate, and oust the movement from the church." The Valentinians did not bother to reply in detail to the charges against them, including one that they were actually "wolves in sheep's clothing." In Bentley's words, "their mythic theology ... foresaw in god's final reckoning a provision for non-Christians to be destroyed; and for ordinary Christians (i.e., the opposition) to enter only a second class paradise and rest forever—not with god the father, but merely with the craftsman of the world."

Most gnostic documents are believed to have been originally written in the Greek language during the time that Irenaeus himself lived—that is, roughly between 100 and 200 CE. Almost all that was known about the gnostics until 1945, when the trove of gnostic documents was discovered at Nag Hammadi, came from their fiercest critics—in particular, Irenaeus, who was also highly critical of the Valentinians.

Yet the gnostics formed a thriving and diverse movement believing wholly in the general truth of their concepts. As Pagels points out:

> The Gnostics who wrote and circulated these texts did not regard *themselves* as "heretics." Most of the writings use Christian terminology, unmistakably related to a Jewish heritage. Many claim to offer traditions about Jesus that are secret, hidden from "the many" who constitute what, in the second century, came to be called the "catholic church."

In those days, who was right about Jesus was far from clear-cut.

When the Nag Hammadi documents were published in the second half of the twentieth century, it was felt that they would significantly alter our understanding of early Christianity. The gnostics could now speak for themselves, so it was no longer necessary to filter their texts through the descriptions of their self-professed enemies. Their thought systems were a revelation. There were at least a few scholars who believed that these manuscripts had the power to threaten centuries-old systems of Christian belief. One of the first books to be published about the new body of Gnostic literature was by French scholar Jean Doresse and was entitled *The Discovery of the Nag Hammadi Texts: A Firsthand Account of the Expedition That Shook the Foundations of Christianity*.

Notwithstanding the hype that the Nag Hammadi texts might counter modern Christianity in any serious way, the perceived challenge fizzled. Conventional Christianity shrugged off the presumed gnostic challenge. "I don't think that any document that appears today is going to destroy faith," Ehrman noted. "I think people will continue to believe—whatever documents appear."

Still, the texts were enormously valuable. They could be seen for the first time and read and judged on their own merits, rather than through the critical eyes of their second-, third- and fourth-century critics such as Irenaeus, who were inevitably presenting a biased view of that world and were fighting their own ideological battles and conflicts of faith.

Gnostic texts had their followers and adherents among modern academics. The world of the second century had been opened up to scholarship, and it offered a tantalizing, new, and above all fuller view of what early Christianity was really like. Classicist Roger Bagnall pointed out what was happening in academia as the gnostic texts began to be read:

> If you think about the state of religious studies as an academic discipline in the 1960s and 1970s, you will recognize that it was heavily populated with people who came out of theological backgrounds, often deep church backgrounds, and who had a highly conflicted attitude toward that part of their background. The Nag Hammadi material was of course heretical in a technical sense, stuff condemned by the orthodox fathers of the church. A scholar who had no personal stake in Christianity would be unlikely to feel a need to come to terms with that, but this was hardly the case. If you read Elaine Pagels, you'll see the result: The gnostics are validated as a direction in which Christianity could have gone and which would have made it warmer and fuzzier, much nicer than this cold orthodoxy stuff.

Historically, the proto-orthodox and the orthodox had won out, and their views dominated the founding of the Church and the broad tradition of faith known as Christianity. The gnostic views were on the whole excluded from that broad avenue of thought and faith. Irenaeus had done his job centuries ago. Irenaeus's work enabled a fusion of the Old and New Testaments. Canonical Christianity had found a balance between the divine and the human, between storytelling and the demands of faith. It had defined the relationship between man and God, between the Jews and the new Christians and ancient prophecy, to the satisfaction of the Church. The Church became an enduring power. Christianity established itself as the primary religion of Western civilization.

Among the gnostic manuscripts Irenaeus railed against was one called the Gospel of Judas:

> Others again declare that Cain derived his being from the Power above, and acknowledge that Esau, Korah, the Sodomites, and all such persons, are related to themselves. On this account, they add, they have been assailed by the Creator, yet no one of them has suffered injury. For Sophia was in the habit of carrying off that which belonged to her from them to herself. They declare that Judas the traitor was thoroughly acquainted with these things, and that he alone, knowing the truth as no others did, accomplished the mystery of the betrayal; by him all things, both earthly and heavenly, were thus thrown into confusion. They produce a fictitious history of this kind, which they style the gospel of Judas.

To understand these comments by Irenaeus, it should be remembered that *Sophia* meant wisdom, or the soul of the world, in gnostic terms.

Judas knew "the truth as no others did." Why? How? Irenaeus

did not feel disposed to elaborate on the precise nature of the gnostic heresy in this regard.

Did Irenaeus ever read the Gospel of Judas? There is no indication in what Irenaeus wrote that he did. But the truth was that the Gospel of Judas did not have to be read by Irenaeus or anybody else to condemn it. The title of the gospel was enough, according to scholarly experts. As the eminent Coptologist Rodolphe Kasser put it, "The title itself reveals it is blasphemous."

Stephen Emmel adds, "The title makes it clear that Judas, the betrayer, should not have written the Gospel.... That's why the suggestion is made that Irenaeus did not have to say too much about it. The title itself condemns it."

Ehrman put the questions into perspective:

> From the earliest times of Christianity, it was understood that Jesus had one of his followers who was a traitor. This is almost certainly a historical tradition. Jesus was almost certainly turned in to the authorities by Judas Iscariot. The reason historians think that is because it's not the sort of story that any Christian would have made up.

For all of Ireneaus's attempts to create an orthodox religion, the faith was still not officially sanctioned. Christians continued to suffer the periodic waves of persecution. These climaxed during Diocletian's reign as emperor of Rome. Diocletian, who was born in 245 and died in 313, started his reign as a moderate, but in later years he oversaw a gruesome wave of the "Great Persecutions" of Christians, beginning in 284. His harsh treatment of

Christians, documented in detail by contemporary Christian scholar Eusebius, created tale after horrendous tale of martyrdom. Although Diocletian abdicated in 305, this spasm of persecution concluded only with the death by execution of Peter, bishop of Alexandria, in 311.

The career of St. Athanasius, who was born in Alexandria about 295, reflects the uncertain times. He followed in the wake of Irenaeus's propagation of proto-orthodox Christianity. By that time the faith was well established among the common people in Egypt. It had spread south from Alexandria through the Nile Valley, and both Copts and many of the Greeks living in Egypt had adopted it. By 313, Emperor Constantine had legitimized the religion, and Christians were allowed to worship freely.

Athanasius, who attended the Council of Nicaea in 325, became a bishop in the summer of 328 and proved himself a vigorous advocate of orthodox Christianity. Constantine, for reasons not fully clear, summoned him to Byzantium in 335 and then exiled him to Trier on the German frontier.

When he returned to Egypt two years later, Athanasius became an acerbic critic of what was referred to as the "Arian heresy," a doctrine that was looked upon with some favor by the new emperor in the East, Constantius, the son of Constantine. It became a continuation of the wars fought by Irenaeus. The Arian heresy was essentially a belief that the birth of Jesus was separate from God, because God preceded Jesus and was all-powerful. It was originally professed by a priest named Arius who, like Athanasius, was from Alexandria. Jesus was the Son of God, but was not God Himself, according to this doctrine—or heresy, as defined by the proto-orthodox—which was bitterly contested within the nascent Catholic Church and had gained numerous adherents.

Athanasius dedicated his life to the fight against whoever or whatever would undo the work of the Council of Nicaea. He was arrested and sent into exile three times. He experienced thirty years of conflict and instability as different forces fought for supremacy within Christianity.

Within this context of turbulence—between 330 and 380—the final framework of the Christian canon crystallized. It represented a significant step toward a defined single body of holy literature that was recognized by all Christians. Athanasius played the critical role in achieving this unified vision. In his thirty-ninth festal letter, written in 367, he basically defined what was acceptable and what was not. He gave a stamp of approval to the New Testament, as it was already generally formulated.

In his letter, which was read throughout Egypt in Christian churches, Athanasius delineated the canon:

> These are the four Gospels, according to Matthew, Mark, Luke, and John. Afterward, the Acts of the Apostles and Epistles (called Catholic), seven, viz. of James, one; of Peter, two; of John, three; after these, one of Jude. In addition, there are fourteen Epistles of Paul, written in this order. The first, to the Romans; then two to the Corinthians; after these, to the Galatians; next, to the Ephesians; then to the Philippians; then to the Colossians; after these, two to the Thessalonians, and that to the Hebrews; and again, two to Timothy; one to Titus; and lastly, that to Philemon. And besides, the Revelation of John.

"These are fountains of salvation, that they who thirst may be satisfied with the living words they contain," Athanasius summed up. "In these alone is proclaimed the doctrine of godliness."

Echoing the spirit of Bishop Irenaeus, he also condemned those who were heretics by the proto-orthodox definition. His words seemed most of all to be a pointed critique of the gnostics, who

> have fabricated books which they call books of tables, in which they shew stars, to which they give the names of Saints.... And therein of a truth they have inflicted on themselves a double reproach: those who have written such books, because they have perfected themselves in a lying and contemptible science; and as to the ignorant and simple, they have led them astray by evil thoughts concerning the right faith established in all truth and upright in the presence of God.

Athanasius added about the scriptures as he had delineated them: "Let no man add to these, neither let him take ought from these. For concerning these the Lord put to shame the Sadducees, and said, 'Ye do err, not knowing the Scriptures.' And He reproved the Jews, saying, 'Search the Scriptures, for these are they that testify of Me.'"

As a result of Athanasius' festal letter, the church had more precisely defined what was acceptable within the churches of Christendom, as well as giving examples of things that were unacceptable. While it is not certain if there was an active campaign to repress dissident and heretical literature, anything that was outside the framework of Athanasius' letter became "apocryphal," in the more mild instances, or something bordering on heresy, if it was in sharp disagreement with prevailing doctrine. Yet there is no clear-cut evidence of book-burning. Scholarly opinions on the question differ. "Athanasius, from what survives, did not order burning of 'heretical' books," David Brakke, author of *Athanasius and the Politics of Asceticism,* contends, "just that they be rejected, never read or used."

For one thing, what means did Athanasius have to enforce his order? Brakke answers:

Not that many, actually. It is true that in his struggles with opponents in the city of Alexandria he seems to have used violence (thugs to beat people up), but such tactics were unlikely to get all Christians in Egypt to use the same Bible and not read or use other writings. As the patriarch of Egypt, Athanasius appointed bishops throughout Egypt, so he would appoint only those men who agreed with him on such issues, and clergy who used "heretical" books could be fired.

Brakke went on:

But above all, Athanasius had his own considerable personal authority. He had been bishop since 328, and he had survived multiple attempts to remove him from his see, including several imperially ordered exiles, e.g., once to Germany. He had been a staunch defender of the Nicene Creed against its "Arian" critics, and very early in his career he worked to forge a close relationship with the prestigious monks of the desert. He was a hero to Egyptian Christians, and thus any success he had in getting people to conform and to get rid of "heretical" books (and it's hard to gauge how much success he really had) primarily came from his own authority.

Brakke has a very simple explanation for why the alternative gospels were forgotten:

The primary reason for the disappearance of these works is that scribes stopped copying them in antiquity and the Middle Ages. Professional scribes reproduced books by hand and only when a customer asked for a book and agreed to pay for it. If a Christian book was declared useless for theology and even dangerous, few people would order such books, and some scribes may have refused to supply them. Most of the manuscripts of Christian works that we have today were not produced by independent professional scribes, but in monasteries, and certainly monastic leaders would not authorize the copying of "heretical" books. Especially in antiquity, quality book materials and scribal services were not cheap, so if there was no demand for a book, it could easily disappear.

Among those texts lost to history was the Gospel of Judas. Apparently, few copies existed, and no one had access to it or them. It was physically nowhere to be found. The copy of it that was miraculously found in the 1970s was a Coptic text, preserved by some kind of accident or what some might believe is an act of God in Middle Egypt.

From the third century on, the Gospel of Judas was hardly mentioned again in the entire vast literature of Christian writing in the centuries that followed. It became one of history's forgotten manuscripts. Yet its powers to shock mainstream Christians has not faded over those hundreds of years because of its alternative account of what led to Jesus' trial and crucifixion. Did it really say that Judas was only carrying out Jesus' wishes? Could it seriously assert that Jesus asked Judas to turn him in to the authorities in order to fulfill his destiny? How could it proclaim that Judas was the favored disciple?

Such questions were for naught unless the long-hidden gospel could be saved from the extensive and continuing damage it had sustained in the two decades since emerging from the Middle Egyptian tomb. Judas's message was steadily turning to dust. And its peril was far from over.

# CHAPTER TWELVE

# THE FERRINI CONFRONTATION

*In the Gospel of Judas, Judas doesn't do an evil thing,
Judas does a good thing. Judas allows Jesus' body to be sacrificed
so that his spirit can be set free. Judas is the only one who
understands who Jesus really is. He understands what Jesus'
mission is and what Jesus' secret revelation is. Based on his
knowledge of the truth, he turns Jesus over to the authorities.
And so it flips the understanding of Judas that you get
from the New Testament Gospels.*
—BART EHRMAN

O n a sunny day in early September 2000, Frieda Tchacos
Nussberger took a train up the coast from New York City. At
Yale University, the precious papyrus texts awaited her in three
big black boxes. The expert consultation was brief. "I didn't even
check what was there. A friend at Yale organized a taxi. He told
me, 'Take these and go.' He was so sorry to see the manuscript
leave. And I left. My heart was bleeding."

"Then I made one of the big mistakes of my life," she recalled later.

Frieda returned to New York with one of the great cultural treasures of our time. She held a physical body of material that was fragile, yet weighty with historical importance. It was up to her to determine the fate of the Judas gospel.

In fact, Frieda had already made a crucial decision that could determine that fate. She had found a potential buyer for the manuscripts. The prospect of selling them caused her considerable anxiety, but she felt she had no choice, knowing that whoever owned them would have to safeguard them as well. The costs of restoration could swiftly mount to financial proportions well beyond her grasp. "For me, it was like a blow to the head. How can I, little Frieda, do this job? It was a gigantic project that I could not afford. Still, I had the manuscript back. That was a relief."

Looking back on it, she laments, "Maybe I should have talked to my friend at Yale about it. He knew, he would have opened my eyes, but Bruce Ferrini, the dealer I was going to meet in Ohio, had asked me to keep it all very secret."

She arrived at Kennedy Airport the next day feeling nervous, all alone. Clutching the three boxes tightly, she produced her ticket and tried to board her flight. The plane, however, had technical problems, and after an hour or two wait, the flight was canceled.

The airline found a replacement aircraft at LaGuardia Airport about a half-hour ride away. The passengers were ferried over on a bus. Frieda, weighted down by history, nervously guarded the boxes she was carrying. "I was holding those three huge black boxes. I was afraid that the bumps up and down would damage the manuscripts or destroy them."

At LaGuardia, the replacement aircraft was a small commuter jet with less than thirty seats, and she was told by security guards that she could not board the plane with the boxes. When she insisted, they assured her that the goods would be safe. In the end, she lost the argument. The Gospel of Judas and its accompanying texts were shoved into the luggage compartment of the plane. She had wanted to sleep, but she could only wonder what further damage was being done to the papyri.

Her destination was Cleveland, Ohio. All along, Frieda Tchacos Nussberger had faced a challenge. She was a known dealer, with clients among the world's largest museums and richest collectors, and she wanted to sell the ancient documents. Naturally, she desired an institution that was suitable—one that could restore, translate, and possibly exhibit the codex. Yale's prestigious Beinecke Library had an impeccable reputation, which was why she had chosen it first.

Then an antiquities dealer based in London, Bill Veres, whom Frieda had known for years, mentioned a possibility. Veres specialized in coinage and ancient objects, not texts, but he told Frieda that he had developed a relationship with an Ohio-based manuscript dealer named Bruce Ferrini and that their collaboration looked promising.

Veres had visited Zurich in June 2000. His meetings with Frieda were exploratory and cordial, and it was then that he told her about Ferrini and asked whether she had anything that she would like to sell. Already aware of Yale's foot-dragging, Frieda mentioned the Coptic manuscripts.

Now, with Yale declining to make an offer, Ferrini's interest appeared to be a stroke of good fortune. Ferrini had excellent financial backing, or so Frieda was told, and would offer a sizable sum for the manuscripts in Frieda's possession.

Bruce Ferrini, of mixed Italian and Native American heritage, was an alumnus of Kent State University in Ohio. He had once been an aspiring opera singer. When he failed to make it in that demanding profession, he turned to old books and Renaissance manuscripts. Ferrini became a leading dealer, one of the few with a base in the American Midwest. Ferrini's reputation was good, Veres assured Frieda, and he was excellently placed to have the manuscripts restored and put on proper display.

Frieda understood Veres to say that Ferrini had as a leading client Bill Gates, the billionaire chairman of Microsoft. She got the impression that Ferrini was Gates's close friend or antiquities provider. Frieda had known Veres a long time and trusted his judgment. She was confident that a good deal, for both her and the codex, could be struck.

Veres did not inform Frieda about one of Ferrini's principal backers, James Ferrell, lest she attempt to go directly to him to explore price and make a sale. Ferrell is a wealthy American business executive also based in the Midwest whose sideline passion was collecting antiquities and art. Ferrell is president and CEO of Ferrellgas, based in Liberty, Missouri, which is one of the leading propane gas companies in America and the world. Ferrell had inherited the business from his father and made a major success of it, going public on the New York Stock Exchange in 1994.

Frieda was met in Cleveland by Ferrini, who was described to her as "looking like an ex-football player." He had been waiting at the airport for hours due to the long delay of her flight. Once they introduced themselves, he drove her in his Mercedes-Benz to his home in Akron. The intermediary, Bill Veres, who had in the meantime become Ferrini's partner, was already on hand to meet them.

Frieda's first view of Ferrini's mansion created a distinctly negative impression. It was huge, but she thought it gaudy and cheap. "It was not the house of a Renaissance manuscripts dealer," Frieda later recalled. "It was a show-off kind of house—a house designed to impress a visitor, but not for living. My first impression was, how the hell could a manuscript dealer, who should be an intellectual, live in a place that resembles Hollywood?

"I saw upstairs, his bedroom. I thought, no one has ever lived in that bedroom. Still, my alarm bells didn't go off."

Ferrini said his client would come in a few days. He was bubbling with enthusiasm, according to Veres. Ferrini, said Veres, was "a hyper personality, who got enormously excited" when a great new deal that was really "hot" was on the way, and this one was as good as they get. Ferrini was extremely eager to close the deal. He set up a conference call with his New York lawyer, Eric Kaufman, and Frieda's family lawyer, who was also based in New York.

Ferrini's company, through which he conducted the deal, was called Nemo. "*Nemo* means 'nobody' in Latin," Frieda later recalled, pointing out that the name was apt.

The negotiations were swiftly concluded. The two dealers agreed on a price of $2.5 million. Veres believed Ferrini could have driven the price down further if he had pressed, since Frieda was eager to sell. The details of the contract were agreed upon, and Frieda and Ferrini went out to dinner to celebrate.

Unfortunately for Frieda, one essential sentence was not included in the signed contract. She did not stipulate that she would keep title of the papyrus manuscripts until she was fully paid. It was a colossal mistake.

The next day, September 9, 2000, Ferrini gave Frieda two post-dated checks: one for $1.25 million dated January 15, 2001, the second for the same amount dated a month later. That payment schedule was designed to give Ferrini enough time to wrap up his deals and sell the manuscript onward.

"There was nothing more for me to do there," Frieda recalled. "I was relieved, but I thought a positive future for the manuscripts was assured. I left everything, except for the checks. I didn't even have a receipt." For a businesswoman with an international reputation in her field, it was a less than stellar performance.

As soon as the deal was signed, Frieda was driven to the airport in Cleveland, and she flew back to New York. From there, she embarked on a plane for home in Zurich. It had only taken a few days to get the manuscripts sold. That alone was a bad sign. A marriage conducted in such haste was bound to be headed for catastrophe.

☥

Ferrini had a grand plan. He was considering a stylish debut for the gospel in Japan. But first he had to negotiate a sale to propane gas billionaire Ferrell. Frieda doubts that Bill Gates was ever really in the picture, as she had been led to believe. For his part, Veres says that Gates was discussed, though no relationship between Ferrini and Gates ever materialized.

Nevertheless, Ferrell was truly intrigued by collecting, and in 1999 he and Ferrini had entered into an agreement "for the purpose of the enhancement of the Ferrell collection of manuscripts." In effect, Ferrell had become one of Ferrini's principal backers in antiquities projects, and their cooperation was extended to encompass opportunities in a wide range of antiquities, from coins to manuscripts to artifacts and pieces of art. A direct system of accounting was set up that assured Ferrell considerable control of the sales process and defined how Ferrell would get the monies owed him.

With Ferrell's encouragement, Ferrini set off to expand into new markets. Veres, with his expertise in ancient coins, offered a whole new aspect of the business to the Ohio manuscript dealer and his backer. Ferrini and Veres had met through the good offices of a curator for ancient coins at the Ashmolean Museum in Oxford, England.

Veres made a special trip to Ohio in February 2000 to crystallize arrangements for what Ferrini and he hoped would be their own lucrative relationship. Veres later summarized his role relating to Ferrini in a memo prepared for Frieda:

> Feb. 18th 2000.
> I arrive in Akron for the 1st time to work out a working arrangement with Ferrell-Ferrini. I will find materials, through my sources, Ferrell will finance and Ferrini would sell.

That September, Veres had arrived in Akron a few days before Frieda so both he and Ferrini could bone up on the subject of the gospels. Veres's memo details the subsequent events. "Ferrini was ecstatic about the deal," he wrote. "Whatever else could be said, the importance of the horde [sic] was mind-blowing."

Veres and Ferrini devised an initial strategy to exploit the purchase. Ferrini had acquaintances at the prestigious Cleveland Museum of Art. Dr. Michael Bennett, a curator for antiquities, paid Ferrini a visit, as did several of the directors of the museum, and Ferrini and Veres responded with a reciprocal visit to the museum.

Veres remained in Akron after Frieda left. As noted in his summary, "I stay on in Akron to see Ferrell arrive and examine the material with the hope of their buying the group."

Ferrini's plans were ambitious. He code-named his new venture "Project First Word." In a memo prepared in the fall of 2000, Ferrini outlined an exacting schedule to get the project off the ground by the beginning of 2002.

In January 2001 he would send out a press release announcing the existence of the Gospel of Judas. Work on photography, conservation, and translation would commence. A press conference would be held in February 2001.

By November or December 2001, a first public exhibition was foreseen. This would be held at the Toppan Printing Museum in Tokyo. A catalogue would be prepared.

In January 2002, the "First Word" would be published, with a facsimile edition to be published sometime later in 2002. Ferrini envisioned enlisting several expert groups who would be drawn from leading individuals and institutions in the world and be convened for specific tasks. These people and institutions might include:

- a "Team to Undertake the Conservation," envisioned to include scholars from the University of Michigan, Duke University, or the British Museum
- a "Team to Do Translation," headed by Elaine Pagels of Princeton University, a leading scholar on the gnostic gospels, along with scholars from Harvard University or the Morgan Library in New York
- a "Team to Do Context and Theological Evaluation, Gnostic, Nag Hammadi," also including Pagels and Harvard University
- a "Team to Do Film Journalism," which would record the entire process
- a "Team to Photograph for Translation" and a "Team to Photograph for Facsimile," the latter projected as coming from the rare-book firm Yoshodo in Tokyo
- a "Team to Sensationalize and Romanticize: Process of Discovery, Recovery, Translation and Dissemination," headed by up Ferrini himself and Dorothy

Shinn, an art and architecture critic for the local *Akron Beacon Journal* newspaper
- a "Team to Prepare Toppan Exhibition and Catalogue," undertaken by Yoshodo and Ferrini
- a "Team to Do Context and Theological Evaluation, Historical Jesus/Judas & Context for Modern Christians," which was projected as coming from Ashland Theological Seminary, although a question mark was added after this institution

Another expert who was consulted was Charles W. Hedrick, a professor at Southwest Missouri State University. A Coptologist who participated in the Nag Hammadi digs and UNESCO supervisory projects of that enterprise, Hedrick was a friend and former colleague of Professor James M. Robinson in Claremont, California.

The ambitious dreams about how the Veres–Ferrini combination would exploit the Gospel of Judas and its accompanying codices lasted only a short time.

James Ferrell arrived a few days later, along with his financial adviser, Theresa Schekirke, president of Ferrell Capital. Someone in the group made a very unusual decision—to put the texts into deep freeze. Mario Roberty says: "Ferrini proudly told me that he had adopted this 'technique' in order to separate the pages 'with no harm to the manuscript'?! Every professional hearing about Ferrini's 'technique' was flabbergasted and shocked." The freezer was later judged to have contributed to the texts' steadily increasing deterioration.

The propane gas magnate had come to Akron with an agenda that was significantly different from what was envisioned by Ferrini. According to Veres, "When Ferrell arrived, it seemed that he was not in a great mood to make any further acquisitions. I found out later this ill humor had to do with problems in Ferrini's bookkeeping that had been discovered by Theresa Schekirke." Ferrell through Schekirke declined to comment on his relationship with Ferrini.

Court documents do not state precisely when Theresa Schekirke discovered what she considered to be financial irregularities in Ferrini's accounting. Veres recorded, in his memo prepared and submitted to Nussberger years later: "Unknown to me at the time"—the time is September 2000—"Schekirke finds problems with Ferrini's handling of Ferrell's portfolio and a purchase of the papyri. [The deal] ... is not concluded." In fact, according to court records, Ferrini and Ferrell would end up suing each other about two years later and breaking off their relationship. Among Ferrell's claims was a demand for proper accounting from Ferrini; Ferrini responded in court documents that he had provided such an accounting.

In fact, many of the court documents were sealed by agreement of the parties, and there is very little that speaks about Frieda Tchacos Nussberger or the Gospel of Judas. What the documents do reveal is that Ferrini's entire relationship with Ferrell was in transition. Bill Veres, who was present in Akron when Schekirke and Ferrell visited, noted that it was unraveling. "Ferrell's opinion of Ferrini had taken a downward turn, and I suspect nothing would have changed his mind, no matter how good a deal was on the table."

Ferrini made other efforts to get sales going. Among the persons he contacted was Martin Schoyen, Robinson's backer, who told Ferrini details of the negotiations that had taken place in 1983, when Robinson had sent Stephen Emmel to Geneva. Schoyen also informed Ferrini that Hanna had agreed, "more or less," in Schoyen's words, to a stipulated sale for $986,000 in 1990—to be concluded at the meeting, scheduled for New York in December 1990, the one that had been cancelled because of Desert Storm. He told Ferrini to check whether everything was still present. Schoyen was paving the way, in Bill Veres' words, to make "a lowball offer" of about the same amount to Ferrini, or one and a half million dollars less than Ferrini had committed to pay Frieda, which would have represented a colossal loss for the Ohio dealer.

Ferrini was in difficult financial straits. He owed hundreds of thousands of dollars to various parties and was depending heavily on the codex deal to stem his losses. Within a few months, memories of the joyous celebration would be replaced by a bitter dispute with Frieda Nussberger and her lawyer, Mario Roberty.

A few days after Schekirke's visit to Akron, Veres informed Frieda that Ferrini's relationship with Ferrell was experiencing strain and that Ferrini was in financial trouble. Frieda began to suspect that Ferrini's two postdated checks would not be honored. She would be out $2.5 million, and Ferrini would retain possession of the ancient texts.

Frieda had already scheduled a meeting with her lawyer, Mario Roberty. The suave Roberty lives and studied law in Basel, a center of art and culture. He is the ultimate Swiss "potpourri," a judiciously flavored combination of French, German, and Italian culture who glides effortlessly among the country's principal languages. A former student at Columbia University in New York, his English is also excellent.

Upon her return to Switzerland, Frieda met Roberty, and on September 15 the two drove together through the heart of Switzerland, from Zurich to a business meeting in Lugano, the beautiful lakeside city in the Italian-speaking southernmost part of the country. The beautiful fall foliage colored their route with tinges of dazzling reds and yellows.

On the way, Roberty looked at the contract Frieda had signed in America. He immediately spotted the problems. Roberty told her, "You have done something stupid."

As they neared the town of Schwyz, Frieda asked, "What shall I do?"

"We have to get the manuscripts back," Roberty replied.

Schwyz was where Roberty had for four years attended high school at a Jesuit college called Maria Hilf, or Mary Help. Here, he and the other students had had to endure long periods of *silencium* every morning, in the faculty's hope that the students would get help from the Virgin Mary in conjuring up visions of the suffering Jesus on his way to crucifixion and resurrection. Ironically, he was here again, now helping to recover the words of Judas the Betrayer that had been condemned by the emerging Catholic Church eighteen hundred years before.

Roberty knew that Frieda might never receive payment from Ferrini, and he realized he had to devise a strategy. As the first step, he pulled out a Dictaphone in order to record Frieda's personal account of the sale. The process of rescuing the gospel from its temporary home in Akron had begun.

Ferrini's financial problems were growing worse, but like many other art and antiquities dealers from throughout the world, he still made the pilgrimage to Basel, Roberty's hometown, which hosts some of the world's most prestigious art and culture fairs. The fall fair was named CULTURA 2000 and was dedicated to ancient art, classical, Asian, pre-Columbian, ethnographical, and European art.

It took place October 14–22, 2000, and Ferrini had a stand on the first floor exhibiting mostly illuminated manuscripts from medieval times. Roberty arranged a meeting with him there.

Roberty thought that cooperation with Ferrini would be preferable to outright confrontation. As a token of friendship, he suggested that Frieda offer a number of objects on consignment. Roberty later noted in a letter that Ferrini had received "a number of objects from Nefer AG [Frieda's company] on consignment bases. Before year ends Nefer AG requires a statement from your side showing which objects have already been sold and for which objects you require a prolongation of consignment."

Although he had his own charitable foundation for projects in the art and antiquity field called Maecenas, Roberty proposed setting up a new and separate charitable foundation specifically to promote the codex project, which would operate under Swiss law with an initial endowment of $100,000, to be funded in equal measure by Frieda and Ferrini. Ferrini's response was not negative, but he was apparently weighing the offer, perhaps hoping to make sales with the material in his possession.

With no results from the conciliatory route, in late 2000 Roberty sought a tougher means of regaining possession of the manuscripts. The interested parties met together in New York in December to work out the deal that would get Frieda her texts back. These meetings were tense. Ferrini was represented by Eric Kaufman, a respected lawyer who himself was passionate about ancient and medieval manuscripts. As the two sides sparred for position, Kaufman probed the provenance of the manuscripts that Frieda had in her possession. He argued that the manuscripts had most likely entered the United States illegally and further argued that selling illegally obtained texts was itself illegal, though it was acknowledged that Frieda was not responsible for their importation: Hanna Asabil had brought the codex into the United States in 1984.

Roberty expanded on the initial concept of a foundation for the codex. Ferrini's original concept for "The First Word" was modified into the "Logos Project."

On December 15, 2000, in a memo to Kaufman, Roberty asked that the points of understanding reached at the New York meeting be put down in writing. He added:

> We first must ascertain that Mr. Hanna Asabil* [sic] had obtained good legal and beneficial title to the manuscripts and that he had the right to sell these documents to Frieda. *Upon my return to Basel, I shall analyze this question and transmit my findings for your examination.*
> *pseudonym

Roberty stressed the need for secrecy.

> It is clearly understood by all persons involved that nobody, not even Bruce and Frieda but only the Foundation, will have the right to promulgate and commercialize any knowledge regarding, concerning, or deriving from the manuscripts. Moreover, for the time being and until all legal aspects are clarified, it is in the best interest of the Project to maintain utmost secrecy about its existence.

By mid-January 2001, a tentative agreement to cancel the original sale to Ferrini was reached. Ferrini would return all manuscripts except two—the mathematical treatise and the Pauline epistles—and the checks provided by Ferrini to Frieda would be voided. An inventory of goods would be made to provide a detailed record of what was being returned. Ferrini would pay a purchase price for the mathematical treatise and the letters of Paul in the amount of $300,000. The new foundation, Logos, would be established and Ferrini would have the option to join it.

Ferrini hesitated, however. Neither Roberty nor Frieda could get an answer that would conclude the deal. The longer they waited, the more likely it was that Ferrini would sell the manuscripts.

Ferrini's delay in responding may have had an ulterior purpose. He was trying hard in late January and February to sell certain texts and realize what he considered to be the essential worth of the papyrus manuscripts. Since he had committed himself to pay $2.5 million, he needed an overall sales price well beyond that number. He believed he had sorted out the different papyri into their respective categories. He was in the process of a deal for the mathematical treatise and thought he had a sale for the Pauline epistles as well, but that latter sale was cancelled.

The proposal to establish the Logos Foundation, in which Ferrini and Frieda would work together, faded into the background and was soon forgotten. From Roberty's standpoint, future cooperation between his client and Ferrini was not desirable. On Frieda's behalf, he wanted to void the postdated checks that had been provided to Ferrini, and to get the precious manuscripts back into his client's hands.

Pressure on Ferrini was building on several fronts. According to court documents, Ferrini and Ferrell entered into another agreement dated February 1, 2001, in which Ferrell imposed strict conditions on Ferrini's representation of illuminated manuscripts, paintings, and other items of art in his personal collection.

Judging by the agreement, Ferrell had lost trust in Ferrini's good faith. Ferrini later alleged that he entered the agreement under some duress.

Roberty decided to play with fire—realizing full well that those who do so often get burned themselves—by leaking information to put pressure on Ferrini. Roberty chose to do this through an Internet blogger named Michel van Rijn, a Dutchman who maintained a scandalmongering "arts and antiquities" website. He and van Rijn had met a year previously on another matter for a Japanese museum. On that occasion, van Rijn had told Roberty that he had been employed by New Scotland Yard, though he had been let go—wrongly, he said—by the British agency. Van Rijn claimed he had damaging information about Roberty's Japanese client and, according to Roberty, asked for money to maintain silence about what he had.

Despite the cloudy nature of such a request, as he interpreted it, Roberty found van Rijn to be an engaging, though eccentric and occasionally irrational, personality: "He is crazy, he is insane, but he is fascinating."

Hoping to apply some pressure on Ferrini, Roberty described Ferrini's dealings with Frieda to van Rijn. Roberty prepared the draft of an article to be published on van Rijn's website under van Rijn's imprimatur, showing Frieda and the project in a favorable light:

> All these manuscripts are priceless historical documents, only comparable to major finds like the Nag Hammadi Library or the Dead Sea Scrolls from Qumran. They belong to mankind and shall be publicly preserved and studied. For this purpose, Frieda has set up a public foundation to which these manuscripts have been donated. But Ferrini wants to turn them into money for the satisfaction of his greedy ambitions.... Buyers beware, a maniac dealer is selling parts of our history.

In an e-mail of February 5, Roberty warmly commended van Rijn for his work.

> You have been doing a genius job. Congratulations. You have updated your site in the best possible way and I am admiring your skills.... The point is, I would like to keep the pressure on B.F. until he really fulfills his (lawyer's) promise. Therefore, probably the best and only possible update on "Bruce on the Loose" is the naked truth. Hopefully B.F. will keep his (lawyer's) word and have the manuscripts returned by February 14/15, 2001.

The relationship proved to be rocky, though, and van Rijn would later turn on Roberty, writing on his website: "As the dealings with Roberty unfolded I was confronted by an even increasingly less attractive picture of his activities." Roberty checked van Rijn's updated site when the article appeared the next day, and found that wording had been changed. He sent van Rijn an e-mail: "Frankly, I am not very happy with it. Your first paragraph reveals such information that obviously could only be fed in by my side and this could make negotiations starting tomorrow (i.e., today) even more difficult."

The truth is that van Rijn was a loose cannon who, in Roberty's later opinion, was "a psychopath with paranoia" who required endless stroking and attention. Roberty's attempts to keep him harnessed were only partly successful.

By early February Ferrini and Kaufman were angry about the accusations on van Rijn's website. Kaufman wrote Roberty on February 8, pointing out that Roberty and Frieda had not yet provided any evidence concerning title. "In all of these circumstances," wrote Kaufman:

> it is particularly troublesome to find your friend van Rijn subjecting Ferrini to public accusations of theft, bouncing checks, failing financial condition, and miscellaneous ad hominem attacks. But it is far more distressing to have you

suggest that it is Ferrini who is guilty of a crime for not paying for or returning the manuscripts....

It is Ferrini who has been injured by events to date. It is Ferrini's reputation that has been sullied by van Rijn based upon information and misinformation communicated to him and it is Ferrini who will suffer substantial economic loss if he cannot satisfy his client that he has good title to the works purchased and sold by Ferrini in good faith.

Meanwhile, van Rijn continued to delight in the information that had come his way. For him, Roberty was a fertile source of information for his website. He wanted to publish what he had. "I think it's time to let 'Bruce on the Loose' have it," he wrote to Roberty on March 6, 2001.

Roberty, who had kept in touch with van Rijn throughout, did not reply by e-mail. By early March he had no further need of van Rijn on the matter of the Gospel of Judas, at least for the moment. By that time the deal was done and he had obtained the return of the ancient manuscripts for his client. Their disposition would be the subject of further debate and discussion. He calmed down the tempestuous van Rijn, to which van Rijn replied by e-mail, "I will not pound more on Bruce, I decided. But if anything else pops up in Frieda's mind I would love to hear it."

Bruce Ferrini's deal with Frieda Tchacos Nussberger was finalized in principle during the second week of February 2001. In the end, only the mathematical treatise would be retained by Ferrini, for a purchase price of $100,000.

On February 15, Frieda and Roberty flew to Cleveland to recover the manuscripts that Frieda had consigned to Ferrini five months earlier. Roberty used the well-known Cleveland law firm of Taft, Stettinius, and Hollister LLP as his representative for the formalities of the transfer. The "voluntary agreement" between the parties was signed and dated February 16.

Frieda remembers the recovery that took place in Akron on February 16 not with gratification or happiness but with mortification:

"The settlement had been reached and signed. My lawyers accompanied us to Akron, they wanted to be sure that everything went smoothly. I had to sign that I was receiving everything, all the manuscripts plus a few rings that I had consigned to Ferrini during the fair in Basel.

"The rings were not a problem. I had photos and descriptions. But the papyri ... how could I have identified anything that may have been missing? I knew I would be unable to identify what Ferrini was giving back as per the manuscripts. I had not even dared to look through them when I took them from Hanna in Brooklyn and left them in Yale. I hadn't even wanted to risk taking photos then, since I knew that the slightest manipulation could result in damage, and that was a terrible loss.

"Ferrini had prepared everything. We were at his house. He spread it all out on the big oak table, which looked like a Renaissance copy of an original, in the impressive library of his villa.

"As I took a glimpse of what was on the table ... the leaves were loose and tiny fragments were floating around ... my head shrank. There was no way to know what I was receiving back after this expensive and extremely painful battle. Never in my career had I had to undergo such a restitution with litigations and legal representatives all around me. Mario Roberty plus three representatives of Taft & Stettinius.... I hated it. I was mortified to the bone.

"Everybody looked at me inquisitively: 'Is it all there?' That is what they were asking me. I nodded sheepishly. How could I know what was there in Coptic and in Greek, in those old manuscripts? I had to sign a paper or a few papers, I don't remember. Then the packing started, and I took photos."

The day before, Roberty and Frieda had prepared themselves by buying packing materials at a large department store just outside Cleveland. They were, in Frieda's words, "super-equipped" to take possession of the manuscripts and return them to Switzerland.

When the packing was finished, Ferrini suggested opening a bottle of champagne. All those who remained there drank a toast. "It tasted awful. It was warm and it tasted sour," Frieda recalls.

The next step was to take the materials to the car and to depart Akron. "We all left that damned villa in Akron. My arms were heavy carrying the manuscripts."

Frieda and Roberty arrived in New York that same evening and immediately booked tickets for Zurich. "I remembered, sitting in our seats with Judas in between us. We were relieved … and after all happy, for having succeeded in that difficult mission, and getting the manuscripts back. We drank a few glasses of good champagne and went to sleep."

Frieda had begun to feel that the sequence of events was abnormal, with no rational explanation. Her personal curse of Judas was continuing. She summed up the experience: "Judas didn't want to let me go. He was holding onto me and was torturing me. The future was gloomy. The future of the manuscripts was looking worse than ever."

But the Gospel of Judas had reached the nadir of its journey and was at long last on its way to proper restoration. Frieda realized that the steps ahead would not be easy, either, and that the strange occurrences which had made this complex and often painful association with the Gospel of Judas such a difficult personal trial would continue. Frieda, up to that point of her life a largely secular person, reflected on what she thought was happening with religiously inspired language that surprised even herself.

"Judas chose me to rehabilitate him," she said. "He was leading me, pulling the strings to put me on the right path. But the unworldly forces who had kept him in the dark for thousands of years were fighting his restitution.

"It had started with the robbery and it continued, following me at every step. It was as if the genie had been released from the magical lamp of Aladdin. It was as if Judas was fighting on my side trying to protect me from the blows, resolving the problems as they arose, leading me through the labyrinth to the final salvation."

There are a number of postscripts to this story.

In the fall of 2002, Bruce Ferrini offered to finance a major building at his alma mater, Kent State University, in his son's name—the Matthew Ferrini Institute for Human Evolutionary Research—with a $6.8 million contribution. Testimonies to Ferrini's sterling character and distinguished career were distributed by the university.

The multimillion-dollar gift was inspired perhaps by his inconsolable despair at losing his son, who had died a year earlier. He was already in considerable debt. According to Professor Owen Lovejoy, who was to head up the project for Kent State—Ferrini had been one of his students years before—the idea behind the center was to memorialize Ferrini's son. A small amount of money did arrive—what Lovejoy called "casual funds," enough to buy some stationery and supplies, but hardly enough to get the project off the drawing board. The full amount never arrived in the university's coffers. By 2005 the widely heralded Matthew Ferrini Institute had disappeared from Kent State's website. Lovejoy lamented its nonfulfillment and said matter-of-factly, "That project is deader than a doornail."

As for the fate of the ancient mathematical treatise acquired by Ferrini, he had two potential clients—and apparently sold portions to both of them. Ferrini found a buyer through a well-known and respected London art and manuscript dealer, Sam Fogg. The new owner of the mathematical treatise is a U.S. citizen who prefers to remain anonymous. This collector is understood to have previously purchased the Archimedes Palimpsest, a well-known mathematical and scientific text from antiquity, which is in the midst of restoration and translation at the prestigious Walters Art Museum in Baltimore, Maryland.

Fogg engaged Alexander Jones of the University of Toronto, a talented up-and-coming Canadian scholar specializing in ancient scientific texts, to study and publish the mathematical treatise that had been purchased. Jones is planning to publish it in 2008, in collaboration with Columbia University's Roger Bagnall.

What is startling about the deal, however, is that Ferrini made an additional, separate sale of at least three pages of the mathematical manuscript, which were not included in what was sold by Fogg. Ferrini sold them directly to a noted Los Angeles–based collector and philanthropist, Lloyd Cotsen, a major donor in the field of art and antiquity. In 1997 Cotsen made a gift to Princeton University, his alma mater, to establish the Cotsen Children's Library. Two years later he made a gift to the University of California at Los Angeles, the largest philanthropic gift up to that point in the history of American archaeology.

Though Cotsen bought the mathematical treatise directly from Ferrini, he did not take physical possession in Los Angeles. Instead, he immediately shipped the pages he had bought to the

Princeton University Archives, according to Lyn Tansey of Cotsen's office. There it came under the overall responsibility of the curator of manuscripts, Don Skemer. Jones, who was a visiting scholar for a year at the Institute for Advanced Study in Princeton, managed to examine the pages at the university in the fall of 2005. He reported, not surprisingly, that they were part of the same manuscript that he and Bagnall were intending to publish.

Bagnall commented later that it was a "scandal" that the treatise had been sold in separate sections. To him, it was a flagrantly irresponsible act.

That was not all that was missing. Frieda Tchacos Nussberger would soon learn that pages and fragments from the Gospel of Judas and the other papyrus texts had also disappeared. Frieda and Roberty suspected a number of those who had held the documents or had had access to them—from Mia in Greece to Bruce Ferrini in Ohio to Bill Veres in London.

Veres responded promptly in a 2004 letter to Frieda, denying that he had ever tampered with the material in any way:

> I understand that a significant quantity of the papyri which I originally had seen in Akron was missing when the group was finally returned. I understand that Ferrini claimed that I was left alone with the material at his home during that period and that I could have stolen/removed some fragments or pages. While it is true that I was allowed access alone at his premises (this was before, and after, Ferrell visited), Ferrini did not make any claims to me at the time that something might have gone missing. I understand from you that a number of fragments in Greek newspaper and a FedEx envelope with other fragments have gone missing. I did witness these being deliv-

ered to Ferrini and being in his possession at the time of my departure from Akron.

Despite his wheeling and dealing, Ferrini plunged in ever deeper financial straits. On September 15, 2005, he filed for bankruptcy in a court in Ohio.

In January 2006, a substantial part of two pages of the Gospel of Judas surfaced; they were identified as pages five and six. These pages had been provided to a private collector in New York subsequent to the return of the papyrus manuscript pages to Frieda Tchacos. The sender was Bruce Ferrini. Efforts to contact the Ohio manuscript dealer were unsuccessful.

All of these sad and even disgraceful shenanigans brought one positive outcome. The Gospel of Judas had been restored to Frieda Tchacos Nussberger, who was now intent on finding the resources and experts to make it a readable document once more. Despite, or because of, her mistake in selling the papyrus codex to Bruce Ferrini, she felt a genuine responsibility for its restoration.

On the flight back to Switzerland, Mario Roberty persuaded her to turn the manuscripts over to the foundation he had established for the benefit of art and antiquity throughout the world: the Maecenas Foundation for Ancient Art. The foundation—named after Maecenas, a benevolent patron of the arts and letters in ancient Rome—had participated actively in supporting several archaeological digs in Egypt, safekeeping the archaeological collection of the Republic of Tajikistan, and cooperating in other archaeological projects in the various countries of the former Soviet Union as well as China. The Maecenas Foundation would donate the codex with its subsections to the Arab Republic of Egypt, while engaging in restoration and publication.

A very long journey had taken a turn for the better.

CHAPTER THIRTEEN

# THE RAVAGES OF TIME

*In the course of my long career, I have had before my eyes
lots of Coptic or Greek documents on papyrus,
but I have never seen one as degraded as this one.*
—RODOLPHE KASSER

The wrenching experience in Cleveland was behind her. Frieda Tchacos Nussberger had returned with the manuscript to the peaceful valleys of Switzerland. She and Mario Roberty had devised a plan that included eventually returning the Gospel of Judas codex to the land where the surviving Coptic copy had originated, Egypt. First, however, they were confronted with the painful, arduous process of sorting out exactly what Frieda had in her possession. Were the texts as complete as they had been when Yale returned them to her less than a year before?

On March 12, 2001, a papyrologist affiliated with an Ivy League university came to Switzerland to help examine what had been returned and what had gone missing. The expert—who had once examined the codex in some depth—found that numerous fragments had been detached from the Coptic book.

After the examination, the ancient manuscripts scholar informed her that, in addition to fragments, nearly four or five nearly complete pages from the Letter of Peter to Philip and the section called "James" seemed to be absent. He could not be certain which, if any, fragments were missing from the Gospel of Judas. The expert summed up his report:

> There were seven manila folders with dozens of fragments in each, that came from the same codex as the Judas Gospel.
>
> Many of these fragments may have belonged to the "Epistle of Peter to Philip" or to the "First Apocalypse of James"; these two works came before Judas in the codex. The fragments varied in size from a postage stamp to 10 cm square. In addition to these fragments in the manila folders, there were 5 larger fragments, nearly full pages, from the same portion of the Judas codex. (About the same size as this resent page) These were wrapped in a Greek newspaper. One of them bears the colophon of "James" (with the name ï d k w B).
>
> There is not a single piece remaining of these many dozens of frames of the Judas codex that were wrapped separately from the main piece of the codex. They are written by the same scribe as the Judas text, and the papyrus is identical in color and quality to the papyrus of the Judas portion.

The expert's findings raised disturbing questions. Selling to Ferrini had been Frieda's decision and therefore her responsibility. Apparently, while in his possession several pages had vanished. She felt she had to track down what had been lost.

The Maecenas Foundation also had to decide how to handle the conservation process and translation. The foundation was ready to accept advice from experts in Coptology and papyrology, but these people had to be absolutely discreet. The recommendation of the expert with whom Frieda discussed the matter was to undertake conservation and translation within an institutional setting, which would be both easiest and probably most successful. The Österreichische Nationalbibliothek—the Austrian National Library—in Vienna was one possibility. The Austrians had excellent in-house capabilities and the scholarly expertise to reconstruct the manuscript. Their conservator was known as one of the best in the field. The suggestion was made to give the Austrians the manuscript in order to conserve it and publish it within five years, reserving the copyright on the publication and translation for the foundation.

Another alternative was to undertake the work in Switzerland. Two options were the Martin Bodmer Foundation, although it was in the process of building a museum and did not have funds readily available, and the Antikenmuseum in Basel. Roberty and Frieda were advised that neither of these institutions had full scholarly or conservation capability without bringing in additional staff. Help might also be obtained from an institution or university in the United States that had the appropriate personnel, for example, graduate students or postdoctoral researchers who could be assigned to the project.

Among the scholars considered capable of handling the project was Stephen Emmel, who had been among those who examined the texts in 1983. Others recommended as possibilities included Tito Orlandi, Anne Boudhors, Bentley Layton, Frederick Wisse, and Charles Hedrick; at least one of these, Layton, had seen and helped identify the text.

Frieda set out independently, together with Roberty, to find the right person for translation. She discovered that one of the world's great Coptologists lived right there in Switzerland:

Rodolphe Kasser. A French-speaking Swiss, he is a professor emeritus of Coptology at the University of Geneva. During the 1970s he was one of the small group of scholars that oversaw the Nag Hammadi discoveries. At that time he came into conflict with the American general secretary, James Robinson. In the context of their long-running personal feud, Kasser translating the Gospel of Judas would represent a tremendous victory.

Kasser grew up in a small city named Yverdon-les-Bains, located on the shores of crystal-clear Lake Neuchâtel. He studied Protestant theology and started his career as a minister in the Free Church of Switzerland, a reformist offshoot formed soon after the Reformation that mixed a touch of Calvinism with old-fashioned Swiss conservatism. Kasser turned from the cloth to the study of the languages and culture of early Christianity. His beliefs were inspired by a vision of the suffering Christ and the Crucifixion and Resurrection.

Kasser initially chose to study Aramaic, the lingua franca of the eastern shore of the Mediterranean in the time of Jesus. Jesus is believed to have preached and conversed with the apostles in Aramaic, the street language spoken by Jewish communities throughout the rocky hills and the small villages of the Holy Land.

In what turned out to be a beneficial twist of fate, Kasser found that a dozen or more students were ahead of him in requesting to study Aramaic; there were far more applicants than places in the halls of academe. An adviser suggested he study Coptic instead, and Kasser was intrigued by the opportunity. He knew that Greek overtook Aramaic and was spoken generally in the entire eastern Mediterranean region in early Christian times. Classicists, however, are a dime a dozen. Coptic, meanwhile, used the basic Greek alphabet with modifications for the Coptic language, including seven extra letters. Kasser was also aware of the intriguing finds of papyri discovered near a then obscure city in Upper Egypt called Nag Hammadi. Partly as a result of his association with that project, he would become one of the great scholars in the field.

On July 24, 2001, Frieda and Roberty met Kasser at a coffee shop in Zurich. Kasser had taken a train to Zurich alone. In his seventies, he was hobbled by Parkinson's disease, which had ravaged his body, so his right hand shook and he was unsteady on his feet. When Frieda saw him, she was initially distressed. Her first thought was, "He will never survive the restoration."

Still, after coffee and cake, they proceeded to where the manuscript was stored, and Kasser had his first look at the manuscript. "As far as I was concerned, my curiosity had got the better of my prudence," he remembered. "I had to see the artifact." Upon seeing how deteriorated it was, he realized immediately that he would need an expert in restoration. He used Frieda's telephone to call Florence Darbre, the chief restorer at the Bodmer Foundation, to see if she was available. She had not seen the texts, but she greatly respected Kasser.

Notwithstanding his encroaching Parkinson's, Kasser was known for his great dedication to and perseverance in his work. From Nussberger and Roberty's point of view, the meeting had gone well. After they learned more about his background, they decided to entrust the codex to him.

At a second meeting two months later, Darbre entered the picture. She had risen from obscurity to become one of Europe's best restorers of ancient papyri. Hailing from Nyon, a small city on Lake Geneva, she had pursued her studies at the University of Geneva and then at an art institute in Bern. She was the restorer in charge of numerous papyrus manuscripts at the prestigious Bodmer Foundation museum located in suburban Cologny, just outside Geneva, where Kasser was a senior adviser.

Conducting the meeting in French, Frieda felt an instant rapport with the scholar and his highly praised restorer. The two visitors and Kasser's wife, Anna, were shocked at the manuscript's condition, but also marveled at the wealth of scholarship it might contain.

As Kasser examined the manuscript a second time, he was sure that it was an ancient work of considerable value. "Destiny, luckily for me, afforded me the opportunity to discover this scroll and meet its owner, who was quite determined to officially give it back to Egypt.... First, the artifact should be repaired, restored, put back in order, brought back if possible to its original pristine state." The Swiss professor, in the twilight of his career, responded with gratitude and delight to this "fortuitous" stroke of luck that had brought the codex to him.

After the meeting, Frieda put the texts inside two solid gray containers and gave them to Kasser and Darbre. Frieda felt these people could be trusted and did not feel the need to ask for a receipt. Kasser was what he appeared: a Swiss scholar of considerable reputation and a person of honor. Anna Kasser said to Frieda later: "You gave us the manuscripts without a receipt, even without insurance. It was unexpected and you were brave."

Kasser and Darbre boarded the train for home. Kasser lived two hours by train from Zurich, while Darbre was another hour south. Darbre, now in charge of the precious, fragile documents, finally reached her studio, where she put them under lock and key.

Three years of careful, assiduous work followed, in which Darbre and Kasser, working in concert and meeting once a month, followed the paths of the fibers in order to put fragments and pages into place and to make sense of what was a horribly deteriorated, glued-together pile of previously undecipherable texts.

"It was ... quite impossible to read some passages," Kasser

commented. "The papyrus was so brittle that it would crumble at the slightest touch, however delicately it was touched, and turn to dust.... In a word, it was a hopeless case if I've ever seen one."

Two other scholars soon joined the endeavor. One was Martin Krause, the retired head of the Coptology program at the University of Münster—where he had been replaced by Stephen Emmel in a refreshingly unorthodox choice for a major German university. Krause was Kasser's former colleague on the technical subcommittee for the Nag Hammadi finds. However, Krause found the trips back and forth to Switzerland too taxing and retired from the project.

In his stead, Krause recommended Gregor Wurst, the number-two man in Coptology at the University of Münster under Emmel. Once he joined the project, Wurst proceeded to apply intricate computer programs with digital imagery that were enormously helpful in identifying the paths of the fibers.

Over the next few years, under this team's painstaking care, what had looked "undecipherable" became, for the most part, readable, providing a startling insight into the world of Christianity in the first few centuries after Jesus.

On July 1, 2004, in Paris, the city of light and love, a gathering of some 150 scholars of the International Coptic Studies Association met in an oversized lecture hall on the grounds of the Institut Catholique, a Catholic university on the Left Bank. Swiss professor Rodolphe Kasser was making an announcement that would provide academic insiders with what one attendee later called "a great scoop."

The old man walked hesitantly toward the podium. He hadn't known if he would make it to this day. As the seventy-eight-year-old mounted the stairs to the stage, his wife, Anna, hoped that he would be able to speak loudly enough to deliver his astonishing news.

He had news of a fabulous discovery. Ancient documents had been resurrected from the sands of Egypt. The documents had lain hidden for nearly two millennia, and the restoration process was nearly complete. Among them, a new gospel had been discovered, the long-lost Gospel of Judas, which had been bitterly condemned as heresy and had disappeared from known history in the second century of the Common Era.

The foundation that was sponsoring the Kasser restoration had prepared a fact sheet, a *feuille volante* in French, which provided those in the audience with insight into the history of the ancient text. The codex that contained the Gospel of Judas comprised three treatises: the Letter of Peter to Philip, of which a different version had been found at Nag Hammadi in 1945; the First Apocalypse of James, somewhat different from a copy also found at Nag Hammadi; and the Gospel of Judas itself, which, it was noted, was "nowadays completely unknown."

The sheet stated that the papyrus was originally a leather-bound papyrus codex composed of at least thirty-one handwritten folios (sixty-two pages) measuring approximately sixteen by twenty-nine centimeters (6.3 x 11.4 inches). The text, written in the Saidic dialect of the Coptic language, was riddled with "linguistic elements hinting to Middle Egypt." The treatises were presumably translations of texts originally written in Greek. Based on the handwriting, the fact sheet stated, the codex could be dated to the fourth or fifth century (carbon dating would subsequently establish an earlier date for the manuscript).

The provenance of the codex had been well documented since

1982. Moreover, it stated, "the prior provenance of the object, from its discovery until 1982, is to a large extent re-traceable."

Time had done its corrosive work, however, blackening the papyri, which had become extremely brittle. About two-thirds of the original text was now readable, after considerable restoration. At least one entire folio as well as a certain number of major and minor fragments were missing.

The codex was being restored in Switzerland by the best specialists in the field, and the publication was entrusted to Professor Kasser. The Swiss foundation backing the project required anonymity for the moment, the document stated, but had agreed to "donate [the codex] to an adequate public institution in Egypt."

The old man read his speech sitting down. Despite his infirmity, the elderly professor wanted to tell his colleagues about what had become the crowning achievement of his life. He was a feisty character with a sense of humor and a determination to get the job done, since his mind was as nimble and sharp as ever.

The hall was silent in respect to a man who had once been its president and was now making what was presumably a farewell address, albeit one that was introducing a startling discovery. No one knew quite what to expect. Kasser titled his brief speech, "A New Coptic Apocrypha Becomes Available to Science," followed by the words "Peuaggelion Nioudas," the Gospel of Judas.

Kasser spoke softly, but his voice vibrated with strong emotion. "Such resurrections are extremely rare," he declared in French. "For it is not every day that a well-known document from antiquity, which, it seemed, had irretrievably disappeared, can finally escape its regrettable fate. Thanks to a happy coincidence, the script comes to light."

He went on, "It is a miracle—this word is not an exaggeration…. Today is a day marked by a white flag because of the resurrection of the famous 'Gospel of Judas.' … This is the same document that scandalized the early church. Copies of it were mercilessly doomed for destruction."

He recounted the painstaking work that, over the course of three years, had rehabilitated the almost destroyed ancient document. He mentioned only obliquely the woman who had been charged with the process of restoration, Florence Darbre, in consideration of security procedures that required keeping the location where the manuscript was stored secret. Together with Gregor Wurst, the trio had meticulously rebuilt what had come to them by merest chance. Kasser glossed over the fact that pages were missing—pages that had been lost as a result of human greed, desperation, or mere negligence.

Professor Kasser described the incredibly complex work involved in the rehabilitation: how the pages had been found or acquired torn in half, with the upper margin in somewhat better condition than the bottom half, giving a possibility of pagination. (Early texts were usually numbered.) "Some leaves were violently shattered," he lamented.

He related how the text of the codex had begun to emerge. "This gnostic treatise had already aroused the wrath of St. Irenaeus, who wrote with contempt about 'Judas the traitor,'" the old professor stated. "The heretics attributed to Judas the quality of being 'the only disciple to possess the "Knowledge of the Truth,"' which had allowed him to perform 'the "Mystery" of treason,' with all its supposedly beneficial consequences. The heretics were both arrogant and gullible, Irenaeus declared. They had 'produced … a manuscript of their own fabrication, which they called the "Gospel of Judas."'"

Kasser explored the title—itself considered heretical at the time the document was created in the first centuries of the Christian era. "It was a controversial title perhaps, but the gnostics have gotten us used to such paradoxes. They restored to favor personalities that were considered by the Church, with its canonical texts, to be 'mediocre.'

"In attempting to reverse the verdict pronounced by the primitive Church twelve [disciples] on the 'traitor' par excellence, the man who was greedy and sly, who sold his beloved Master for a kiss (what a stigma!), the author of the berated treatise was flagrantly drawing attention to his doctrines. This is the reason for the impatience of the researchers of yesterday and today. Beyond the curses of the Church leaders, who burned and still burn for having had direct contact with the *ipsissima verba* [own words] of the pseudo-Judas himself.

"Their patience will soon be satisfied," he concluded. "This mutilated manuscript, in any case, has been greatly ill treated by these recent vicissitudes. This precious manuscript will be published."

Among those sitting in the hall of academics were Coptologists, papyrologists, classicists, some nuns, at least half a dozen Coptic priests adorned in their long robes and stitched head coverings, a considerable number of Egyptians, an Israeli, and a collection of Arabists.

Unknown to the venerable professor, a few of those in the hall had a passing acquaintance with the document, though none of them had had the time, the rights, or the authority to study it. Some of them had not yet put two and two together: That the document they were hearing about was the same one they had seen briefly so many years ago.

Twenty-one years had passed since Stephen Emmel had first seen the manuscripts in a dingy hotel room in Geneva in 1983 when the codex had first made an enigmatic appearance on the antiquities markets of the Western world.

Also in the audience was Bentley Layton, Emmel's Ph.D. adviser, who had been the first to be given the time and resources necessary to accurately identify the gospel. He had seen it in 2000, when his institution, Yale University, had held the precious ancient texts for close to half a year. Yale's refusal to purchase the manuscript because of unanswered questions about its past meant it had surrendered pride of first translation to Kasser.

Marvin Meyer was in attendance as well. The chair of New Testament Studies at Chapman College in California, he was a gnostic scholar of note and had written several highly regarded books on early Christianity.

Also present was Meyer's former mentor—and one of Professor Kasser's longtime rivals—James M. Robinson. Even after nearly three decades, the two men of approximately the same age, in their late seventies or approaching eighty, remained estranged.

The Columbia University classicist, Roger Bagnall, who was now also on the board of the International Coptic Studies Association, was by chance attending another session at the conference and was not aware that what was being discussed was that intriguing text he had had the opportunity to briefly examine in 1984.

Sitting quietly in the back, unobserved among the world's most brilliant scholars in the related fields was Frieda Tchacos Nussberger. She had transferred her title in the Gospel of Judas to the Maecenas Foundation. She had brought a tape recorder with her and recorded the session.

Frieda looked about warily, trying to determine what reactions would be elicited from this august body. This was the first public exposure of the ancient text, though few details of its contents would be provided. Few people had even known that the Gospel of Judas had ever existed, and those few who did know something about it feared it had been lost to scholarship forever. No one could have imagined that this obscure ancient text would surface in Switzerland.

⚦

Kasser mused on the meaning of Destiny and Fate, concepts that, he pointed out, were common in the world of early Christianity, influenced as it was by Greek doctrine. "The Ancients, who knew what they were talking about, used to say that Destiny—*Moira* in Greek—is 'weaved' together, fiber by fiber. Likewise human destiny, where paths cross each other unexpectedly and are built fiber by fiber. In an entirely unexpected way, quite unplanned, human destinies crossed paths. This is what occurred in Switzerland a few years ago."

He then offered hints on what the codex said, how it might "contradict the 'canonic' assessment of biblical personalities, that is, the accounts of Judas and Jesus that were integrated into the four Gospels that had become the basis of the New Testament of Christianity. Judas, this greedy fellow, a thief even ... a scoundrel, who goes as far as selling his best friend to his worst enemies, for the sake of a hypocritical and vile kiss.... We will certainly be sure not to jump to hasty conclusions as a result of having started to read but, we can expect to find in EvJud [the Gospel of Judas] the very opposite of the neo-testament Judas: [Here is] a secret friend of Jesus, maligned by his disciples.

"Paradoxically, all this is possible, in spite of the truthfulness of facts: the apparent 'treason,' the price of absolution, with its dramatic consequences...."

"But, is there really a crime, according to the gnostic perception?

"Saint Irenaeus himself confirms that the gnostic who wrote the Gospel describes the deed, a despicable one—where we are concerned—as mysterious treason. However, in the religious context, 'mystery' is a fact that is central to cults, mystery re-creates, and is ultimately a positive....

"How can we not mention, at this point, some unsettling facts, which have been borne out by the New Testament itself? The traditional interpretation of which could be challenged (and has been, by a few rare authors): in particular, the ambiguity surrounding the words uttered by Jesus, whom he addressed to Judas at the last Supper, 'Whatever you have to do, do it fast.' This might lead us to believe that, at that moment, Jesus was ordering Judas to take the responsibility of performing a special mission, which is at once subtle, surprising, and paradoxical.

"It is wise to be prudent at the start of this exploratory attempt. The research ... is not yet at such an advanced stage to the point that we can now describe with precision a new profile of the 'traitor,' whom we now find ourselves to be dealing with. In addition to the facts that underpin the final title, which is entirely self-explanatory, different pointers previously known, but, of late, gathered more efficiently, would suggest that the path to be followed should be that of logic."

The Kasser speech had earthshaking implications, yet the reaction of the assembled scholars was muted. The information given was just too sparse. In discussions beforehand with Frieda, the professor and his sponsors had decided to carefully restrict what information went public.

Only one man asked a question: Jim Robinson. Unknown to Kasser, Robinson had been on a twenty-year hunt for the same ancient texts that were now in Kasser's hands. Now, Robinson had conclusively learned today that he had failed in his quest. According to those who watched him closely, he seemed baffled, a bit angry, even somewhat insulted. Robinson challenged the Swiss professor, asking Kasser if he knew that Emmel had seen this same document twenty years earlier and that some photographs had been taken.

Robinson's challenge was a classic attempt at a put-down. "It was embarrassing," one of Robinson's closest colleagues said later. "Jim lost his dignity. It was totally unprofessional."

Yet Kasser was shaken. The venerable Swiss professor had not realized that this newly discovered ancient manuscript had also involved a contest for its possession.

But Robinson was not done railing against the loss of the Gospel of Judas to the European scholars. On November 20, 2005, he erupted again in a packed room for a symposium at the annual meeting of the Society for Biblical Literature, held in Philadelphia. The subject of the symposium was "How Nag Hammadi Changed the World of Early Christianity." There were four panelists: Robinson; Harry Attridge, by now the dean of the Yale Divinity School; John Turner; and Marvin Meyer. Robinson and Meyer had recently finished coediting a revised and updated version of the Nag Hammadi library.

Robinson reiterated his position that nothing should be kept "private" or be monopolized by individual scholars. He would forbid "private" publications in favor of facsimile editions, where the text in the original language was published in full, from which all scholars could then translate and publish as they might wish. That would prevent any single professor from holding a monopoly on publishing rights. Robinson is not a Coptologist, but a theologian by training. Since he did not qualify as a Coptic translator, it was easy enough for him to advocate a free-for-all on publication and translation matters.

Privately, Meyer, who was working with professors Kasser and Wurst on an English-language translation of the gospel, tried to assure Robinson that there was no conspiracy, no "European attempt at monopoly," but an ongoing publication process that would soon see the light of day. Still, Robinson decided to publish his own book on the Gospel of Judas, in which he revived claims about scholarly monopolies and indirectly asserted what he believed to be his own central and proprietary role in Gnostic scholarship.

CHAPTER FOURTEEN

# THREAT OF EXPOSURE

*Jesus said to the disciples: "{Let} any one of you who is {strong enough}*
*among human beings bring out the perfect human and stand before my face."*
*They all said, "We have the strength."*
*But their spirits did not dare to stand before {him},*
*except for Judas Iscariot.*
—THE GOSPEL OF JUDAS

Although the papyrus documents had returned to Switzerland, the characters left behind had not entirely abandoned the stage. In particular, the Dutch blogger Michel van Rijn—a gadfly eager to expose on his website all the alleged scandal and corruption possible within the world of antiquity trading—had been a very busy man in the years after Bruce Ferrini gave up the codex to Frieda Tchacos Nussberger.

On his website, van Rijn's outrageously self-centered, chatty personality was insistently on display, as he attempted to convey his "inside" knowledge. His know-it-all pose was accompanied by vicious attacks on personalities, some of whom he had never met, others who had crossed him personally. He liked to refer to himself as the "inkslinger." He would often refer to readers as "dahlink" (a derivation of "darling"), and he would spew forth as much as he could recount about any particular incident, often claiming that he was withholding extraordinary information that would be revealed next week, next month, or sometime later. He had a certain crusading moral stance—to expose the profession of which he himself had been and still was a part—but his purposely provocative and often reckless accusations earned him the enmity of a number of powerful figures.

During 2002, van Rijn gained Ferrini's confidence. He detailed his feelings in an article titled "La Bête Humaine" published on his website. In it, van Rijn recalled how he had met Ferrini in 2002 at Ferrini's house in Pietrasanta, Italy.

> Ferrini had then recently lost his only son and learning from my sources in the trade that Ferrini's biggest client, the American billionaire art collector, had been stolen away from him by some of his "loyal" colleagues.... I decided to pick up the glove for what at that time was a plainly beaten man.

Van Rijn wrote that Ferrini had become his friend. "Ferrini was good company, a passionate aficionado of opera and literature and seemed as straight as one could expect from a mainstream art dealer nowadays."

Taking up Ferrini's cause, van Rijn traveled to Ohio and wound up moving into Ferrini's Akron home for four months. He wrote about Ferrini's pain in grieving for his son, how Ferrini refused to go upstairs in the house because that was where he had found Matthew dead, and how the Ohio dealer hesitated to go to sleep and also prayed often not to wake up. He also claimed privately to have found out where Ferrini's secret safe was located, and managed to extract considerable information about Ferrini from Ferrini's own website and from Ferrini's employees.

Van Rijn's next target was billionaire collector James Ferrell, Ferrini's former backer. Van Rijn had begun to attack Ferrell on his website. The accusations he made against Ferrell did not specifically concern the Gospel of Judas or illuminated manuscripts, but rather coins imported from Turkey and other hard objects as well. His charges were wild and unsupported, however, and Ferrell clearly had enough ammunition and financial muscle behind him to fight back, which he decided to do against both Ferrini and van Rijn. The blogger became an integral part of the court claims and counterclaims between Bruce Ferrini and James Ferrell, and van Rijn was specifically named in Ferrell's counterclaims filed on December 12, 2002, in an Ohio court. Ferrell's complaint noted, "Ferrini and van Rijn have published defamatory material aimed at Ferrell's personal and business reputations and practices, thereby causing damage and for the purpose of extorting money from Ferrell." Ferrell further asserted, "Ferrini and van Rijn have demanded that Ferrell pay them $6,000,000 ... in order to stop the publishing and spreading of this defamatory material." Ferrell also contended, "By demanding payment as a condition to ceasing their other illegal conduct, Ferrini and van Rijn have committed, attempted to commit, and continue to commit an underlying crime, including, but not limited to extortion." Ferrini denied these allegations in court papers.

The upshot of the charges and countercharges was that the three—Ferrell, Ferrini, and van Rijn—entered into a court-backed settlement on March 8, 2003, in which van Rijn promised to remove Ferrell's name from his website. Additionally, van Rijn, for a period of twenty years, would not make reference in any form to Ferrell on any website "managed or created" by him and would not engage "in any form of communication (written or oral)" about Ferrell.

By signing the agreement, van Rijn legally committed himself to silence that could be enforced in a court of law. He nonetheless perceived the settlement as a victory, writing that he received payment of $180,000 for "expenses" because of the case. Because the settlement agreement was filed under seal, this detail and other particulars of the agreement are not part of the public record and, thus, cannot be verified. Van Rijn then returned to England from the United States.

As time marched on, however, the terms of the agreement proved increasingly difficult for van Rijn to obey. With his main website closed down, he searched for other avenues of self-expression. Apparently he could not restrain himself. He moved his website to Holland, kept articles flowing, and fed information to journalists whenever he felt it appropriate. A lot of that information concerned the activities of James Ferrell, whom he scathingly criticized, often in language that would never ordinarily appear in a mainline publication, but was scurrilous and often threatening. For example, according to court documents, van Rijn wrote a "Last Word" to Ferrell as follows: "Dear Jimbo I have taken an interest in you.... Welcome to my web, I will be your worst... nightmare. I am going to take you down...."

Ferrell and his lawyers remained on the alert, ready to crack down on any violation of what had been agreed, and he eventually sought and obtained an injunction from the court to restrain van Rijn.

In messages sent to the Ohio court, van Rijn claimed that the Dutch website was not among those that had been included in the earlier ban. He asserted that he could continue to publish because his new venue was not officially a website, and the specific websites lacked a direct connection to any of the main search engines on the Internet. Van Rijn contended that his First Amendment rights to freedom of speech had been violated.

Magistrate Judge George J. Limbert of the U.S. District Court in the Northern District of Ohio disagreed. He ruled that the gag order to which van Rijn had agreed was valid because "the gag provision standing alone is not a prior restraint on speech because there is no government action involved. The alleged restraint stems from a clear and unambiguous private agreement between two private parties and government action is not involved or implicated in any way." In a judgment issued on October 29, 2004, the federal court declared that van Rijn was guilty of contempt of court, warned that his conduct was "flagrant and contemptuous," and cautioned van Rijn that he was subject to arrest. "The Court admonishes Mr. van Rijn once again that even stronger sanctions are at the Court's disposal for his continuing contemptuous conduct."

On November 3, 2004, the court ordered van Rijn to pay compensation at the rate of $1 per contemptuous act—a total of $10,590 for 10,590 individual contemptuous acts—plus an additional $10,000 fine. Van Rijn, back in England, ignored the court-imposed judgment and order to pay the fine.

Van Rijn was officially silenced, at least in the United States.

Still, the punitive action against van Rijn had caused him considerable financial pain. He soon complained that he lacked adequate funds to support his children properly and send his children to the English school they attended. Nonetheless, he said he would soldier on, that he would not be intimidated by court orders or financial distress. Through his scandal sheet, he declared himself to be a crusader in the cause of righteousness and truth. Under considerable financial pressure, he needed a way to make some money. He soon grasped at the slim reed that the Gospel of Judas represented to make another big payday.

$$\frac{\female}{}$$

Despite Rodolphe Kasser's caution in his announcement of the gospel's existence in July 2004, the loose ends that remained from Ferrini's involvement threatened public exposure of the Gospel of Judas before Kasser could complete his complex restoration work—potentially exposing the gospel's content to misinterpretation or inaccurate speculation. Leaking the news before Kasser had completed his years of translation could compromise years of painstaking scholarship.

Michel van Rijn struck again on December 5, 2004. During the process of authenticating the significant ancient documents in Florence Darbre's studio, Mario Roberty's cell phone rang. Van Rijn was on the line.

He had considerable information, he said, on the Gospel of Judas. Roberty did not reject discussion out of hand. He and Frieda frankly thought that van Rijn was a "nutcase," but he did often have access to good information. In this case, the information he claimed to possess could destroy the impact of all of the hard work done to restore the ancient texts.

The call was the culmination of a bizarre month that began when Bill Veres, Bruce Ferrini's former partner, had been approached by people claiming to have once worked for Ferrini. They said they had documents and photographs of Ferrini's archives and secret deals, intimating that they had penetrated

Ferrini's hard disc. The people maintained that they had invested $90,000 with the dealer and had not been paid another $50,000 for work they had done for him. They showed Veres some of what they had, and he believed it was genuine. The people wanted to contact Roberty and Frieda to work out a deal.

From the evidence he was shown, Veres was persuaded that Ferrini had, in Veres' words, "massacred" several of the texts in his possession and would derive benefit from the sale of individual pages and fragments. As Veres examined the materials in the strangers' possession, he saw contracts and other documents that were, in his view, indisputably authentic.

Even more alarming, the mysterious visitors had pictures that they said were taken from Ferrini's hard disc—photographs of the text of the Gospel of Judas. A Coptology professor in Missouri, Charles Hedrick, had apparently already received copies of these photographs, had undertaken a translation, and was planning to publish. According to their information, sixty to ninety images of the Gospel of Judas had been sent by Ferrini to Hedrick. It was a grave breach of the settlement agreement between Ferrini and Frieda.

Ferrini had been obligated by his agreement with Frieda to return not only the codices and their fragments but also all pertinent documents, including all photographs and electronic copies of materials in his possession. After Nussberger and Roberty weighed the potential of damage to the Gospel of Judas project, they concluded that the risk for the project was high.

Their first step was to contact Hedrick at Southwest Missouri State University, who had received photographs of the Gospel of Judas. Through the offices of their Cleveland-based law firm, the same one that also represented Ferrell, a lawyer for Frieda and Roberty had an exploratory first conversation with the Missouri-based professor. Hedrick said he intended to publish a rough translation of what he had. He believed he had come upon the photographs legally. According to correspondence between the law firm and Hedrick, Hedrick initially declined to confirm precisely what he had or did not have.

A dialogue by letter and e-mail between professors Kasser and Hedrick ensued. The Maecenas Foundation and Kasser wanted to know precisely what Hedrick had in his possession, especially any of the missing pages and fragments that could complete the text that he, Darbre, and Professor Gregor Wurst from Germany were restoring and translating. Hedrick proved to be a congenial colleague, and he promised cooperation. Hedrick said that he had never met Ferrini personally, and he did not have a business relationship with Ferrini, but the professor agreed to provide Kasser with copies of the photographs he had, though that had to be at Maecenas's expense.

All this negotiating took time to work out, yet the two professors enjoyed a healthy exchange of information, and the crisis was averted.

The other threads that had unraveled due to Ferrini's involvement were not so easily tied together.

A trip to London to inspect other fragments Ferrini was alleged to have retained revealed that the documents on offer indeed appeared to be genuine. Mario Roberty did not like or trust Bill Veres, and was uncomfortable working through him as an intermediary with the people who had initially contacted Veres, whom Roberty did not know and could not adequately trace.

It was in the midst of these delicate proceedings that Michel van Rijn called Roberty on December 5. According to Roberty, van Rijn told him that he had relevant documents and information about Ferrini in his possession. Roberty and Frieda traveled to London on December 10 to meet with van Rijn. They related that Van Rijn said he had been pulling the strings behind the attempt to derive money from the information obtained from Ferrini's private files. He said he was going to publish whatever he had. His threat was credible. He was going to try to destroy the Judas project. He bragged on his website that, in his opinion, Frieda would never have agreed to donate the gospel to Egypt if not for his having exposed the project in the first place. He further proclaimed that she was not going to profit from her venture if he had anything to do with it.

Roberty and Frieda met van Rijn at the latter's apartment, and while they were there, Bill Veres called. Veres and van Rijn discussed a deal for an object, and from the conversation Roberty somehow became convinced that van Rijn and Veres were conspirators.

Veres said later, "Van Rijn is diabolical. He tried to convince Mario that I was in league with him." But he insisted, "My interests were to help Frieda get back the stuff."

Veres was in frequent telephone contact with Frieda. "Veres would telephone me every hour, he was so excited, so hyper," she said.

Looking back on it, Veres acknowledges that he had overstepped his position by attempting to play the role of intermediary. In the end, he was not trusted by either side. He speculated, "I fully admit it could all have been organized by van Rijn."

In any case, Roberty wanted Veres out of the deal, and from that point on Veres was not consulted.

That left Frieda and Roberty to strike a deal with van Rijn. Roberty wanted to know the answers to one question: What did Michel van Rijn know? Van Rijn claimed to have the same set of photographs of the Gospel of Judas that Hedrick had, but Roberty could not know how many he actually possessed.

That left Frieda and Roberty to strike a deal with van Rijn. It was ultimately agreed that van Rijn would deliver information and materials in his possession to Roberty. He said he would do this in person. For these services, van Rijn would receive a fee of 71,000 Euros. Van Rijn promised to come to Basel directly after the New Year. After an endless series of telephone calls between van Rijn and Roberty, Michel van Rijn was finally scheduled to fly in to Basel on January 19, 2005. Mario Roberty waited, but van Rijn did not show up.

Roberty considered van Rijn an erratic, untrustworthy sort, so he says he was not totally surprised when van Rijn was a no-show. Yet the reason for his absence became apparent only late that evening, when Roberty got a call from van Rijn's son, who was worried because he had not heard from his father. He asked Roberty if he knew where van Rijn was.

Roberty made a few calls and discovered that van Rijn had been arrested by the Swiss police at Basel Airport by order of the Geneva prosecutor's office. He was being held in a Basel jail pending a transfer to the city of Geneva, where charges were to be lodged against him. It turned out that a family of art dealers sometimes represented legally by Roberty, believing themselves maligned on van Rijn's site, had independently brought charges against van Rijn. Having been under sporadic assault from van Rijn for several years, they had filed complaint against him, and the Swiss police responded to that alert when van Rijn entered the country. Roberty says he did not know of these charges.

A few days later, Roberty hurried to Geneva to testify before the investigating magistrate. He related honestly that van Rijn had been contracted to deliver materials to him and was in the process of doing so when he was arrested. After more than a week in prison, van Rijn was released. He later accused Roberty of betraying him. Veres commented, "Van Rijn believes Mario joined with the art dealers to grab him."

It was not true, but there have been many betrayals in this story of the most famous betrayal of all.

Meanwhile, on January 21, 2005, the American court entered an additional judgment against van Rijn to the tune of a hefty $157,377.98.

Within a few weeks, van Rijn decided to publish much or all of what he had on the Gospel of Judas, including photos and Charles Hedrick's translation, with a big "THANK YOU, CHARLIE!" posted on his website.

In a 2006 interview, Hedrick said he provided some translations to van Rijn, but he did not give him permission to publish them. "It was a foolish mistake," said Hedrick.

Luckily for Frieda Tchacos Nussberger and everyone else involved in the Judas project, the published document was incomprehensible, full of obscure Coptic allusions to gnostic levels of heaven, to Allogenes and people of a different race. The document garnered little press coverage because it was too obscure for any layperson to understand. Most important, it was not the Gospel of Judas.

The truth was, much of what Charlie Hedrick had translated came from a fourth part of the codex that was separate from the Gospel of Judas, the Apocalypse of James, and the Letter of Peter to Philip. It focused on a gnostic figure called Allogenes. That text had been discovered as being a separate part of the codex's text by Rodolphe Kasser and his colleague, Gregor Wurst, a few months before, and it did not, strictly speaking, belong to the Gospel of Judas at all.

Michel van Rijn had himself been fooled.

Later, van Rijn chose to read this section of what he thought was the Gospel of Judas on a BBC-2 television film about himself. He announced, "This is the only surviving Gospel of Judas, which has been suppressed for two thousand years by the Catholic Church. I have the translation and now I'm exposing the whole thing."

With a lighted cigarette in his fingertips, and his right arm slung casually in a kind of existential defiance around a large chest-high statue of Jesus, van Rijn read a few lines that were almost all from the Allogenes section of the codex. Unfortunately for the Dutchman, no one paid attention. The translation was too obscure. BBC chose to run their end credits over the scene. Van Rijn never realized that what he was reading was not the Gospel of Judas.

The van Rijn saga has continued. Van Rijn has deliberately ignored and sometimes even verbally flaunted his defiance of the judgments imposed by the American court. On January 27, 2006, a criminal investigation was authorized by the Ohio court after a complaint by Ferrell's attorneys. The court appointed "disinterested counsel to investigate and prosecute Mr. van Rijn for criminal contempt due to his continued contemptuous refusal to obey this Court's Orders." In the following months Ferrell continued to press for van Rijn's strict compliance with the earlier court judgment.

The detective work in tracking down the Gospel of Judas to make as complete a publication as possible had not come to a conclusion. Still, the main part of the arduous process was proceeding apace at Florence Darbre's restoration studio. All those years of painstaking work were reaching a point that the way was clear for its unveiling to the world. More than twenty-five years after it had first been discovered, the Gospel of Judas was finally coming to light.

# CHAPTER FIFTEEN

# A FIBER PUZZLE

*When Jesus observed their..., {he said} to them,*
*"Why have you been incited to anger? Your god who is within*
*you and ... have become angry in your souls ... you ...*
*let one ... bring out the perfect human and stand before my face."*
—BROKEN FRAGMENT FROM THE GOSPEL OF JUDAS

The early December gusts that swept off Lake Geneva brought the windchill factor to zero, though the thermometer registered forty degrees. On the lake, white caps rippled at the crest of waves. Before an alabaster-white chateau that overlooked the harbor of Nyon, seagulls shivered on the shore.

Nyon was a major town of the Roman Empire, and two columns from Roman times still watch over the lake. The town lies on a narrow plain stretching toward Geneva on one side and Lausanne on the other. Vineyards grace the rolling slopes that stretch back toward the dramatic Jura mountain range where Switzerland meets France.

Outside town is a small industrial zone, marked by a high

mound out of which two air filters resembling chimneys emerge. Across the street from this installation of the local water company is an ordinary pizzeria. On the second story of the building is a compact studio belonging to Florence Darbre, the art and antiquities conservation expert in paper and papyrus.

That studio, including a small laboratory, as ordinary as it looks, examines goods whose worth cannot be calculated in monetary terms. On December 5, 2004, the contents of this obscure laboratory were top secret. Only a few people knew of its treasure.

The experts arrived at eleven o'clock. They had come from all over the world to gather at this innocuous setting in Nyon. They came one by one, hunched in overcoats and jackets. One American expert on the early years of Christianity wore a full-brimmed hat that covered much of his face. All had been made to sign a restrictive secrecy agreement before they could come. They could not relate, for a period of five years, what they were about to see.

One of them was Bart Ehrman, the handsome, slightly balding, straight-talking academic with a mounting reputation as America's, and possibly the world's, leading scholar on early Christianity. He was head of the Department of Religion at the University of North Carolina, Chapel Hill.

A second figure, the burly British-born A. J. Timothy Jull, had built a name as the world's most renowned expert in carbon-14 dating. He was director of the prestigious National Science Foundation–Arizona Accelerator Mass Spectrometer Facility in Tucson.

The third expert was the bespectacled, American-born Stephen Emmel, one of the world's leading experts in the Coptic language and culture. These days he headed the Department of Coptology at the University of Münster in Germany.

What these three came to view had been hidden for seventeen

centuries or more. This scriptural text could shatter some of the interpretations, even the foundations, of faith throughout the Christian world. It was not a novel. It was a real gospel straight from the world of early Christianity.

The document was an assemblage of shriveled, sometimes brittle ancient papyri with writing on them that Darbre kept under lock and key in a safe in a small room off her main studio.

The ancient manuscript had defied time. It had defied most biological rules on the disintegration of matter. Few had known about it. No one suspected it still existed. No one could have realistically believed that it would survive. Nonetheless, it did not survive unscathed. It arrived in the twenty-first century beaten and battered, with many of its pages stuck together.

The manuscript was created on papyrus. Papyrus has great staying power—far more than modern paper. The tenacity of the manuscript in making its journey through time was dependent on the qualities of the papyrus itself. It was made from a water plant that once flourished by the lush banks of the Nile River. To make papyrus writing materials, narrow strips were removed from the pith of the plant. These were laid on a flat surface, and a layer of similar strips was laid perpendicularly across them. Then they were pressed together, dried, and sanded. This process gave the Egyptians their writing "paper."

This particular papyrus manuscript was a codex, a group of folios (in this case, of papyrus, though they could have been parchment or paper) folded together and sewn at the spine to make a book such as we use today (as opposed to a scroll). This codex had thirty-three folios, or sixty-six pages, of papyri. From afar, a number of the pages looked like weather-beaten maps of the ancient world or a jigsaw puzzle that was nearly complete but still had significant gaps. They were accompanied by occasional missing pieces, odd conjunctions of ancient papyrus, and possibly a few missing folios—not to mention an abundance of tiny fragments.

The pages of the papyri in Darbre's studio had an ancient script scrawled on them. The language was Coptic. The letters rose and fell in complex, barely distinguishable patterns. Some of it was initially unreadable because of the gaps. Much of it, however, could be delineated.

The codex had somehow journeyed through the centuries and emerged in this unlikely spot in mountainous Switzerland. It had arrived in poor shape, with considerable damage. Its leather binding, though also withered and weathered, had made its way through the centuries partially intact and still linked many pages of the codex into a single whole.

The codex contained a story, a biblical account. Its message was one of faith and belief. The fresh and innovative narrative, with a revolutionary message, had survived the journey across time. That in itself was a minor miracle.

A bank of windows faced east, letting in the drab morning light, as ten people crowded into Darbre's small studio. The meeting was convened by the National Geographic Society, which had assembled the team of scholars and experts to start the assessment process. Those present included Emmel, Ehrman, and Jull; representatives from National Geographic; and John Huebesch, who headed up Gateway Computer's investment programs and its Waitt Institute for Historic Discovery, which controls tens of millions of dollars.

Completing the group of visitors were the two Swiss who actually owned the mysterious codex: Mario J. Roberty, the president of the Maecenas Foundation, which was its legal owner, and Frieda Tchacos Nussberger, the previous owner who had turned over her interest in the manuscript to the foundation.

Roberty thanked everyone for coming. He related how his foundation had come into the possession of a priceless manuscript. "The codex came out of Egypt more than twenty years ago," he said. "It was found in Middle Egypt, that is, somewhere between Cairo and Luxor, in the Muhafazat Al Minya Province. We've had it for the last four years."

"The codex actually consists of four separate documents," Roberty elaborated. "The first one is the Epistle of Peter to Philip. The second part of the codex is the First Apocalypse of James. Third is the Gospel of Judas. The last is Allogenes."

"Nowadays," Roberty explained, "this manuscript is completely unknown."

The room was filled with suppressed tension. This was the great prize. Questions hung in the air: Had the gospel survived the ravages of time? And if so, what specifically did it say?

Roberty confirmed that the foundation had made a commitment to the government of Egypt to donate the Gospel of Judas and the entire codex to that country—where it had originally been found—several years after its first publication in the West.

Roberty then introduced Florence Darbre. The Martin Bodmer Foundation Library and Museum, where she worked as the chief restorer, was conceived as a kind of "spiritual edifice" for original manuscripts of the ancient and modern world. The museum includes Akkadian cylinder seals; cuneiform inscriptions from Mesopotamia; books of the dead from Thebes in Egypt; ancient Bibles in Coptic and Greek, including a Coptic manuscript of the Gospel of Saint Matthew from the fourth or fifth century in the Sahidic dialect; and other treasures.

Darbre observed that ancient manuscripts each have their own character, which she, as a conservator, comes to know intimately. "Sometimes there are manuscripts that create an atmosphere of calm," she said, "and sometimes the documents fight you. Not this document. This document was a calm one. I was—spiritually—in accord with this document. This work has been calm, precise, gentle.

"In order to best understand it you have to be close to the manuscript itself. I became immersed in it."

Darbre stressed that hers was a team effort. "I work well with Professor Kasser, the chief translator. We are often in touch. We speak by telephone. He visits here in Nyon about once a month, perhaps more." Restoring a codex is like solving a puzzle, she explained. She and Professor Rodolphe Kasser regularly exchanged ideas. He would suggest a particular fragment for a particular page. She would fit it. She also had to match the fibers. The fibers showed how the parts of a page could fit together.

Some of that work could be handled by visual matchups using the naked eye. Not all fibers, however, could be seen. A high-powered microscope stood in one corner of her studio. She used it whenever the human eye was not capable of delineating the intricate details of the tiny fibers. Once she made a match, the work of determining full letters, words, and sentences could proceed.

This work, she said, had been one of the great challenges of her professional life. So far she had spent more than four years on it. The papyrus was unquestionably ancient. About two-thirds of the document was recoverable and readable, but significant obstacles remained.

Professor Kasser was also in attendance. His demeanor reflected the suffering afflicted on his aging body by Parkinson's disease.

Despite his physical handicap, though, Kasser's mind was as sharp as that of a much younger man, and he was single-minded in his pursuit: to complete a translation of the long-lost document, which would represent the greatest achievement in his professional life.

The one expert in the room whom Kasser knew was Emmel.

They had last met five months before at the International Coptic Studies Association meeting in Paris in July, when Kasser had made his public announcement of the codex and its contents. For Emmel, a brilliant Coptologist, Professor Kasser was a mentor. In this way, Emmel bridged the European and American camps, having also studied under James Robinson in California.

Kasser watched as the experts examined his "baby," the treasure that had fallen like manna several years before to provide him with an unparalleled opportunity.

Darbre brought out certain pages of the codex. Ehrman, Emmel, Jull, and the others strained to have a look. Much of the manuscript was stabilized. That is, it was already in a state of advanced preservation due to Darbre's diligent attention to minute detail. Most important, much of it was readable. The codex had been put under glass and could be examined page by page.

On the negative side, it was missing sizable pieces and literally several hundred tiny fragments. Some of the pages lacked substantial sections. The codex was a puzzle in the process of being assembled, though it was near the final stage in terms of available materials.

Darbre loosened the clips on one side of the frame, but did not entirely remove the glass, so the experts could look closely at the restored manuscript. Stephen Emmel perused the first page for a full few minutes. Genuine excitement sparked his voice as he explained that this was his second visit to Geneva. The first one had been in 1983 to examine an unknown ancient Coptic document. "This is the same manuscript!" he exclaimed.

He proceeded to tell the story of the earlier trip. He had been invited to a Geneva hotel and met two men, one of them European, one an Arab who only spoke Arabic. The European spoke Arabic as well. He could not now remember the name of the hotel or the names of either of the men; it was possible that they had not fully identified themselves. He had had only a limited amount of time, two hours, to examine the artifact. He had used tweezers to pull back folio after folio, page after page. Many of the pages were stuck together. He had identified one of the documents as the James epistle, the second as Peter. However, he had failed to identify the third document, placed at the back of the manuscript.

As Emmel proceeded to examine the restored codex, he offered a step-by-step analysis. The first page showed a similarity with many gnostic documents. "These manuscripts are based on a dialogue between the resurrected Jesus and one or more of his disciples. This codex is roughly within that tradition." However, it seemed to offer some variations on the theme. He needed more time and more folios to better examine the text.

Darbre delivered additional photos of pages of papyrus. Could it be certified that this was the Gospel of Judas?

Emmel perused the last page of the manuscript, titled "The Gospel of Judas." He said it was.

The next question was obvious: "How can we be confident that this Gospel of Judas is that of Judas Iscariot, and not some other Judas?"

By way of reply, Emmel turned to Kasser. The older man searched out the name within photographic copies of the codex. Finally, he pointed out the name within the body of text, that of Judas Iscariot. Emmel scanned the section himself and nodded in agreement.

"Could this be a modern forgery?" was one question.

"Absolutely not," Emmel declared categorically.

"How many people could create a modern forgery?"

"Maybe twenty-five," Emmel speculated. Then, after a moment's consideration, he amended his estimate. "No, I'd say four, and two are in this room."

A modern forgery was not a serious possibility. "What about an ancient forgery?"

It was almost definitely a Coptic translation from an early document written in Greek, probably one dating from the second or third century. Many gnostic documents stemmed from that period. The authenticity could also be judged by the epigraphy, the analysis of the handwriting on the papyri. "There is no question," said Emmel, "the handwriting is that of an ancient Coptic scribe."

The first page indicated that the dialogue took place after Jesus' crucifixion. Jesus had risen from the dead, and he was engaged in a conversation with his disciples. It then continued with a dialogue between Jesus and Judas. That pattern is typical of ancient gnostic manuscripts.

"The epigraphy itself is marked by the kinds of indentations that are characteristic of Coptic writing," Emmel related. A careful study of the use of language would reveal more.

"Can you tell when it was written?"

"That is more of an open question."

"What are the chances that the Coptic author could have created the document on his own?"

"No chance," said Emmel. This was a copy and almost certainly a translation—most likely from Greek—and the original document from which it had been translated would date most likely back to the second century, when gnostic writing began.

Emmel wavered on precise dating. That was too uncertain. He preferred to await carbon-14 testing of the manuscript.

Bart Ehrman then offered his initial assessment. He provided general background rather than any specific analysis of a document he had not yet had time to study.

A native of Kansas, Ehrman had received his B.A. at Wheaton College in Illinois and a Master of Divinity and Ph.D. at the Princeton Theological Seminary, where he had studied under Bruce M. Metzger, whom he regarded as the icon of American expertise on early Christianity. Ehrman's scholarship into the complexities and diversity of early Christianity was supplemented by something rare among academics: an ability to express his expertise in English a layperson can understand.

Ehrman was careful not to make statements about a manuscript where no authoritative translation yet existed. He wanted to wait until Kasser finished his work, though that could take another year. Like Emmel, he also awaited the results of the radiocarbon dating. He was, however, ready to put the gospel within the context of the general history of early Christianity.

"What we apparently have here in the Gospel of Judas is perfectly consistent with Irenaeus's condemnation of it," Ehrman said. "It was written after the Gospel of John was written. The Gospel of John is the youngest of the canonical Gospels, but it [the Gospel of Judas] would have been in circulation prior to the time the canonical Gospels were selected.

"This is a document associated with the Cainites. The Cainites were named after Cain. It was a contrary movement—this would have been part of their New Testament. The Cainites wanted to show their allegiance to the one true God. This meant they had to break from what they considered the inferior God of the Old Testament. The Cainite doctrine was that you had to break every law there was in order to have salvation.

"The fact is that Irenaeus specifically cited this one, the Gospel of Judas, as heretical. But his criticism is very general."

Tim Jull, the radiocarbon-dating expert, had his turn to speak next. Jull's family had moved to Canada when he was eleven, and he did his original training in chemistry at the University of British Columbia and in geochemistry at the University of Bristol in England, with postdoctorate studies first at Bristol, then at the University of Cambridge, and later at the world-famous Max-Planck-Institut für Chemie at Mainz, Germany. He joined the University of Arizona and its prestigious NSF-Arizona Accelerator Mass Spectrometer Facility in Tucson in 1981 and had been promoted through the ranks to become director of the lab in 2001.

Jull explained why radiocarbon dating is considered the most accurate way to date ancient artifacts derived from living specimens. "It's a method of looking at the amount of radioactive-isotope carbon 14 produced in the atmosphere, which is accumulated in all living things equally," he recounted. "When the plant or animals die, the radioisotope decays. It has a half-life of 5,700 years. That is, in 5,700 years one-half of it is steadily removed. That gives us a clock against which we can measure the age of just about anything.

"We're dating the age of the papyrus—the age when the papyrus was cut down.... If there's a sample that dates from 400 A.D., that can give us a plus or minus of fifty years. There are some fluctuations in the amount of carbon 14 at the time the plant is growing. So you have to correct for that, through calibration."

Other methods of analyzing ancient materials may offer additional information about the provenance of an artifact—for example, details about where the papyrus came from, or what materials were used in the manufacture of a certain paper or ink. However, when dating a manuscript or any ancient object derived from living materials, Jull contended that the carbon-14 method remains the best.

There is at least one drawback, however. "The process [of radio-carbon dating] is destructive," Jull cautioned. "The samples we take are destroyed. If there's any material left over we return it to the owners."

With the afternoon pushing on, outside light began to fade. Three of the group, Florence Darbre, Tim Jull, and Rodolphe Kasser, went to work selecting the pieces from the codex that would be sacrificed for radiocarbon dating. They were looking for fragments from the text that would not hamper the work of translation when they were destroyed. They wanted to select pieces from different parts of the codex, but ones that would not harm its future preservation.

A significant part of the actual leather binding of the manuscript had also survived along with the manuscript. Parts of it were attached to the papyri. Testing this would help corroborate the radiocarbon dating of the papyrus itself.

"We're taking samples from both the manuscript and the leather binding," Jull said. "That will help a lot. It's easy to date the contents of an ancient binding. We'll also date the papyrus inside the binding." The leather binding in ancient days was often stuffed with old papyrus.

"We want to take those [fragments] that will do the least damage," Jull explained. "But we want to know that the three texts are contemporary and come from the same period, even though there doesn't seem to be much doubt about it, judging by the people here."

Jull explained that he needed samples at least half a centimeter square in dimension weighing at least ten milligrams. "That will enable us to get a clean sample and convert it to graphite."

Altogether, the trio chose five samples:

- A piece from the papyrus interior of the binding of the outside leather cover
- A fragment of loose papyrus from the hundreds of fragments in the file box
- A piece of leather from the binding, with attached papyrus
- A sample from page 9 of the codex, the James epistle, with page 10 on the reverse
- A fragment from page 33 of the Codex, part of the Gospel of Judas, with page 34 on the reverse

Darbre took over the technical work of cutting out the samples from the papyri. Not wanting to create additional damage, she worked precisely, chiseling out the fragments with great care and placing each of them in a tiny nylon sack.

Jull remembered a famous previous client: "Our laboratory dated a number of scrolls from the Dead Sea Scrolls. They were mostly parchment. This involves many of the same issues. In the case of parchment that's two thousand years old, the parchment degrades along the edges. What I've seen of this papyrus, it doesn't look that it should be too difficult."

Jull recalled that, when actually cutting out fragments from the Dead Sea Scrolls, the Israeli woman in charge had suddenly begun to cry. The process was too painful emotionally. Absorbed in cutting the valuable papyrus neatly and precisely, Florence Darbre showed a hint of the same kind of distress.

Jull and his associate Greg Hodgkins promised the results as soon as possible. The radiocarbon dating involved the use of an accelerator mass spectrometer. An accelerator has a series of magnetic and electric lenses that focus the carbon beams on detectors about the size of a quarter.

The analysis took place the week of January 10, 2005. The detectors registered the beams and recorded the effect.

"Sometimes things fall into place beautifully. This is one of them," Greg Hodgkins e-mailed the team. "The samples have been measured, and I've just finished calibrating them."

The night of January 11, Jull was traveling to Israel from Glasgow, where he was on a study-program leave of absence, to give two lectures and several seminars at the Weizmann Institute of Science in Rehovot, Israel's premier scientific institution. He received the results from Hodgkins via e-mail at London's Heathrow Airport, but had difficulty opening the attachments. After he reached the San Martin guesthouse on the Weizmann Institute campus, he managed to turn on his computer and display the attachments. He caught a few hours' sleep and then, with his computer, constructed intricate graphs of statistical possibilities for the Judas gospel.

He couched his results in probabilities and likelihoods; the range of the samples was amazingly similar. It was one of the better runs he'd seen. "These are excellent results," he reported. "Basically, the samples, from the leather and the codex itself, with the exception of the loose papyrus, have come in with statistical equivalency."

He had 95 percent confidence that both the leather binding and the codex fragments fell between the broad range of 220 and 340 CE. "Statistically, there's only a 2.5 percent chance the document was written before 220, and similarly only a 2.5 percent chance it was written after 340," he explained.

Carbon-14 dating is reported in "radiocarbon years," which differ from calendar years and must be adjusted using a calibration factor. Universal calibration—a standard agreed to by all laboratories working in the field of radiocarbon dating—derives from research studies undertaken primarily by nuclear laboratories in Seattle, Heidelberg, and Belfast, with some handled at the Arizona facility, over more than two decades. It reflects analyses of the fluctuation of carbon-14 levels in the atmosphere. Every instance of radiocarbon dating has to be adjusted by at least 1 percent and sometimes up to 3 or 5 percent or even more. The size of the calibration factor varies based on factors such as weather measured over years and centuries, cosmic-ray flux change, and the oscillation of the Earth's magnetic field.

The graphs that Jull created showed the following results:

- Papyrus from interior of outside cover: 1,796 radiocarbon years. That would make the radiocarbon age 209 CE, with a variation factor of plus or minus 58.
- Loose papyrus in file box: 1,672 radiocarbon years, or radiocarbon age 333 CE, plus or minus 48.
- Leather with attached papyrus: 1,782 radiocarbon years, or radiocarbon age 223 CE, plus or minus 51.
- Manuscript, from page 9 of the codex, the James epistle: 1,739 radiocarbon years, or 279 CE, plus or minus 50.
- Manuscript, page 33, the Gospel of Judas: 1,726 radiocarbon years, or radiocarbon age 279 CE, plus or minus 47 years.

"It is unusual and very exciting to get such consistency in the results," Jull said.

The loose piece of papyrus that was tested was apparently not part of the manuscript and could be discounted. The overall range of dates for it, when adjusted for calibration, was much later than what was indicated by the radiocarbon dating of the other samples.

Combining the results for the other four samples, Jull reported that the odds were greatest—a 68.1 percent probability—that the Judas document had been created between 240 and 320 CE. There was roughly a 15 percent probability that it had been written before 240, and a 15 percent chance that it came from after 320. Adding twenty years on either side of the 240–320 range increased the probability factor to 95.4 percent, statistically a near certainty.

Averaged out, with all sorts of input from statistical methods, the mean year of the measurements was 280 CE. "Give or take sixty years on either side and I can say with confidence that is the age of the codex," Jull declared.

Professor Kasser had told his close associates that, in his view, judging on the basis of the ancient handwriting and the use of Coptic language in the codex, the document had been transcribed no later than the first quarter of the fifth century. He suspected it was even earlier.

The results of the radiocarbon dating were dramatic confirmation of Kasser's conservative instincts. What was clear, according to Jull, was the following: The date the codex was copied could have been as early as 220, when many gospels were competing for dominance in the new religion called Christianity. It could have been written painstakingly on its papyrus before Emperor Constantine, who decreed Christianity the official religion of the Roman Empire, was born.

Looking at the other extreme, the date could also be the early fourth century—possibly after 315, when Constantine embraced Christianity. It was statistically less likely that it was copied as late as 325, when the Council of Nicaea took place. And it was statistically quite unlikely that the papyrus text derived from any time much later than 340.

If the statistical mean, 280, was in fact its date of origin, then it was created just about a century after Irenaeus's comments on the Greek original, issued around 180. It could have been copied only forty or sixty years after Irenaeus had condemned the gospel in his *Against Heresies*.

The Gospel of Judas and the rest of the Coptic language codex was far older—by a century or more—than anyone had anticipated. The codex, written originally in Greek during the very heart of the early Christian era, was one of the earlier intact Christian documents known to man. This dating of the Coptic translation of the original Greek text makes the gospel's message even more compelling. If an entire sect believed that the great betrayal had in fact been ordered by Jesus and carried out by his favored disciple, that interpretation could, after study, become as valid as the version told in the New Testament.

# CHAPTER SIXTEEN

# THE GOSPEL

*Jesus said to Judas, "{Come}, that I may teach you about*
*{secrets} no person {has} ever seen. There is a great and boundless*
*realm ... which no eye of an angel has ever seen,*
*no thought of the heart has ever comprehended,*
*and it was never called by any name."*
—THE GOSPEL OF JUDAS

The Gospel of Judas is unlike anything that you have read before. Within its pages, Judas is not the betrayer of Jesus but Jesus' most faithful friend and disciple. Judas is the person who is asked to make the greatest of all sacrifices—to hand Jesus over to his executioners. And this request is made by Jesus himself.

The Gospel of Judas, almost certainly created in the second century, is fresh, it is different, and it is now making its first public appearance in modern times. We know that the text was condemned by the emerging church, along with other gnostic texts, and that it disappeared from history.

One copy of this text has miraculously survived. A team of

scholars have tirelessly restored and translated it over a period of four years. Now its message can be related to everyone.

As bitterly as it was attacked in ancient times, the Gospel of Judas does not seem threatening today. It was written by someone who revered Jesus. He communicates that adoration with fervor and good humor. Jesus appears to be a less suffering, more joyful figure than in the canonical Gospels, and he has the capacity to laugh. He does so four times. The unknown writer of the Gospel of Judas took particular joy in telling the story. It is a document that brims with love and affection, both for Judas and for Jesus. "In the Gospel of Judas, Jesus laughs a great deal," says Marvin Meyer. "He sees a great deal of humor in the human condition, in all the foibles and all the unusual features of our life upon this Earth."

Judas is different in this gospel, unlike the faithless traitor scorned in the canonical Gospels of Matthew, Mark, Luke, and John. So, too, is Jesus different from the savior in those Gospels. Jesus is called "master" and "rabbi," as in the canonical Gospels, but he is not a suffering martyr nailed to a cross. Rather, Jesus is a friendly, benign teacher who radiates divine wisdom.

The Gospel of Judas is a "Christian" text in the sense that the author believed in the divinity of Jesus and wrote from within a tradition that recounts the story of a teacher who came to save first his people and then humanity at large, and then was handed over to the authorities and passed from death to eternal life.

Some scholars think that texts like the Gospel of Judas were part of a collection of secret knowledge—not meant to be read in public. Elaine Pagels believes that it was meant to have been read in conjunction with other Gospels. "You could take the Gospel of Mark, which is widely the favorite of Christians, and read it with the Gospel of Thomas or with the Gospel of Judas. You could read one as the text read publicly and the other as the text that is read as advanced-level teaching. So it's not that these are necessarily opposites; you don't have to choose Mark or the Gospel of Thomas or Judas. They would probably have been read together by the people who were interested in all of them."

Pagels goes on to make a very interesting point about who might have copied the Gospel of Judas that was discovered. The many gospels "were loved probably by monks, who are likely to have copied them and treasured them and kept them in the monastery library, because they were for people who were going into a deeper level of spiritual discipline and understanding."

In the Gospel of Judas, Judas is Jesus' favorite and his chosen disciple. "The star that leads the way is your star," Jesus tells his loyal follower. Judas is asked to hand over Jesus to the authorities—by none other than Jesus himself. Jesus promises his faithful disciple: Your star, the star of Judas, will shine in the heavens.

A different image of Judas Iscariot emerges. Rather than Judas the Betrayer, he is a special person who stands above the other disciples. He becomes "the thirteenth" among the group, standing apart from the others, the only one who can stand tall in Jesus' presence, though he cannot look Jesus directly in the eye.

A reader can disagree with the themes of the Gospel of Judas. Some may think it blasphemy. But what cannot be denied is that the writer accords Judas a new place in history.

Because the Gospel of Judas was written in the century that followed Jesus' life, it is a startling text that provides fresh insight into early Christianity and its varied movements. It falls within a different tradition than that of the canonical Gospels. The writer believes in the divinity of Jesus from within a gnostic framework. The Gospel of Judas offers an alternative narrative, but does not challenge the bases of Christian faith. Instead, it may augment that faith by providing an additional view of the personality of Jesus.

Many of the cosmological concepts in the Gospel of Judas are strange to the modern reader. The author was clearly familiar with what became the canonical gospels and knew their stories of Judas intimately. Yet the Gospel of Judas is neither a reply to, nor a denial of, the four canonical gospels. It does not refute. It does not attempt to shatter belief or destroy the meaning of what was written elsewhere. It is its own independently told story, claiming secret knowledge of the real relationship between Judas and Jesus.

The author could have lived almost anywhere. The document might have been created in a number of places in the Near East—in Jerusalem or Caesarea or Alexandria, perhaps. Most likely he heard a story, and that story was part of a tradition. It was believed by certain people who genuinely regarded Jesus as the true messiah because of the shining example he set and because he could lead each person to the god inside himself or herself. The author was clearly determined to tell Judas's side of the story as Jesus' most faithful servant. He proclaimed it proudly in his title. This was the "Gospel of Judas," revealing the "good news" about Judas.

While the story is contrary to what had been written in other Christian texts, it is not illogical. Jesus came to save the world, and he predicted his own death. Jesus, bluntly put, needed to die in order to fulfill his mission. Judas Iscariot was an instrument in that process. He was an essential part of the narrative—both for those who wrote the canonical texts and for the writer of the Gospel of Judas. The twist on the narrative is different, but the factual outlines of the story remain the same.

The author wrote in Greek, the lingua franca of culture and

enlightenment within the Roman Empire. It was the language of philosophy and of faith, including the spreading Christian faith. Almost beyond doubt, he knew the writings of the great Greek philosopher Plato. In *Timaeus,* Plato says that each person has his soul and his own star. The author was apparently influenced by Plato's thought, as were all gnostics. Judas has his own star. In the gospel, Jesus tells Judas:

> "Lift up your eyes and look at the cloud and the light within it and the stars surrounding it. The star that leads the way is your star."
>
> Judas lifted up his eyes and saw the luminous cloud, and he entered it.

Communication during the time of the Roman Empire was good, given its excellent roads, and news of the document traveled far. It gained the attention of Irenaeus in the far west, nearly a thousand miles from the Holy Land. Irenaeus condemned it thoroughly, if for nothing else than its title. It was outrageous that someone would take up the cause of Judas, he who had betrayed Jesus. Irenaeus castigated the document as being "Cainite," although given beliefs stated in the gospel, the author might have been a Sethian, a sect named after the biblical Seth, Adam's son. The author was certainly gnostic, a prime target of Irenaeus's condemnation.

The author was influenced by the Jewish idea of the messiah and the concept of a future day of judgment. His was a vision of the apocalypse, and he shared a primary gnostic belief that the material world is not a "fallen" place, imbued with sin, but is itself inherently evil. He rejected that Old Testament god who causes suffering and created this lesser world on earth.

The person who wrote the specific papyrus codex found in Al Minya was a scribe, in ancient times a craftsman who worked laboriously, word by word. He was a highly specialized figure, because back then only a few select individuals could use the technology called writing. In today's world, when our daily life takes for granted the general ability to read or write, it is hard to imagine that people who were able to write could be so scarce or so valuable. In ancient Egypt, scribes were often highly prized members of the royal administration, not least because they tallied the pharaoh's taxes on the yearly totals of grain. They were also responsible for writing such key religious texts as the Book of the Dead.

Their enormous importance had not waned by the time of the Christian bishop Irenaeus in the second century. As quoted by Bruce M. Metzger in *The Text of the New Testament,* Irenaeus appended a succinct note to a scribe who was copying one of the bishop's own written essays:

> I adjure you who shall copy out this book, by our Lord Jesus Christ and by his glorious advent when he comes to judge the living and the dead, that you compare what you transcribe, and correct it carefully against this manuscript from which you copy; and also that you transcribe this adjuration and insert it in the copy.

The scribe who wrote down the extant manuscript of the Gospel of Judas was almost undoubtedly a Copt, since the language he used was Coptic. Since the document was originally written in Greek, this scribe or one of his predecessors possibly translated it at the same time he copied it. If there were words he could not find in his own language, he used the Greek original.

There is no way to know which scribe copied the copy of the Gospel of Judas that has survived. Many scribes were attached to monasteries, but some were employed by other religious authorities or private individuals, and others worked for civil administrations or educational institutions. "The Gospel of Judas is clearly the work of a professional scriptorium," Stephen Emmel states. "Whoever wrote this was highly trained and highly experienced in copying literary manuscripts."

The scholars who write about the dramatic finds in the Egyptian desert are sometimes puzzled by the finding of such extensive ancient literature written in the obscure Coptic language, almost all of it believed to derive from original Greek language texts and found in obscure places where barely scraping out a living is often a challenge.

Emmel notes, "As a Coptologist, one of the greatest mysteries for me remains who produced this Coptic-language gnostic literature. We have no secondary sources that tell us who made the translations from Greek to Coptic of works like the Gospel of Judas or the Gospel of Thomas or the Apocrypha of John. All we have is mostly individual copies of those translations. The copies that we have are certainly not the original translations. They have long since been lost. We have third-, fourth-, fifth-, sixth-generation copies of these translations produced for people of whom we know nothing about."

We are also certain about some of the more practical aspects of the papyrus manuscript. The copy that we have was found in Egypt. The original text was translated from Greek to Coptic. Numerous

Greek words exist within the document, and it is likely that the translation into Coptic was done at an early stage in the development of the Coptic language and its writing system. That would place the copy in the third or fourth century. The radiocarbon dating indicates the same.

We also know that the codex contains three other parts: the Letter of Peter to Philip; a statement of or by James, who is also known in history as James the Just; and an untitled section titled "Allogenes" by the translator.

The Letter of Peter to Philip was first within the binding. A separate version of this letter was found at Nag Hammadi. In the Codex Tchacos, Peter, one of the apostles of Jesus Christ, writes to Philip, his dear friend and fellow apostle, and to the other Brethren—that is, the disciples. The last paragraphs sum up the message of Peter's letter: "He rose from the dead, my Brothers! Jesus is a stranger to death, but we are the ones who have died through the transgr[e]s[sion] of our Mother."

After a gap of eighteen lines, the text resumes with these words:

> Jesus appeared [and] he said: "Peace to you and glory to
> those w[ho be]lieve in my name. Walk [and] go! Joy will
> [be] to you and grace [a]nd power. Be not afraid! [I a]m with
> you forever." Then the Apostles parted [from each other into
> four words, [so as to preach]. [So] they went [in the power
> and] peace of Jesus.

This is not "dissident" writing, but writing from within a particular tradition of Christian belief.

A second part of the codex is a separate text regarding James, similar to a document found at Nag Hammadi called "The (First) Apocalypse of James." Jesus addresses James on a number of points, including what is "femaleness." Jesus says, "Femaleness existed, but it did not exist from the beginning."

The resurrected Jesus explains to James that he did not die. He tells James to say that he is from "the Father who exists from the beginning, and the Son who exists in Him-Who-Is from the beginning." This statement reflects debates within early Christianity concerning whether the Son coexisted with and was part of the Father, or was a son of God born on Earth.

James the Just, either the apostle James or a second man named James, is eventually persecuted, much like Jesus. He says at the end of the text: "My Father [who is in heaven], forgive them, for they are i[gno]rant of what they are doing." Here, the parallels to the wording in the canonical gospels is clear.

The "Allogenes" section is far more fragmentary. No official title exists from the time. Allogenes was a Coptic figure who is literally a foreigner, or a person of a different race. The name Allogenes was invented by the authors of the Septuagint. He was a figure who overcame ignorance and fear and entered into the multilayered gnostic realm in heaven.

The primary interest of the discovery was the Gospel of Judas. As opposed to the scanty mentions of Judas Iscariot in the four Gospels of Matthew, Mark, Luke, and John, the new gospel, as its title would indicate, is filled with references to Judas and Jesus both. There are twenty references to Judas Iscariot, the same number of times that Judas is mentioned by name in all four canonical Gospels combined.

The Gospel of Judas presents a picture of Judas that is significantly at odds with that presented in the New Testament. Rather than a traitor whose soul is invaded by Satan. Judas is the favorite disciple, called upon by Jesus to "sacrifice the man that clothes me," in Jesus' words.

The portrait of Jesus is different as well. Jesus is not a tormented figure who will die in agony on the cross. Instead, he is a friendly and benevolent teacher with a sense of humor. Jesus never ridicules others with his laughter. Often, he laughs as he teaches.

The gospel is marked by a striking image. It occurs at the very beginning of the text. Jesus "began to speak with them [the disciples] about the mysteries beyond the world and what would take place at the end. Often he did not appear to his disciples as himself, but he was found as a child among them." The word for "child" may also be rendered as "apparition," but, according to Marvin Meyer, that translation is less likely.

The idea that Jesus would appear not as himself but as a child is both provocative and unexplained. It is part of the enchantment of the text. Meyer notes, "The fact that Jesus could appear as a child on occasion is in fact paralleled in other gospels, too." Elaine Pagels offered this interpretation: "It's often the case in these texts that when it says Jesus appeared to them as a child, it's not meant to be taken literally. It means that his teaching appears in a more naïve form than the mature teaching. So much in these texts, particularly in the secret texts, are understood to be taken as metaphor."

The Gospel of Judas opens with a dialogue. The setting is Judea, though it is not specified where, and it need not have been Jerusalem. Jesus finds his disciples sitting together in pious observance. It is three days before Passover.

As they are seated, the disciples offer a prayer of thanksgiving. Jesus approaches, and he laughs.

"Master, why are you laughing at our prayer of thanksgiving? We have done what is right," the disciples say.

Jesus answers: "I am not laughing at you. You are not doing this because of your own will but because through this your god is praised."

Jesus is referring not to God above in the heavenly realm but rather to the ruler of the material world. In some gnostic texts, the creator of the world was even regarded as Satan.

The disciples tell him, "Master, you ... are the son of our god."

He answers: "How do you know me? Truly [I] say to you, no generation will know me among humans."

According to certain gnostic sects, Seth, the son of Adam, fathered an immortal race of people who would be marked out by the special relationship to the Divine. The Sethians saw themselves as the fulfillment of the divine race. Meyer elaborates: "In the Gospel of Judas and other Sethian texts, the human generations are distinguished from 'that generation,' the great generation of Seth, that is, the gnostics. Only those of 'that generation' know the true nature of Jesus."

The disciples start to become angry. Jesus asks, "Why have you been incited to anger? Your god who is within you.... Bring out the perfect human and stand before my face."

They all say, "We have the strength." But they don't. The gospel says, "Their spirits did not dare to stand before him."

Regarding this passage, Meyer notes, "Jesus issues a challenge to the disciples. He says, let the perfect person inside of you step forward and face me. And that perfect person within is that spiritual person that truly knows. That person ought to have a knowledge of God and a knowledge of oneself."

Only one of the disciples has the moral strength to stand before Jesus: Judas Iscariot. Yet Judas, too, lacks a second level of strength—that is, the spiritual fortitude to look Jesus in the eyes, and he turns his face away.

Judas says, "I know who you are and where you have come from. You are from the immortal realm of Barbelo." Barbelo, in Sethian texts, Meyer says, is the divine mother of all. To say that Jesus is from the realm of Barbelo is to believe that Jesus is from the divine realm above and is the son of God.

Judas, aware of his own limitations, continues: "And I am not worthy to utter the name of the one has sent you."

Jesus then asks Judas to "step away from the others," promising to tell him about "the mysteries of the kingdom."

Pagels explains: "When we consider the claim that Jesus had secret teachings that he taught only to some people, we should consider two things. First of all, how did Jewish teachers teach in the first century? How do they teach today? They will often teach the congregation one thing, and they'll teach their own disciples a deeper level of the teaching. Jesus, if he was like other Jewish teachers, would have probably taught one way to the crowd and other things to his disciples in secret." She points out that in the Bible, he sometimes tells parables to the public and then explains their meaning to the disciples in private.

In a private conversation, Jesus tells Judas, "It is possible for you to reach [the kingdom], but you will grieve a great deal."

Judas responds with a question: "When will you tell me these things, and [when] will the great day of light dawn for that generation?"

Jesus does not answer the question. As mysteriously as he came, he suddenly departs.

Jesus returns the next morning and appears to the disciples again. They ask him, "What is that generation that is superior to us and holier than us, that is not now in these realms?"

Jesus laughs for a second time in the text, and then recounts to the disciples the great difficulties in attaining the secret place or time. "No person of mortal birth can go there."

He then offers what Meyer calls "an allegorical interpretation of the Temple." There is a mention of sacrifice, which was practiced in the Temple when it still stood. "The cattle you have seen brought for sacrifice are the many people you lead astray before that altar," Jesus says. Meyer suggests that this is a subtle attack by the author of the Gospel of Judas on the emerging orthodox Christians who were spreading Jesus' word.

Jesus cautions that there are those who make "use of my name…. [They] plant trees without fruit, in my name, in a shameful manner." He reminds the disciples that "the Lord who commands, who is the Lord of all, will judge them on the last day." Here is a reference to an end of days—a final Day of Judgment.

Finally, Jesus says to the disciples: "Stop struggling with me. Each of you has his own star."

Much of the following text is lost. Bart Ehrman notes about this exchange: "Jesus reveals these truths to Judas and Judas alone. Among these truths are that people in this world have a divine spark trapped within them that needs to be set free. Jesus himself represents a divine spark that needs to be set free."

In the next section, Judas asks Jesus, "Rabbi, what kind of fruit does that generation produce?"

Jesus answers: "The souls of every human generation will die. When these people, however, have completed the time of the kingdom and the spirit leaves them, their bodies will die, but their souls will stay alive, and they will be taken up."

"And what will the rest of the human generations do?" Judas asks.

Jesus replies, "Seed cannot be sown on rock, so as to be

fruitful." Much of what directly follows is incomplete and unclear. It deals with Sophia, the symbol of wisdom, a central figure in gnostic texts.

Jesus, having said what he had to say, departs.

Time passes. Judas and Jesus meet yet again. Judas has made a great discovery. "Master, as you have listened to all of [the other disciples] now also listen to me. For I have seen a great vision."

Jesus laughs again. Judas is for him no longer one of the twelve disciples but someone very special, the "thirteenth spirit." He is a spiritual being above and beyond the more common disciples. "You thirteenth spirit," Jesus says, "why do you try so hard? But go ahead and speak, and I shall support you."

Judas recounts a vision: "The twelve disciples were stoning me and persecuting [me severely]. I saw [a great house].... Great people were running toward it ... and in the middle of the house was [a crowd]. Master, take me in along with those people," Judas pleads.

Jesus' response is poignant. "Judas, your star has led you astray. No person of mortal birth is worthy to enter the house you have seen, for that place is reserved for the holy."

Judas then asks about his own fate. "Master," he asks, "could it be that my seed [i.e., the spiritual part of a person] is under the control of the rulers [i.e, the rulers of this world]?"

Jesus answers, "Come ... but you will grieve much when you see the kingdom and all its generation."

"What good is it that I have received it?" Judas asks. "For you have set me apart for that generation." Judas has become the leading faithful follower and disciple of Jesus, a man recognized by Jesus as a special spiritual human being.

Jesus tells him, "You will become the thirteenth, and you will be cursed by the others, because you reign over them. In the last days they will curse your [departure?] up to the holy generation."

Pagels shows how this passage aligns with the negative interpretation offered in the Bible: "It is something that we could have expected from the clues given by the Gospel of John in the New Testament. That Judas betrays Jesus is a despicable act elsewhere, and he is hated and kills himself for that because he sacrifices Jesus for money. In the Gospel of Judas, Jesus instructs him that although he will be hated, he has a special mission. He has to participate in the divine plan by bringing about the sacrifice of Jesus' form. He has to bring Jesus' life on this earth to an end."

Jesus then offers to teach Judas about secrets that "no person [has] ever seen.... There is a great and boundless eternal realty, whose extent no generation of angels has seen ... since it is great ... invisible ... no thought of the heart has ever comprehended, and it was never called by any name."

The following pages are filled with gnostic cosmology: about the aeons and their secrets. The universe is created, then the Earth is created, and finally human beings. Saklas, one of the angels, but one who is considered a fool, is the one who decides to create a human being; Meyer notes that similar accounts of the creation are cited in other Sethian texts. Adam and Eve are created. Eve is also called Zoë, which is Greek for "life." "For by this name all the generations seek the man, and each of the generations calls the woman by these names ... And the ruler said to Adam, 'You shall live long, with your children.'"

In the section of text that follows, Judas asks Jesus, "Does the human spirit die?"

Jesus replies, "This is why God ordered Michael to give the spirits of people to them as a loan, so that they might offer service, but the Great One ordered Gabriel [Michael and Gabriel are two archangels, as in the Bible] to grant spirits to the great generation with no ruler over it—that is, the spirit and the soul."

Somewhat later in the text, Jesus undertakes to destroy the wicked. Unfortunately, words are missing and the phrases are incomplete here.

Judas asks Jesus, "What will those generations do?"

Jesus replies, "Truly, I say to you, for all of them, the stars bring matters to completion. When Saklas completes the span of time assigned for him, the first star will appear with the generations, and they will finish what they said they would do."

Lamentably, there are additional missing words, which makes comprehension of the next sentences difficult.

"For they will fornicate in my name and slay their children … .and they will … and … my name, and … will … your star on the … -teenth aeon." Meyer notes that "the references to the stars, their influences, and their eventual destruction are astronomical and apocalyptic."

After this description, Jesus laughs yet again—a fourth time.

Judas asks, "Master, why are you laughing at me?"

Jesus answers, "I am not laughing at you, but at the configuration of the stars, because these six stars wander about with these five combatants, and they all will be destroyed along with their creatures."

Judas then asks: "Look, what will those who have been baptized in your name do?"

Jesus' response is not clear. This paragraph, however, leads into what Bart Ehrman regards as the key phrase in the entire gospel:

"But you [Judas] will exceed all of them. For you will sacrifice the man that clothes me."

Jesus is asking Judas to hand him over and sacrifice him. The reasons become clearer. Jesus' life on Earth is only in the guise of a man. The man provides clothes for the spirit within. Jesus is an eternal figure; he is part of the higher God, he is greater than and separate from man, he is eternal. The clothes and the man are Jesus' trappings only while he is on Earth. They are ephemeral, a temporary phenomenon. The man who is clothed, who is disguised, hides the holy spirit of the infant Jesus. It is the body of the man that is being sacrificed—but not the soul of Jesus, not God himself.

Jesus goes on: "Look, you have been told.... Lift up your eyes and look at the cloud and the light within it and the stars surrounding it. The star that leads the way is your star." Judas is thus assured of his special place. Then comes a great moment, equal in dramatic power to much that is in the canonical Gospels:

"Judas lifted up his eyes and saw the luminous cloud, and he entered it."

This passage, with its powerful imagery, "may be described as the transfiguration of Judas," according to Meyer. It is both Judas's vindication and his glorification.

A voice speaks from the cloud. Unfortunately, those words are lost. Meyer notes that about six lines of Coptic text are missing. He speculates that this voice "may have praised Judas or offered conclusions about the meaning of the events described." Further, he points to the comparisons between this scene and Jesus' own transfiguration, as well as the baptism of Jesus, described in the canonical Gospels (Matthew 3:13–17, Mark 1:9–11, Luke 3:21–22).

The final scene is handled in a matter-of-fact manner. Yet it contains high drama. As opposed to a long narrative covering the trial, crucifixion, and resurrection of Jesus, the conclusion of the Gospel of Judas is short and to the point:

> The high priests murmured because [Jesus] had gone into the guest room to pray. But some scribes were there watching carefully in order to arrest him during the prayer, for

they were afraid of the people, since Jesus was regarded by all as a prophet.

As in the canonical Gospels, the word about Jesus has spread.

"They [the high priests] approached Judas and said to him, 'What are you doing here? You are Jesus' disciple.'"

It is immediately clear that Judas did not come to them wanting money to betray Jesus. There is no conspiracy. Judas is already a willing partner, but he is a partner with Jesus, not the high priests, in this telling.

"Judas answered them as they wished," the text goes on, without stating precisely what Judas said or what the high priests may have wished.

Then comes the final line of the gospel:

"And Judas received some money and handed him over to them."

There are no second thoughts, no agonizing pangs of conscience. There is no weeping. There are no suicides looming in the future. The deed is done simply. Judas has acted on behalf of Jesus, sacrificing the man that clothes Jesus so that Jesus may fulfill his destiny.

Ehrman explains why this ending made so much sense to gnostic believers. "In the early Gospels, it's the death and resurrection of Jesus that really matters for salvation. His body dies and then God raises his body from the dead. This resurrection of the body is very important, and Jesus in the Gospels of Matthew, Luke, and John actually appears to his followers to show that he's still living. His body is still alive.

"That stands completely at odds with what happens in the Gospel of Judas, where there's no account of his death because his death isn't what really matters. There especially is no account of his resurrection. Because in the Gospel of Judas, Jesus is not going to be resurrected. What matters for Judas is not that the body is going to come back to life. What matters is that the body is going to die and the spirit is going to live on."

What the gospel does not say may be as important as what it says.

It does not directly criticize or contradict the canonical gospels—which were not yet accepted as the New Testament at the time the Gospel of Judas was written. It takes no direct issue with anything factual written in the New Testament narratives.

The Gospel of Judas does not mention the theme of betrayal, because Judas does not betray his master. Instead, he fulfills Jesus' wish. He is above the other disciples, who fade into the background. Judas is Jesus' chosen instrument of fulfillment.

The Gospel of Judas mentions neither crucifixion nor salvation. It evinces no indication or even the slightest hint of collective guilt. The Gospel of Judas offers no blood libel that will course through history, causing vilification of Jews, pogroms, and even the Holocaust. As the favored disciple, Judas obeys his beloved master's wishes.

Although a modern reader might wish for a more detailed account of what happened, for less complex gnostic cosmology, for fewer gaps in the text, the message nevertheless comes through clearly. Here is a view of a key act in the life of Jesus that turns the traditional interpretation of Judas on its head. Judas is Jesus' chosen instrument. Through Judas, Jesus will be liberated from "the man that clothes me" and will achieve his rightful place through all of eternity.

EPILOGUE

*In the Gospel of Judas, he does nothing Jesus himself does not ask him to do, and he listens to Jesus and remains faithful to him. Judas Iscariot turns out to be Jesus' beloved disciple and dear friend.*
— MARVIN MEYER

The Gospel of Judas is its own unique story. It has lived two distinct, eventful existences. The first took place between the first and fourth centuries, when Christianity separated itself from Judaism. Christianity began as a diverse religion because its different believers had developed competing viewpoints and doctrines, all vying for dominance. The document some have called "The Lost Gospel" was branded as heretical by the developing Church because it failed to conform with the orthodox politico-religious agenda. It was labeled "a fictional account" by Bishop Irenaeus, who was later designated a saint. By the fourth century, the text, with its startlingly different narrative of ancient events, essentially disappeared from history.

In modern times, the Gospel of Judas traveled a long road toward discovery. Along its journey, there were instances of mishandling, of human greed, of deception, of individuals exhibiting cruelty towards others. It was part of a prized package to be bought and sold—and stolen. These moments remind us not only of the frailty of any single man or woman but of flawed humanity in general.

Columbia University, dominating the cliffs of Morningside Heights, was where the priest Gabriel Abdel Sayed, Hanna Asabil, and an Egyptian colleague went in 1984 to have their texts appraised by a young but already distinguished classicist named Roger Bagnall. Twenty-one years later, in his office in Hamilton Hall, Professor Bagnall sat down at his computer and pulled up a document referred to as the mathematical treatise, now scanned into his computer. This was the same document that Professor Ludwig Koenen had examined twenty-two years earlier in Geneva, a year before Bagnall had first seen it.

Bagnall scrolled down until he found a small mark on a page of Greek writing, designating its origin as relating to a certain "Pagus 6." Bagnall did not have a map available, but he pointed out a book by Jane Rowlandson of King's College London called *Landowners and Tenants in Roman Egypt: The Social Relations of Agriculture in the Oxyrhynchite Nome,* which has maps showing the administrative districts of Egypt under Roman rule.

Pagus 6 was a strip in the Oxyrhynchite Nome stretching across toward Maghagha. Pagus 6, Bagnall explained, came into being only in 307 or 308 CE, replacing the toparchies that had previously been the bureaucratic nomenclature. Therefore the mathematical document could not have been made before that year, because Pagus 6 did not exist any earlier.

Were the ancient papyrus documents that were being sold together—including this treatise—actually found together? That was a logical assumption, though not an absolute certainty. Certain witnesses have claimed that they were all found together, but witnesses are fallible, and at least one key person involved in the discovery has already passed away.

Even if the documents were discovered in a single burial place, each text may have had its own special history. The codex containing the Gospel of Judas might have been created considerably earlier than other documents with which it was found. That's not to mention that it was a Coptic copy of an earlier Greek document.

Who was the person with whom the documents were buried? What kind of person would choose to be buried with a biblical text, Paul's letters, the Gospel of Judas, and a text for teaching ancient mathematics? The quest for answers about this tantalizing codex continues—and is likely to go on for years.

The painstaking work of Rodolphe Kasser, along with Florence Darbre, Gregor Wurst, and others, has reconstructed a document from the ancient past for the benefit of humankind for eternity. Professor Kasser, sitting in his cramped study by his own computer, recalled that moment when he first saw the gospel: "I experienced what one always does when one is confronted with a mystery. In my profession we know many things and yet we know nothing. We find things, theories and explanations all the time that completely surpass the previous blueprints. and we have to be receptive to changing our mind about the manuscript. It is the manuscript that is the master of the situation.

"It is as if I paid a visit to a stranger and tried to listen to him but knew that it would take me a very long time to understand the depths of his soul…. If the text were really complete, it would be easier, but we have many gaps."

The effort to fill out the Gospel of Judas with its fragments continued into 2007. Bruce Ferrini, the Ohio art dealer, had gone bankrupt, and his papers were in the possession of a court-appointed receiver in his home state. Experts were brought in to see if any of the fragments would match up with the existing lacunae, or gaps, in the text. At least one half page—a part of pages 41 and 42 in the Gospel of Judas—that had been included in one of Charles Hedrick's photographs was somehow lost. Only the photograph remained, and it showed only one side of the page. Whether the original of that precious piece of papyrus, once almost certainly in Ferrini's possession, would ever be found was an open question. Still, some 80 percent of the historical treasure known as the Gospel of Judas could, almost miraculously, be read and studied.

What we do know is that the Gospel of Judas is a fresh and authentic witness of an early era in Christianity. Its message turns the long-accepted belief that Judas betrayed his master on its head, and in so doing, it invites all of us to reexamine what Jesus tried to teach. Following our own star is an idea that is as relevant today as it was back then. Rather than cast out the betrayer, perhaps we should look more deeply for the goodness inside ourselves.

The unknown persists, waiting alluringly to be discovered as we learn more about times when a new faith was born. No matter how far we journey, mysteries always seem to remain.

# THE GOSPEL OF JUDAS

*Translated by*
*Rodolphe Kasser, Marvin Meyer, and Gregor Wurst,*
*in collaboration with François Gaudard*

# THE GOSPEL OF JUDAS

## INTRODUCTION: INCIPIT

The secret account[1] of the revelation[2] that Jesus spoke in conversation with Judas Iscariot during a week[3] three days before he
celebrated Passover.[4]

---

[1] Or, "treatise," "discourse," "word" (Coptic, from Greek, *logos*). The opening of the text may also
be translated to read "The secret revelatory word" or "The secret explanatory word." A substantial number of words of Greek derivation are included in the Coptic text of the Gospel of Judas
as loanwords.

[2] Or, "declaration," "exposition," "statement" (Coptic, from Greek, *apophasis*). In his *Refutation of All
Heresies* (6.9.4–18.7), Hippolytus of Rome cites another work, attributed to Simon Magus, that
employs the same Greek term in its title: *Apophasis megalē*—Great Revelation (or, Declaration,
Exposition, Statement). The incipit, or opening of the present text, reads "The Secret Account of the
Revelation of Jesus" (or the like). The titular subscript, "The Gospel of Judas," is found at the end
of the text.

[3] Literally, "during eight days," probably intended to indicate a week.

[4] Or, perhaps, but much less likely, "three days before his passion." The Gospel of Judas chronicles
events described as taking place over a short period of time leading up to the betrayal of Jesus by
Judas. In the New Testament, cf. Matthew 21:1–26:56; Mark 11:1–14:52; Luke 19:28–22:53;
John 12:12–18:11.

# The Earthly Ministry of Jesus

When Jesus appeared on earth, he performed miracles and great wonders for the salvation of humanity. And since some [walked] in the way of righteousness while others walked in their transgressions, the twelve disciples were called.[5]

He began to speak with them about the mysteries[6] beyond the world and what would take place at the end. Often he did not appear to his disciples as himself, but he was found among them as a child.[7]

SCENE 1: *Jesus dialogues with his disciples: The prayer of thanksgiving or the eucharist*

One day he was with his disciples in Judea, and he found them gathered together and seated in pious observance.[8] When he [approached] his disciples, [34] gathered together and seated and offering a prayer of thanksgiving[9] over the bread, [he] laughed.[10]

The disciples said to [him], "Master, why are you laughing at [our] prayer of thanksgiving?[11] What did we do? [This] is what is right."[12]

---

[5] On the calling of the twelve disciples, cf. Matthew 10:1–4; Mark 3:13–19; Luke 6:12–16.

[6] Coptic, from Greek, *emmustērion*, here and in subsequent text.

[7] Sahidic Coptic *hrot*, which we take as a form of the Bohairic Coptic word *hrot*, "child." Much less likely is the possibility that *hrot* may be a form of the Bohairic Coptic word *hortef*, "apparition." On Jesus appearing as a child, cf. Secret Book of John (Nag Hammadi Codex II), 2; Revelation of Paul 18; Hippolytus of Rome *Refutation of All Heresies* 6.42.2, where Hippolytus reports a story that the Word (*Logos*) appeared to Valentinus as a child; Gospel of Thomas 4. On Jesus appearing as an apparition, cf. the Acts of John, the Second Discourse of Great Seth, and the Nag Hammadi Revelation of Peter.

[8] Literally, "training (or practicing) their piety" (Coptic, partly from Greek, *eergumnaze etmntnoute*; cf. 1 Timothy 4:7).

[9] Coptic, from Greek, *eureukharisti*.

[10] The scene recalls, in part, accounts of the Last Supper, particularly the blessing over the bread, or descriptions of some other holy meal within Judaism and Christianity. The specific language used here calls to mind even more the celebration of the eucharist within Christianity; cf. additional criticisms within the Gospel of Judas of forms of worship within the emerging orthodox Church. On Jesus laughing, cf. Second Discourse of Great Seth 56; Revelation of Peter 81; several other passages in the Gospel of Judas.

[11] Or, "eucharist" (Coptic, from Greek, *eukharistia*).

[12] Or, "Have we not done what is right?"

He answered and said to them, "I am not laughing at you. <You> are not doing this because of your own will but because it is through this that your god [will be] praised."[13]

They said, "Master, you are [...] the son of our god."[14]

Jesus said to them, "How do you know me? Truly [I] say to you,[15] no generation of the people that are among you will know me."[16]

## THE DISCIPLES BECOME ANGRY

When his disciples heard this, they started getting angry and infuriated and began blaspheming against him in their hearts.

When Jesus observed their lack of [understanding, he said] to them, "Why has this agitation led you to anger? Your god who is within you and [...][17] [35] have provoked you to anger [within] your souls. [Let] any one of you who is [strong enough] among human beings bring out the perfect human and stand before my face."[18]

They all said, "We have the strength."

---

[13] Or, "[will receive] thanksgiving." It is also possible to translate this clause as a question: "But is it through this that your god [will be] praised?" The god described as the god of the disciples is not the exalted deity above but rather the ruler of this world.

[14] Cf. the confession of Peter in Matthew 16:13–20, Mark 8:27–30, and Luke 9:18–21. Here, however, the disciples mistakenly confess that Jesus is the son of their own god.

[15] Or, "Amen I say to you." This is the standard introductory statement of authority in sayings of Jesus in early Christian literature. Here and elsewhere in the Gospel of Judas, the statement is given with the Coptic *hamēn* (from the Hebrew *'amen*).

[16] In the Gospel of Judas and other Sethian texts, the human generations are distinguished from "that generation" (Coptic *tgenea etᵉmmau*), the great generation of Seth—that is, the gnostics. Only those of "that generation" know the true nature of Jesus. Elsewhere in Sethian literature—for example, in the Revelation of Adam—the people of Seth can similarly be described as "those people" (Coptic *nirōme etᵉmmau*).

[17] Perhaps "[his powers]," or the like.

[18] The restoration is tentative. Here Jesus indicates that the anger rising within the hearts of the disciples is being provoked by their god within them. Jesus challenges them to allow the true person—the spiritual person—to come to expression and stand before him.

But their spirits[19] did not dare to stand before [him], except for Judas Iscariot. He was able to stand before him, but he could not look him in the eyes, and he turned his face away.[20]

Judas [said] to him, "I know who you are and where you have come from. You are from the immortal realm[21] of Barbelo.[22] And I am not worthy to utter the name of the one who has sent you."[23]

## JESUS SPEAKS TO JUDAS PRIVATELY

Knowing that Judas was reflecting upon something that was exalted, Jesus said to him, "Step away from the others and I shall tell you the mysteries of the kingdom.[24] It is possible for you to reach it, but you will grieve a great deal. [36] For someone else will replace you, in order that the twelve [disciples] may again come to completion with their god."[25]

---

19 Here and elsewhere in the text, "spirit" apparently means "living being"; cf. Gospel of Judas 43, 53.

20 Of the disciples, only Judas has the strength to stand before Jesus, and he does so with modesty and respect. On Judas averting his eyes before Jesus, cf. Gospel of Thomas 46, where it is said that people should show a similar form of modesty by lowering the eyes before John the Baptizer.

21 Or, "aeon," here and in subsequent text.

22 In the Gospel of Judas, it is Judas himself who provides the true confession of who Jesus is. To confess that Jesus is from the immortal realm (or aeon) of Barbelo is to profess, in Sethian terms, that Jesus is from the divine realm above and is the son of God. In Sethian texts, Barbelo is the divine Mother of all, who often is said to be the Forethought (*pronoia*) of the Father, the infinite One. The name of Barbelo seems to be based on a form of the tetragrammaton, the holy four-letter name of God within Judaism, and it apparently comes from Hebrew—perhaps "God (compare *El*) in (*b-*) four (*arb(a)*))." For presentations of Barbelo in Sethian literature, see Secret Book of John II:4–5; Holy Book of the Great Invisible Spirit (also known as the Egyptian Gospel; Nag Hammadi Codex III) 42, 62, 69; Zostrianos 14, 124, 129; Allogenes the Stranger 51, 53, 56; Three Forms of First Thought 38.

23 The one who has sent Jesus is the ineffable God. The ineffability of the divine is also asserted in Gospel of Judas 47, and it is emphasized in such Sethian texts as the Secret Book of John, the Holy Book of the Great Invisible Spirit, and Allogenes the Stranger. In Gospel of Thomas 13, Thomas similarly declares to Jesus, "Teacher, my mouth is utterly unable to say what you are like."

24 Or, "reign"—that is, the kingdom or reign of God.

25 Cf. Acts 1:15–26, on the selection of Matthias to replace Judas in the circle of the twelve in order to complete the twelve once again.

Judas said to him, "When will you tell me these things, and when will the great day of light dawn for the [...]²⁶ generation?"

But when he said this, Jesus left him.²⁷

SCENE 2: *Jesus appears to the disciples again*

The next morning, after this happened,²⁸ Jesus [appeared] to his disciples again.²⁹

They said to him, "Master, where did you go and what did you do when you left us?"

Jesus said to them, "I went to another great and holy generation."³⁰

His disciples said to him, "Lord, what is the great generation that is superior to us and holier than us, that is not now in these realms?"³¹

When Jesus heard this, he laughed and said to them, "Why are you thinking in your hearts about the strong and holy generation? [37] Truly³² [I] say to you, no one born [of] this aeon will see that [generation], and no host of angels of the stars will rule over that generation, and no person of mortal birth can associate with it, because that generation does not come from [...] which has become [...]. The generation of people among [you] is from the

---

²⁶ Only faint traces of ink remain.

²⁷ Judas asks questions about the promised revelation from Jesus and the ultimate glorification of that generation, but Jesus abruptly leaves.

²⁸ Or, "At dawn of the next day."

²⁹ The word "again" is implied in the text.

³⁰ Jesus maintains that he went beyond this world to another realm, apparently the spiritual realm of that generation.

³¹ These realms or aeons are the ones, here below, that are mere copies or reflections of the realms or aeons above. This theme is discussed more fully later in the text. The Platonic character of this theme is clear, but the Platonic concept of the realm of ideas and the reflections of ideas in our world is interpreted in a gnostic manner in the Gospel of Judas and other texts, especially Sethian texts.

³² Amen.

generation of humanity [...] power, which [... the] other powers [...] by [which] you rule."³³

When [his] disciples heard this, they each were troubled in spirit. They could not say a word.

Another day Jesus came up to [them]. They said to [him], "Master, we have seen you in a [vision], for we have had great [dreams ...] night [...]."³⁴

[He said], "Why have [you ... when] <you> have gone into hiding?"³⁵ [38]


## The Disciples See the Temple and Discuss It

They³⁶ [said, "We have seen] a great [house with a large] altar [in it, and] twelve men—they are the priests, we would say— and a name;³⁷ and a crowd of people is waiting at that altar,³⁸ [until] the priests [... and receive] the offerings. [But] we kept waiting."

[Jesus said], "What are [the priests]³⁹ like?"

---

³³ In this passage Jesus seems to say, among other things, that the great generation comes from above and is indomitable, and that people who are part of this world below live in mortality and cannot attain that great generation.

³⁴ Here the text may be restored, tentatively, as follows: "for we have had great [dreams of the] night on which they have come to [arrest you]," in which case the disciples may be referring to premonitions of the arrest of Jesus in the Garden of Gethsemane.

³⁵ If the restoration proposed in the last note is accepted, this may be a reference to the disciples running away to hide, in terror, when Jesus is arrested. Cf. Matthew 26:56; Mark 14:50–52.

³⁶ Here the text suggests that the disciples have a vision of the Jewish Temple in Jerusalem—or, less likely, that they have gone to visit the Temple—and then they report on what they have seen (cf. pronouns in the first-person plural "we" in this passage). In the section that follows, Jesus refers explicitly to what the disciples "have seen"; this provides part of the justification for the restoration of lacunae proposed in this section. In the New Testament gospels, cf. the accounts of the visits of Jesus and the disciples to the Temple in Matthew 21:12–17, 24:1–25:46; Mark 11:15–19, 13:1–37; Luke 19:45–48, 21:5–38; and John 2:13–22.

³⁷ Apparently the name of Jesus; cf. Gospel of Judas 38 ("your [name]") and 39 ("my name"). In the context of the Jewish Temple in Jerusalem, the reference to "a name" could also be understood to refer to the ineffable name of God (Yahweh) in Judaism.

³⁸ Here the text seems inadvertently to repeat "at that altar" (a case of dittography).

³⁹ The restoration is tentative but reasonable in the context.

They [said, "Some[40] ...] two weeks; [some] sacrifice their own children, others their wives, in praise [and][41] humility with each other; some sleep with men; some are involved in [slaughter];[42] some commit a multitude of sins and deeds of lawlessness. And the men who stand [before] the altar invoke your [name], [39] and in all the deeds of their deficiency,[43] the sacrifices are blazing [...]."

After they said this, they were quiet, for they were troubled.

## JESUS OFFERS AN ALLEGORICAL INTERPRETATION OF THE VISION OF THE TEMPLE

Jesus said to them, "Why are you troubled? Truly[44] I say to you, all the priests who stand before that altar invoke my name. Again I say to you, my name has been written on this [...] of the generations of the stars through the human generations. [And they] have planted trees without fruit, in my name, in a shameful manner."[45]

Jesus said to them, "Those you have seen receiving the offerings at the altar—that is who you are.[46] That is the god you serve, and you

---

[40] On this section, cf. the polemical description of leaders of the emerging orthodox Church in the allegorical interpretation of the vision of the Temple given by Jesus in Gospel of Judas 39–40.

[41] Or, "[or]."

[42] The restoration is tentative.

[43] "Deficiency" (Coptic *šōōt*) is a technical word in Sethian and other texts for the lack of divine light and knowledge that can be traced to the fall of the Mother—usually Sophia, the Wisdom of God—and the subsequent loss of enlightenment. Cf., for example, Letter of Peter to Philip 3–4 (Codex Tchacos), 135 (Nag Hammadi Codex VIII). This passage is quoted in the commentary of this book. On corruptible Sophia, cf. Gospel of Judas 44.

[44] Amen.

[45] The reference to planting trees without fruit, in the name of Jesus, seems to be an indictment of those who preach in the name of Jesus but proclaim a gospel without fruitful content. The same image of trees bearing or not bearing fruit is found in Revelation of Adam 76, 85; cf. Gospel of Judas 43. Also compare, perhaps, the withered fig tree in Matthew 21:18–19 and Mark 11:12–14.

[46] Throughout this section, Jesus interprets what the disciples have seen at the Temple as a metaphor for erroneous religious instruction, apparently in the emerging orthodox Church. The priests are the disciples, and perhaps their successors in the Church, and the animals led to the slaughter are the victims of the improper religious observance in the Church.

are those twelve men you have seen. The cattle brought in are the offerings you have seen—they are the many people you lead astray [40] before that altar. [...][47] will stand and make use of my name in this way, and generations of the pious will remain loyal to him. After him[48] another man will stand there from[49] [the fornicators], and another [will] stand there from the slayers of children,[50] and another from those who sleep[51] with men, and those who abstain,[52] and the rest of the people of pollution and lawlessness and error, and those who say, 'We are like angels'; they are the stars that bring everything to its conclusion. For to the human generations it has been said, 'Look, God has received your sacrifice from the hands of the priests'— that is, a minister of error. But the Lord who commands is the Lord of the universe.[53] On the last day they will be put to shame."[54] [41]

Jesus said [to them], "Stop sac[rificing ...] which you have [...] over the altar, since they are over your stars and your angels and have already come to their conclusion there.[55] So let them be [ensnared][56] before you, and let them go [—*about 15 lines*

---

[47] Perhaps "[The ruler (or archon) of this world]"; cf. 1 Corinthians 2:8.

[48] Or, but less likely, "After that."

[49] Coptic, from Greek, *parista* (two lines later, *parhista*). The people who stand may be leaders in the emerging orthodox Church who are judged, in this polemical section, to be working as assistants of the ruler of this world. The verb may also be translated as "represent," here and in the passages that follow, rather than "stand there from."

[50] Here the text seems to suggest that the leaders of the emerging orthodox Church are immoral in their own lives and are endangering the lives of the children of God and leading them into spiritual death. This image may recall the comparison with cattle being led to death in temple sacrifice.

[51] Here we read *nrefnkotk* for the *nrefnkokt* of the manuscript. The accusation of sexual impropriety is a standard feature of polemical argumentation. One's opponents are frequently said to be immoral people.

[52] Or, "fast." For a similar negative view of fasting, cf. Gospel of Thomas 6.

[53] Or, "All," that is, the fullness of the divine realm above (Coptic *ptēr*ᶠ*f*).

[54] At the end of time, the leaders of the emerging orthodox Church will be punished for their acts of impiety.

[55] Here Jesus seems to indicate that the leaders of the emerging orthodox Church are strong, but their time is coming to an end.

[56] Or, "entrapped," "upbraided." The reading and meaning of the text are uncertain. The Coptic (perhaps *šōnt*, literally "entwined") may also be translated "quarreling" or "in a struggle." The reading *šōōt*, "deficient" or "diminished," is also possible.

*missing—]*[57] generations [...]. A baker cannot feed all creation [42] under [heaven].[58] And [...] to them [...] and [...] to us and [...].

Jesus said to them, "Stop struggling with me. Each of you has his own star,[59] and every[body—*about 17 lines missing*—] [43] in [...] who[60] has come [... spring] for the tree[61] [...] of this aeon [...] for a time [...] but he[62] has come to water God's paradise,[63] and the [generation][64] that will last, because [he] will not defile the [walk of life of] that generation, but [...] for all eternity."[65]

## JUDAS ASKS JESUS ABOUT THAT GENERATION AND HUMAN GENERATIONS

Judas said to [him, "Rabb]i,[66] what kind of fruit does this generation produce?"[67]

Jesus said, "The souls of every human generation will die.

---

[57] An extant photograph from an earlier inspection of the codex, though lacking in clarity, reveals a few words and expressions.

[58] This statement may be an ancient proverb about setting reasonable goals for what people can accomplish—in this case, readers of the Gospel of Judas who face the opposition of the emerging orthodox Church. Conversely, the statement may also be intended as a critique of the eucharist as it is celebrated in the emerging orthodox Church.

[59] The teaching here and elsewhere in the Gospel of Judas that each person has a star seems to reflect Plato's presentation in his *Timaeus*. After a statement by the creator of the world, it is said there that the creator "assigned each soul to a star" and declared that "the person who lived well during his appointed time was to return and dwell in his native star" (41d–42b; the passage is quoted at length in the commentary of this book). On the star of Judas, cf. Gospel of Judas 57.

[60] Or, "which."

[61] The reference to a tree, in this fragmentary portion of the text, may indicate one of the trees in paradise. The trees of the Garden of Eden are frequently discussed in gnostic texts, and the tree of the knowledge (Greek *gnōsis*) of good and evil is often thought to be a source of the knowledge of God. Cf. Secret Book of John II:22–23.

[62] Or, "it." The identity of the pronominal subject here and in the next lines is uncertain.

[63] Cf. Genesis 2:10.

[64] Or, "race." Here and elsewhere in the text, rather than the Coptic *genea*, which is usually employed, the Coptic reads *genos*. Both words derive from Greek.

[65] Literally, "from everlasting to everlasting."

[66] The title "rabbi" (largely restored) is the Hebrew term for a Jewish teacher or master.

[67] Compare and contrast Gospel of Judas 39, on those who plant trees without fruit.

When these people, however, have completed the time of the kingdom and the spirit[68] leaves them, their bodies will die but their souls will be alive, and they will be taken up."

Judas said, "And what will the rest of the human generations do?"

Jesus said, "It is impossible [44] to sow seed on [rock] and harvest its fruit.[69] [This] is also the way [...] the [defiled] generation[70] [...] and corruptible Sophia[71] [...] the hand that has created mortal people, so that their souls go up to the eternal realms above. [Truly][72] I say to you, [...] angel [...] power[73] will be able to see that [...] these to whom [...] holy generations [...]."

After Jesus said this, he departed.

SCENE 3: *Judas recounts a vision and Jesus responds*

Judas said, "Master, as you have listened to all of them, now also listen to me. For I have seen a great vision."

When Jesus heard this, he laughed and said to him, "You thirteenth spirit,[74] why do you try so hard? But speak up, and I shall bear with you."

Judas said to him, "In the vision I saw myself as the twelve disciples were stoning me and [45] persecuting [me severely]. And I

---

[68] The spirit or breath of life? On spirit and soul, cf. also Gospel of Judas 53.

[69] Cf. the parable of the sower in Matthew 13:1–23, Mark 4:1–20, Luke 8:4–15, and Gospel of Thomas 9. According to the parable, seed that is sown and lands on rock cannot take root and thus cannot produce heads of grain.

[70] Or, "race," as above.

[71] Or, "Wisdom," that part of the divine, in gnostic tradition, that falls through a lapse of wisdom and is eventually restored to the fullness of the divine once again. Sophia is often personified as a female figure in Jewish and Christian literature, and she plays a central role in many gnostic texts, including Sethian texts. Cf., for example, the account of the fall of Sophia in Secret Book of John II:9–10, which is cited in the commentary of this book. The child of Sophia, according to gnostic accounts, is the demiurge Saklas or Yaldabaoth. Cf. Gospel of Judas 51.

[72] Amen.

[73] Perhaps, "angel [of the great] power."

[74] Or, "thirteenth demon" (Coptic, from Greek, *daimōn*). Judas is thirteenth because he is the disciple excluded from the circle of the twelve, and he is a demon (or daemon) because his true identity is spiritual. Compare tales of Socrates and his *daimōn* or *daimonion*, in Plato *Symposium* 202e–203a.

also came to the place where [...] after you. I saw [a house ...],[75] and my eyes could not [comprehend] its size. Great people were surrounding it, and that house <had> a roof of greenery,[76] and in the middle of the house was [a crowd—*two lines missing*—], saying,[77] 'Master, take me in along with these people.'"

[Jesus] answered and said, "Judas, your star has led you astray." He continued, "No person of mortal birth is worthy to enter the house you have seen, for that place is reserved for the holy.[78] Neither the sun nor the moon will rule there, nor the day, but the holy will abide[79] there always, in the eternal realm with the holy angels.[80] Look, I have explained to you the mysteries of the kingdom [46] and I have taught you about the error of the stars; and [...] send it [...] on the twelve aeons."

## JUDAS ASKS ABOUT HIS OWN FATE

Judas said, "Master, could it be that my seed[81] is under the control of the rulers?"[82]

---

[75] Judas reports a vision in which he is harshly opposed by the other disciples (cf. Gospel of Judas 35–36, 46–47). In the vision, Judas approaches a place and makes mention of Jesus ("after you"); there is a great heavenly house there, and Judas asks that he may be received into that house along with the others who are entering. On the heavenly house or mansion, cf. John 14:1–14. On the eventual ascension or transfiguration of Judas, cf. Gospel of Judas 57–58.

[76] The reading is conjectural and corrects a possible scribal error.

[77] The word "saying" is implied in the text.

[78] Or, "the saints," here and in subsequent text.

[79] Or, "stand."

[80] On this apocalyptic description of heaven, cf. Revelation 21:23. According to Secret Book of John II:9, the souls of the holy or the saints dwell in the third eternal realm, with the third luminary Daveithai, the home of the offspring of Seth. Cf. also Holy Book of the Great Invisible Spirit III:50–51.

[81] The seed is the spiritual part of a person, the spark of the divine within, and, collectively, the offspring of those who come from the divine. Thus, in Sethian texts gnostics can be called the seed or offspring of Seth.

[82] Or, "archons," here and in subsequent text—that is, the rulers of this world, especially the cosmic powers who collaborate with the demiurge. This clause may also be translated "that my seed subdues the rulers?"

Jesus answered and said to him, "Come, that I [—*two lines missing*—], but that you will grieve much when you see the kingdom and all its generation."

When he heard this, Judas said to him, "What good is it that I have received it? For you have set me apart for that generation."

Jesus answered and said, "You will become the thirteenth,[83] and you will be cursed by the other generations—and you will come to rule over them.[84] In the last days they will curse your ascent[85] [47] to the holy [generation]."

JESUS TEACHES JUDAS ABOUT COSMOLOGY:
THE SPIRIT AND THE SELF-GENERATED

Jesus said, "[Come], that I may teach you about [secrets][86] no person [has] ever seen. For there exists a great and boundless realm, whose extent no generation of angels has seen, [in which] there is [a] great invisible [Spirit],[87]

> *which no eye of an angel has ever seen,*
> *no thought of the heart has ever comprehended,*
> *and it was never called by any name.*[88]

---

83 On Judas as the thirteenth, cf. Gospel of Judas 44, where Judas is said to be the thirteenth spirit or demon.

84 On Judas being cursed, compare the assessments of Judas in Matthew 26:20–25, 27:3–10; Mark 14:17–21; Luke 22:21–23; John 13:21–30; and Acts 1:15–20. Here it is suggested that Judas is despised by the other disciples, but he is to be exalted over them as the preeminent disciple.

85 Or, "return up." The translation is tentative. The text seems to allude to some kind of transformation or ascent, as in Gospel of Judas 57 (the transfiguration of Judas) or 2 Corinthians 12:2–4 (the ecstatic ascent of a man—Paul—to the third heaven).

86 Or, "hidden things." The restoration is tentative. For a full account of Sethian cosmology, cf. Secret Book of John and Holy Book of the Great Invisible Spirit.

87 Or, "[the] great invisible [Spirit]." In many Sethian texts—for example, the Secret Book of John and the Holy Book of the Great Invisible Spirit—the transcendent deity is called the great invisible Spirit.

88 Cf. 1 Corinthians 2:9; Gospel of Thomas 17; Prayer of the Apostle Paul A. The parallel text in the Valentinian Prayer of the Apostle Paul is close to part of the formulation in the

"And a luminous cloud[89] appeared there. He[90] said, 'Let an angel[91] come into being as my attendant.'[92]

"A great angel, the enlightened divine Self-Generated,[93] emerged from the cloud. Because of him, four other angels came into being from another cloud, and they became attendants[94] for the angelic Self-Generated.[95] The Self-Generated said, [48] 'Let [...] come into being [...],' and it came into being [...]. And he [created] the first luminary[96] to reign over him. He said, 'Let angels come into being to serve [him],'[97] and myriads without number came into being. He said, '[Let] an enlightened aeon[98] come into being,' and he came into being. He created the second luminary [to] reign over him, together with myriads of angels

---

Gospel of Judas: "Grant what eyes of angels have not [seen], what ears of rulers have not heard, and what has not arisen in the human heart, which became angelic, made in the image of the animate god when it was formed in the beginning." The ineffability and transcendence of the divine is emphasized in many gnostic texts, especially Sethian texts. Cf. Secret Book of John II:2–4; Holy Book of the Great Invisible Spirit III:40–41; Allogenes the Stranger; Irenaeus of Lyon *Against Heresies* 1.29.1–4, on the "gnostics" or "Barbelognostics" ("gnostics of Barbelo"); Gospel of Judas 35. Lines from the Secret Book of John illustrating such descriptions of divine transcendence are quoted in the commentary of this book.

[89] Or, "cloud of light." The luminous cloud is a manifestation of the glorious heavenly presence of the divine, and clouds of light often appear in ancient descriptions of theophanies. In the accounts of the transfiguration of Jesus in the New Testament gospels, for instance, luminous clouds accompany the revelation of glory (Matthew 17:5–6; Mark 9:7–8; Luke 9:34–35). In the Holy Book of the Great Invisible Spirit, heavenly clouds also play an important role; in the Secret Book of John, there is light surrounding the Father of All.

[90] The Spirit.

[91] Or, "messenger," here and in subsequent text.

[92] Or, "as my assistant," "to stand by me" (Coptic, from Greek, *parastasis*). Compare the verb *parista/parhista* in Gospel of Judas 40.

[93] Or, "Self-Begotten," "Self-Engendered," "Self-Conceived," "Autogenes" (Coptic *autogenēs*, from Greek), here and in subsequent text. Typically the Self-Generated is the child of God in Sethian texts; cf. Secret Book of John II:7–9; Holy Book of the Great Invisible Spirit III:49, IV:60; Zostrianos 6, 7, 127; Allogenes the Stranger 46, 51, 58.

[94] Again, Coptic, from Greek, *parastasis*.

[95] In Secret Book of John II:7–8, the Four Luminaries, named Harmozel, Oroiael, Daveithai, and Eleleth, come into being through the Self-Generated. Cf. also Holy Book of the Great Invisible Spirit III:51–53; Zostrianos 127–28; Three Forms of First Thought 38–39.

[96] Coptic, from Greek, *phōstēr*, here and in subsequent text.

[97] Or, "offer adoration," "offer worship" (Coptic *šemše*, here and in subsequent text).

[98] Or, "an aeon of light."

without number, to offer service. That is how he created the rest of the enlightened aeons. He made them reign over them, and he created for them myriads of angels without number, to assist them.[99]

## ADAMAS AND THE LUMINARIES

"Adamas[100] was in the first luminous cloud[101] that no angel has ever seen among all those called 'God.' He [49] [...] that [...] the image [...] and after the likeness of [this] angel. He made the incorruptible [generation] of Seth[102] appear [...] the twelve [...] the twenty-four [...]. He made seventy-two luminaries appear in the incorruptible generation, in accordance with the will of the Spirit. The seventy-two luminaries themselves made three hundred sixty luminaries appear in the incorruptible generation, in accordance with the will of the Spirit, that their number should be five for each.[103]

"The twelve aeons of the twelve luminaries constitute their father, with six heavens for each aeon, so that there are seventy-two heavens for the seventy-two luminaries, and for each [50] [of them five] firmaments, [for a total of] three hundred sixty [firmaments ...]. They were given authority and a [great] host of angels [without number], for glory and adoration, [and after that

---

[99] According to the text, the divine realm is filled with luminaries, aeons, and angels brought into being by the creative word of the Self-Generated, to serve and adore the divine.

[100] Adamas is Adam, the first human of Genesis, here understood, as in many other gnostic texts, to be the paradigmatic human of the divine realm and the exalted image of humanity. Cf., for example, Secret Book of John II:8–9.

[101] The first luminous cloud is the initial manifestation of the divine; cf. Gospel of Judas 47.

[102] This is Seth, son of Adam, also in the divine realm; cf. Genesis 4:25–5:8. The role of Seth as the progenitor of the generation of Seth ("that generation") is well established in Sethian texts; cf. also Gospel of Judas 52.

[103] Everything finally happens in accordance with the will of the divine, the Spirit.

also] virgin[104] spirits,[105] for glory and [adoration] of all the aeons and the heavens and their firmaments.[106]

## THE COSMOS, CHAOS, AND THE UNDERWORLD

"The multitude of those immortals is called the cosmos— that is, perdition[107]—by the Father and the seventy-two luminaries who are with the Self-Generated and his seventy-two aeons. In him[108] the first human appeared with his incorruptible powers. And the aeon that appeared with his generation, the aeon in whom are the cloud of knowledge[109] and the angel, is called [51] El.[110] [...] aeon [...] after that [...] said, 'Let twelve angels come into being [to] rule over chaos and the [underworld].' And look, from the cloud there appeared an [angel] whose face flashed with fire and whose appearance was defiled with blood. His name was

---

[104] In Sethian texts, the term *virgin* is used as an epithet for a variety of divine manifestations and powers in order to stress their purity. In the Holy Book of the Great Invisible Spirit, for example, the great invisible Spirit, Barbelo, Youel, and Plesithea are described as virgins, and additional mention is made of more virgins.

[105] Eugnostos the Blessed includes a passage on the aeons that also mentions virgin spirits, and this passage (Nag Hammadi Codex III:88–89, cited in the commentary) is very close to the text under consideration. Cf. also Wisdom of Jesus Christ (Nag Hammadi Codex III), 113; On the Origin of the World, 105–6.

[106] These aeons and luminaries, the spiritual powers of the universe, represent aspects of the world, especially time and units of time. On the twelve aeons, compare the months of the year or the signs of the zodiac. On the seventy-two heavens and luminaries, compare the traditional number of nations in the world, according to Jewish lore. On the three hundred sixty firmaments, compare the number of days in the solar year (thirty days per month, for twelve months), without five intercalary days. This passage in the Gospel of Judas is paralleled in Eugnostos the Blessed III:83–84 (cited in the commentary), and in the lines that follow in Eugnostos the Blessed, the author discusses a similar number of aeons, heavens, and firmaments.

[107] Our cosmos, unlike the divine realm above, is susceptible to decay and hence may be termed a realm of perdition.

[108] Or, "In it"—that is, in the cosmos.

[109] Coptic, from Greek, *gnōsis*.

[110] El is an ancient Semitic name for God. In Sethian texts, related names, such as Eloaios, are used for powers and authorities of this world. The Secret Book of John also refers to Elohim, the Hebrew word for "God" in the Jewish Scriptures.

Nebro,[111] which means 'rebel';[112] others call him Yaldabaoth.[113] Another angel, Saklas,[114] also came from the cloud. So Nebro created six angels—as well as Saklas—to be assistants, and these produced twelve angels in the heavens, with each one receiving a portion in the heavens.[115]

## THE RULERS AND ANGELS

"The twelve rulers spoke with the twelve angels: 'Let each of you [52] [...] and let them [...] generation [—*one line lost*—] angels':

The first is [Se]th, who is called Christ.[116]
The [second] is Harmathoth, who is [...].

---

[111] In Holy Book of the Great Invisible Spirit III:57, Nebruel is a great demoness who mates with Saklas and produces twelve aeons; cf. also the role of Nebroel in Manichaean texts. Here the name Nebro is given without the honorific suffix -el (also "God" in Hebrew; cf. the name El, above). In Secret Book of John II:10, the demiurge Yaldabaoth has the appearance of a snake with the face of a lion, and his eyes are like flashing bolts of lightning. In Holy Book of the Great Invisible Spirit III:56–57, Sophia of matter is bloody in appearance: "A cloud [named] Sophia of matter appeared .... [She] surveyed the regions [of chaos], and her face looked like ... in her appearance ... blood."

[112] Or, "apostate" (Coptic, from Greek, *apostatēs*). Nebro most likely derives from Nebrod in Genesis 10:8–12 (cf. 1 Chronicles 1:10) of the Septuagint, where Nebrod (Hebrew Nimrod) reflects the tradition of a well-known legendary figure in the ancient Middle East. The word Nimrod may be related to the Hebrew word for "rebel."

[113] Yaldabaoth is a common name for the demiurge in Sethian texts. Yaldabaoth probably means "child of chaos" (or, less likely, "child of (S)abaoth") in Aramaic.

[114] Saklas (or Sakla, as in Gospel of Judas 52) is another common name for the demiurge in Sethian texts. *Saklas* (or *Sakla*) means "fool" in Aramaic.

[115] The syntax of this sentence is not entirely clear, so that the role of Saklas and his relationship with Nebro remain uncertain. If Nebro and Saklas each create six angels, that accounts for the twelve angels that are produced. Cf. Holy Book of the Great Invisible Spirit III:57–58: "Sakla the great [angel observed] Nebruel the great demon who is with him. [Together] they brought a spirit of reproduction to the earth, and [they produced] angelic assistants. Sakla [said] to Nebruel the great [demon], 'Let twelve realms come into being in the ... realm, worlds ....' Through the will of the Self-Generated, [Sakla] the great angel said, 'There shall be ... seven in number ....'"

[116] Here, as in other Christian Sethian texts, Christ is described as the manifestation of Seth in this world. In Holy Book of the Great Invisible Spirit III:63–64, the text refers to "the incorruptible one, conceived by the Word [*Logos*], the living Jesus, with whom great Seth has been clothed." In Three Forms of First Thought 50, the Word, or Logos, declares, "I put on Jesus. I carried him from the accursed wood [the cross] and established him in the dwelling places of his Father." Cf. Gospel of Judas 56.

The [third] is Galila.

The fourth is Yobel.

The fifth [is] Adonaios.

These are the five who ruled over the underworld, and first of all over chaos.[117]

## THE CREATION OF HUMANITY

"Then Saklas said to his angels, 'Let us create a human being after the likeness and after the image.'[118] They fashioned Adam and his wife Eve, who is called, in the cloud, Zoe.[119] For by this name all the generations seek the man, and each of them calls the woman by these names. Now, Sakla did not [53] com[mand ...] except [...] the gene[rations ...] this [...]. And the [ruler] said to Adam, 'You shall live long, with your children.'"[120]

## JUDAS ASKS ABOUT THE DESTINY OF ADAM AND HUMANITY

Judas said to Jesus, "[What] is the long duration of time that the human being will live?"

---

[117] In Holy Book of the Great Invisible Spirit III:58, through Nebruel and Sakla twelve angels are produced, several of which have names similar or identical to the names here, and mention is made of Cain (this passage is quoted in the commentary of this book). The reference to Cain may bring to mind the claim of Irenaeus of Lyon (*Against Heresies* 1.31.1) that the people who composed the Gospel of Judas appealed to the authority of Cain, though Cain is not mentioned in the extant text of the Gospel of Judas. In Secret Book of John II:10–11, a similar list of names is given, and it is said that seven rule over the seven spheres of heaven (those of the sun, moon, and five planets then known—Mercury, Venus, Mars, Jupiter, and Saturn) and five rule over the depth of the abyss.

[118] Cf. Genesis 1:26. Similar accounts of the creation of a human being are found in other Sethian texts, and sometimes it is said, in more fully developed traditions, that the human is created after the image of God above and with a likeness to the rulers of this world. Cf. Secret Book of John II:15, cited in the commentary of this book.

[119] Zoe, Greek for "life," is the name of Eve in the Septuagint.

[120] Cf. Genesis 1:28, 5:3–5. The demiurge seems true to his word: The people described in the early chapters of Genesis are said to have lived extraordinarily long lives.

Jesus said, "Why are you wondering about this, that Adam, with his generation, has lived his span of life in the place where he has received his kingdom, with longevity with his ruler?"[121]

Judas said to Jesus, "Does the human spirit die?"

Jesus said, "This is why God ordered Michael to give the spirits of people to them as a loan, so that they might offer service, but the Great One ordered Gabriel[122] to grant spirits to the great generation with no ruler over it[123]—that is, the spirit and the soul.[124] Therefore, the [rest] of the souls [54] [—*one line missing*—].[125]

## JESUS DISCUSSES THE DESTRUCTION
## OF THE WICKED WITH JUDAS AND OTHERS

"[...] light [—*nearly two lines missing*—] around [...] let [...] spirit [that is] within you[126] dwell in this [flesh] among the generations of angels. But God caused knowledge[127] to be

---

121 This sentence is difficult and the translation tentative, but it seems to mean that Judas is wondering about Adam in his world with his length of life and his god—all of which is irrelevant for Judas. At the end, the sentence reads, literally, "in a number with his ruler?"

122 Michael and Gabriel are two prominent archangels.

123 Or, "the kingless generation," a reference to the generation of Seth, using a description familiar from Sethian texts to indicate that the people of Seth are indomitable.

124 God, apparently the god of this world, gives the spirit of life (the breath of life? Perhaps cf. Genesis 2:7) to people, through Michael, as a loan, but the Great Spirit gives spirit and soul to people, through Gabriel, as a gift. Genesis 2:7 can be interpreted creatively in other gnostic texts, including Sethian texts; cf. Secret Book of John II:19: "They [five luminaries from above] said to Yaldabaoth, 'Breathe some of your spirit into the face of Adam, and the body will arise.' He breathed his spirit into Adam. The spirit is the power of his mother [Sophia], but he did not realize this, because he lives in ignorance. The Mother's power went out of Yaldabaoth and into the psychical body that had been made to be like the one who is from the beginning. The body moved, and became powerful. And it was enlightened." On spirit and soul in the present text, cf. also Gospel of Judas 43.

125 Here the Coptic reads, in part, *toou*, which means "mountain"; it may also be restored to read {*<sup>e</sup>n}toou*, "they." In the following fragmentary section, second-person plural pronominal forms appear, and this seems to indicate that Jesus is in the company of more people than only Judas. Probably the other disciples are also included in this discussion.

126 Plural.

127 Again, Coptic, from Greek, *gnōsis*.

[given] to Adam and those with him,[128] so that the kings of chaos and the underworld might not lord it over them."

Judas said to Jesus, "So what will those generations do?"

Jesus said, "Truly[129] I say to you,[130] for all of them the stars bring matters to completion.[131] When Saklas completes the span of time assigned for him, their first star will appear with the generations, and they will finish what they said they would do. Then they will fornicate in my name and slay their children[132] [55] and they will [...] and [—*about six and a half lines missing*— ] my name, and your star will rule over the [thir]teenth aeon."

After that Jesus [laughed].

[Judas said], "Master, [why are you laughing at us]?"[133]

[Jesus] answered [and said], "I am not laughing [at you] but at the error of the stars, because these six stars wander about with these five combatants, and they all will be destroyed along with their creatures."[134]

## JESUS SPEAKS OF THOSE WHO ARE BAPTIZED, AND JUDAS'S BETRAYAL

Judas said to Jesus, "Look, what will those who have been baptized in your name do?"[135]

---

128 This passage suggests that *gnōsis*, or knowledge, is given to Adam and thus to humanity. The way in which Adam and humanity come to possess knowledge is explained in detail in other gnostic texts, including Sethian texts, and in these texts it is asserted that humanity has knowledge but the megalomaniacal rulers of this world do not.

129 Here and in subsequent text, the Coptic word *alēthōs* (from Greek) is used rather than *hamēn*, as earlier in the text.

130 Plural.

131 The references to the stars, their influences, and their eventual destruction are astrological and apocalyptic.

132 Cf. Ezekiel 16:15–22, as well as Gospel of Judas 38 and 40, on slaying children and committing fornication.

133 The restoration is tentative.

134 The wandering stars are probably the five planets (Mercury, Venus, Mars, Jupiter, and Saturn) along with the moon. According to ancient astronomical and astrological theory, such wandering stars can rule over us and influence our lives in unpleasant ways. Cf. also Gospel of Judas 37.

135 These are Christians baptized in the name of Christ. Whether this is meant as a criticism of ordinary Christian baptism, as in other Sethian texts, is unclear.

Jesus said, "Truly I say [to you], this baptism [56] [...] my name [—*about nine lines missing*—] to me. Truly [I] say to you, Judas, [those who] offer sacrifices to Saklas[136] [...] God [—*three lines missing*—] everything that is evil.

"But you will exceed all of them. For you will sacrifice the man that clothes me.[137]

*Already your horn has been raised,*
*your wrath has been kindled,*
*your star has shown brightly,*
*and your heart has {become strong}.*[138] [57]

"Truly [...][139] your last [...] become [—*about two and a half lines missing*—] grieve [—*about two lines missing*—] the ruler, since he will be destroyed. And then the image[140] of the great generation of Adam will be exalted, for prior to heaven, earth, and the angels, that generation, which is from the eternal realms, exists.[141] Look, you have been told everything. Lift up your eyes and look at the cloud and the light within it and the stars surrounding it. The star that leads the way is your star."[142]

Judas lifted up his eyes and saw the luminous cloud[143], and he

---

[136] On offering sacrifices to Saklas, perhaps cf. Gospel of Judas 38-41.

[137] Literally, "that bears me" (Coptic, from Greek, *etrphorei* <sup>e</sup>*mmoei*). Jesus tells Judas that he will do what no other disciple does: He will help Jesus by sacrificing the fleshly body ("the man") that clothes or bears the true spiritual self of Jesus. The death of Jesus, with the assistance of Judas, is taken to be the liberation of the spiritual person within.

[138] On the poetic lines depicting how Judas is prepared for his act of salvific betrayal, cf. passages from the Psalms.

[139] Perhaps restore to read "Truly [I say to you ]," or the like.

[140] Coptic, from Greek, *tupos*. The text, restored to read [*tu*]*pos,* may also be restored as [*to*]*pos,* "place" (also from Greek).

[141] That is, the generation of Seth is a preexistent generation that comes from God.

[142] Judas is literally the star of the text.

[143] This passage may be described as the transfiguration of Judas. He is vindicated by being glorified in the luminous cloud, and a voice speaks from the cloud. As in accounts of the transfiguration

---

entered it. Those standing on the ground[144] heard a voice coming from the cloud, saying, [58] [...] great generation [...] image [...] and [—*about five lines missing*—].[145]

## CONCLUSION: JUDAS BETRAYS JESUS

[...] Their high priests murmured because [he][146] had gone into the guest room[147] for his prayer.[148] But some scribes were there watching carefully in order to arrest him during the prayer, for they were afraid of the people, since he was regarded by all as a prophet.[149]

They approached Judas and said to him, "What are you doing here? You are Jesus' disciple."

Judas answered them as they wished. And he received some money and handed him over to them.[150]

## THE GOSPEL OF JUDAS[151]

---

of Jesus (Matthew 17:1–8, Mark 9:2–8, Luke 9:28–36; cf. Book of Allogenes 61–62, just after the Gospel of Judas in Codex Tchacos), here Judas enters a luminous cloud, on high, and a divine voice speaks.

[144] Or, "below."

[145] Most of the words of the divine voice from the cloud are lost in the lacuna in the manuscript, but it may have praised Judas and the great generation or offered conclusions about the meaning of the events described. On a divine voice in the New Testament gospels, compare the accounts of the transfiguration of Jesus as well as the baptism of Jesus (Matthew 3:13–17; Mark 1:9–11; Luke 3:21–22).

[146] Jesus. The restoration "[they]"—that is, Jesus and the disciples—is also possible.

[147] Coptic, from Greek, *kataluma*. The same word is used in Mark 14:14 and Luke 22:11 for the guest room where the Last Supper was celebrated.

[148] This clause may also be translated as direct speech: "Their high priests murmured, '[He] has (or [They] have) gone into the guest room for his prayer.'"

[149] Cf. Matthew 26:1–5; Mark 14:1–2; Luke 22:1–2; John 11:45–53.

[150] Cf. Matthew 26:14–16, 44–56; Mark 14:10–11, 41–50; Luke 22:3–6, 45–53; John 18:1–11. The conclusion of the Gospel of Judas is presented in subtle and understated terms, and there is no account of the actual crucifixion of Jesus.

[151] Here the wording of the titular subscript is not "The Gospel According to [*pkata* or *kata*] Judas," as is the case in most gospel texts, but "The Gospel of [*ᵉn-*] Judas." It is possible that the title means to suggest that this is the gospel, or good news, about Judas and the place of Judas in the tradition. What he accomplished, the text concludes, is not bad news but good news for Judas and for all who would come after Judas—and Jesus.

PUBLISHER'S NOTE

When Zurich antiquities dealer Frieda Tchacos Nussberger acquired the ancient codex that included the Gospel of Judas in 2000, it had been for sale for nearly twenty years and carried from Egypt to Europe to the United States. Rodolphe Kasser, a Swiss expert in such Coptic texts, says he had never seen one in worse shape. "The manuscript was so brittle that it would crumble at the slightest touch." Alarmed by its deterioration, Tchacos turned it over to the Maecenas Foundation for Ancient Art, which will restore and translate the manuscript and ultimately give it to Cairo's Coptic Museum. The codex project, which combined archaeology, cutting-edge science, and a subject of cultural interest, was a natural for National Geographic. The Society enlisted the support of the Waitt Institute for Historic Discovery, a foundation created by Gateway founder Ted Waitt to support projects that improve mankind's knowledge through historical and scientific exploration. The Society and the Waitt Institute would work with the Maecenas Foundation to authenticate the document, continue the restoration process, and translate the contents of the codex. But first, conservator Florence Darbre, assisted by Coptic scholar Gregor Wurst, had to resurrect the tattered text.

Someone had rearranged the pages, and the top of the papyrus (with the page numbers) had broken away. A greater challenge: Almost a thousand fragments lay scattered like crumbs. Darbre picked up the fragile pieces with tweezers and laid them between sheets of glass. With the help of a computer, she and Wurst were able to reassemble more than 80 percent of the text in five painstaking years. Kasser and other scholars translated the twenty-six page document, a detailed account of long-hidden gnostic beliefs. Scholars of early Christianity say it is the most dramatic textual discovery in decades. Says Kasser, "This script comes back to light by a miracle."

In order to be certain of its age and authenticity, the National Geographic Society put the codex through the closest scrutiny possible without doing it harm. This included submitting minute samples of the papyrus to the most rigorous radiocarbon dating process available and consulting with leading Coptic scholars well versed in the fields of paleography and codicology.

In December 2004, the National Geographic Society hand-delivered the five minuscule samples to the University of Arizona's radiocarbon-dating Accelerated Mass Spectrometry (AMS) lab in Tucson, Arizona.

Four samples were papyrus pieces from the codex, while a fifth was a small section of leather book binding with papyrus attached. No portion of the text was damaged in this process.

In early January 2005, scientists at the AMS lab completed their radiocarbon-dating testing. While individual samples calibrated ages varied, the mean calendar age for the collection was between CE 220 and 340, with an error margin of +/- sixty years.

According to AMS Lab Director Dr. Tim Jull and research scientist Greg Hodgins, "the calibrated ages of the papyrus and leather samples are tightly clustered and place the age of the Codices within the Third or Fourth centuries A.D."

Since its discovery in the late 1940s, radiocarbon dating has been the gold standard for dating ancient objects and artifacts in fields ranging from archaeology to paleoclimatology. The development of accelerated mass spectrometry technology has enabled researchers to sample many tiny fragments of an artifact, as was done in the case of the codex.

The University of Arizona's AMS Lab is world-renowned for its work—including precision-dating the Dead Sea Scrolls, which enabled scholars to place the scrolls accurately within their correct historical context.

The content and linguistic style of the codex is further evidence of its authenticity, according to leading scholars who have studied it. These experts included Drs. Rodolphe Kasser, former professor of the University of Geneva, and a leading translator of the Nag Hammadi library; Marvin Meyer of Chapman University (Orange, CA); Gregor Wurst of the University of Augsburg (Germany); and Stephen Emmel, professor of Coptic studies at the University of Münster (Germany).

According to these scholars, the codex's theological concepts and its linguistic structure are very similar to concepts found in the Nag Hammadi library, a collection of mostly gnostic texts discovered in Egypt in the 1940s that also date to the early centuries of Christianity.

"This text coheres very well with known ideas of the second century of the common era. Even in its fragmentary form it is very interesting—it fits very well into the second century, nicely into a certain part of the second century," Dr. Meyer said.

Emmel concurs with Meyer's view that the content of the codex reflects a unique gnostic worldview prevalent in the second century. "[To fabricate such a document] you would have to reflect a world that is totally foreign to any world we know today. A world that is fifteen hundred years old ... That is very difficult for scholars even who spend their lives studying these things to understand, let alone to create for other people. It would take a real genius to produce an artifact like this and personally I don't think it possible," he said.

"I have no doubt whatsoever that this codex is a genuine artifact of late antique Egypt and that it contains evidence for genuine works of ancient Christian apocryphal literature," Emmel added.

In addition to reflecting a gnostic world view, the paleographic evidence also supports the codex's authenticity. Dr. Emmel—an expert in Coptic paleography—or handwriting, gave this assessment: "It is carefully written by someone who is a professional scribe. The kind of writing reminds me very much of the Nag Hammadi codices. It's not identical script with any of them. But it's a similar type of script."

"The question of whether or not someone in modern times could fake an object like this is for me a non-question—it's out of the question. One would not only have to have genuine material, papyrus, and not simply any papyrus, but ancient papyrus. One would also have to know how to imitate Coptic script from a very early period. The number of specialists in Coptic that know that in the world is very small. You would also have to compose a text in Coptic that is grammatically correct and convincing. The number of people who could do that is even smaller than the number who could read Coptic."

In a further effort to absolutely ensure the codex's authenticity, samples of the ink were sent to McCrone and Associates—a firm well known for its work in forensic ink analysis. This analysis again confirmed the document's authenticity.

Transmission electron microscopy (TEM) confirmed the presence of carbon black as a major constituent of the ink, and the binding medium is a gum—which is consistent with inks from the third and fourth centuries CE.

Using a method known as Raman spectroscopy, McCrone and Associates was further able to establish that the ink contained a metal-gallic ink component consistent with the iron gall inks used in the third century.

# AUTHOR'S NOTE

I first heard about the Gospel of Judas in the fall of 2000. A friend who is a major collector was a client of Bruce Ferrini, the Ohio dealer. Ferrini was looking to evaluate the potential worth of The Gospel of Judas and develop it as a television property. A meeting between us was arranged in New York. Nothing came of it. Ferrini mysteriously cut off all contact after that first meeting and about two or three weeks' worth of e-mail exchanges. I did not know why at the time, and had no idea that Ferrini had gotten himself into all kinds of problems that would lead to his returning most of the papyri to Frieda Tchacos Nussberger.

As there was no way to evaluate the papyri's importance or worth as a media project or to pursue the project at the time without Ferrini's cooperation, I dropped it.

I heard in 2004 that the Gospel of Judas had somehow made its way to Switzerland, and heard it might be with a dealer, Frieda Tchacos Nussberger, who I learned was well-known. At that moment I was trying to develop a project that was more Old Testament-based for National Geographic Television. However, the possibility that the Gospel of Judas might be real fired up the imagination of one executive there and led to a research contract.

I undertook research about Frieda, Mario Roberty, and the Maecenas Foundation. However, it was extremely difficult to find Frieda to talk with her directly. But the closer I got to the two Swiss personalities, the more credible I found them personally, and the more I began to realize that the Gospel of Judas was a true artifact that might contribute enormously to history.

On June 30, 2004, I had dinner with Roberty in Basel. It was the evening before Professor Kasser was to make his announcement in Paris. Soon negotiations commenced that led to this project.

During the writing of this book, I tried to contact all living participants. This narrative reflects those interviews. Some individuals could not be reached. Some chose to be identified by pseudonym only.

## ACKNOWLEDGMENTS

I would like to thank National Geographic, and its exceptional personnel, for being inspired to take on this story, and for being able to bring to the broad public a rare document of great historical importance. By doing so, it is fulfilling its own historic role.

More specifically, Kevin Mulroy, Publisher of National Geographic Books, has played an outstanding role, as has editor John Paine, who helped immeasurably in forming this book, and editor Ellen Beal.

On the television side, John Bredar has proved an enormously talented executive producer; James Barratt an inspired and efficient producer and writer working, like myself, within an extremely limited time framework; and Michael Rosenfeld, Executive Vice President at National Geographic Television and Film, a leader of truly outstanding sensitivity, intelligence and ability. I should also mention Maryanne Culpepper, whose business acumen helped get the entire project going; Cheryl Zook, a dedicated and persistent associate producer; Bruce Brown, whose advice was both practical and insightful; and above everybody, Terry Garcia, who proved himself to be his own kind of shooting star in the otherwise sometimes murky Washington night.

In the United Kingdom, I would thank Ray Bruce, whose knowledge of early Christianity and helping hand at the beginning of this project was both useful and welcome; and my agent, Jonathan Harris, whose negotiating talent enabled this project to be skillfully put together.

In Egypt, I mention Magdy el Rashidi and other Egyptian friends who were instrumental in developing the story for National Geographic and in guiding us how to work within the framework of Egyptian reality; and the hospitable and kind people of Egypt in general.

In Israel, I would thank Sy Gittin, director of the WF Albright Institute of Archaeological Research, affiliated with ASOR, the American School of Oriental Research; the unparalleled Trude Dothan, Israel's venerated senior archaeologist; the versatile and talented archaeologist, Shimon Gibson; and a superb historian, Doron Mendels whose expertise on Eusebius, the father of church history, helped lead into other areas of research.

In Switzerland, Mario Roberty and Frieda Tchacos Nussberger were always there, trying to rescue an historical artifact from the darkness to which it had been condemned, as well as Professor Rodolphe Kasser and his team, especially conservator Florence Darbre and colleague Gregor Wurst. I enjoyed meeting the far-flung Tchacos family in their various lives.

In the United States, I would thank my own far-flung family, and in addition all the superb scholars and personalities whom I had the good fortune to meet. I should also point to that Ivy League scholar who has played an enormously positive role in bringing the manuscript to light and who deserves a medal for his still largely unknown efforts. I thank Bart Ehrman of the Department of Religion, University of North Carolina-Chapel Hill, who wrote the introduction to this book. Bart's insight and wisdom concerning the early centuries of the Christian era provided a compass for ongoing exploration. Marvin Meyer from Chapman College in Orange County, was a person whose company I particularly enjoyed and whose scholarship has been so instrumental in creating a readable literary translation in English of the Coptic codex. He just happens to live near one of my sisters who is, like Meyer, herself a

Ph.D. from Claremont. I should not forget Jordan Ringel, the attorney who was so instrumental in getting it all off the ground.

Mary Stewart Krosney has been a constant companion who has shared this journey of discovery and its excitement with me.

It has been a great adventure and great fun to undertake this exploration. I hope that the knowledge we gain will help to promote understanding of those earlier times when Christianity diverged from its Judaic origins, and that it will somehow bring not a sense of betrayal, not a breaking of faith, but an increased sense of brotherhood on this increasingly crowded planet.

ABOUT THE AUTHOR

**H**erbert Krosney is an award-winning writer and documentary film-maker specializing in investigative and historical projects. He has worked for TV networks throughout the world, including the BBC, PBS, and the History Channel as well as National Geographic. He is the author of *Beyond Welfare: Poverty in the Supercity* (Holt, Rinehart & Winston); *Deadly Business: Legal Deals and Outlaw Weapons* (Four Walls Eight Windows); and the co-author, with Steve Weissman, of *The Islamic Bomb: The Nuclear Threat to Israel and the Middle East* (Times Books). A Harvard graduate, he began his career in newspaper reporting before going into TV documentaries. Married with three children and five grandchildren, he divides his time between homes in New York and Jerusalem.

RODOLPHE KASSER, PH.D., a professor emeritus on the Faculty of Arts at the University of Geneva, is one of the world's leading Coptologists. He has organized the restoration and prepared the *editio princeps* of Codex Tchacos, containing the Gospel of Judas and three other Coptic Gnostic texts.

MARVIN MEYER, PH.D., Griset Professor of Bible and Christian Studies at Chapman University and Director of the Chapman University Albert Schweitzer Institute, is one of the foremost scholars on Gnosticism, the Nag Hammadi Library and texts about Jesus outside the New Testament.

GREGOR WURST, PH.D., is a professor of Ecclesiastical History and Patristics at the University of Augsburg, Germany.

FRANÇOIS GAUDARD, PH.D., is an Egyptologist and Research Associate at the Oriental Institute of the University of Chicago.

BART D. EHRMAN is the James A. Gray Distinguished Professor of Religious Studies at the University of North Carolina at Chapel Hill, and is an expert on the history of early Christianity. He is the author of 19 books, including the bestselling *Misquoting Jesus: the Story Behind Who Changed the Bible and Why*.

This book is set in Garamond 3, designed by
Morris Fuller Benton and Thomas Maitland Cleland in
the 1930s, released digitally by Adobe. This book also
features HTF Requiem, designed by Jonathan Hoefler
in the 2000s and released digitally by
Hoefler & Frere-Jones.

Printed by R. R. Donnelley and Sons on
Gladfelter 60-pound Thor Offset smooth
white antique paper.

Cover printed by Moore Langen Printing.
Color separation by Quad Graphics.

This symbol that is used throughout the book is a
digital recreation of a symbol found on the original
Gospel of Judas papyrus manuscript.